Lecture Notes in Computer Science 10181

Commenced Publication in 1973
Founding and Former Series Editors:
Gerhard Goos, Juris Hartmanis, and Jan van Leeuwen

More information about this series at http://www.springer.com/series/7409

David Brosset · Christophe Claramunt
Xiang Li · Tianzhen Wang (Eds.)

Web and Wireless Geographical Information Systems

15th International Symposium, W2GIS 2017
Shanghai, China, May 8–9, 2017
Proceedings

 Springer

Editors
David Brosset
Naval Academy Research Institute
Brest
France

Christophe Claramunt
Naval Academy Research Institute
Brest
France

Xiang Li
East Normal China University
Shanghai
China

Tianzhen Wang
Shanghai Maritime University
Shanghai
China

ISSN 0302-9743   ISSN 1611-3349 (electronic)
Lecture Notes in Computer Science
ISBN 978-3-319-55997-1   ISBN 978-3-319-55998-8 (eBook)
DOI 10.1007/978-3-319-55998-8

Library of Congress Control Number: 2017935018

LNCS Sublibrary: SL3 – Information Systems and Applications, incl. Internet/Web, and HCI

Preface

These proceedings contain the papers selected for presentation at the 15th edition of the International Symposium on Web and Wireless Geographical Information Systems held in Shanghai in May 2017 and hosted by the Shanghai Maritime University. This symposium is intended to provide an up-to-date review of advances in both theoretical and technical development of Web and wireless geographical information systems (W^2GIS). It is the 15th in a series of successful events beginning with Kyoto 2001, and mainly alternating locations annually between East Asia and Europe. It provides an international forum for discussing advances in theoretical, technical, and practical issues in the field of wireless and Internet technologies suited for the dissemination, usage, and processing of geo-referenced data.

W2GIS is organized as a full two-day symposium, recognized as a leading forum for the dissemination and discussion on the latest research and development achievements in the Web GIS and wireless domains. The submission process was successful this year attracting papers from almost all continents. This demonstrates not only the growing importance of this field for researchers but also the growing impact these developments have in the daily lives of all citizens.

Each paper received at least three reviews and was ranked accordingly. The accepted papers are all of excellent quality and cover topics that range from Web technologies and techniques, paths and navigation, Web visualization, and novel applications.

We wish to thank the authors who contributed to this workshop for the high quality of their papers and presentations and the support of Springer LNCS. We would also like to thank the Program Committee for the quality and timeliness of their evaluations. Finally, many thanks to the Steering Committee for providing continuous advice and recommendations.

February 2017

David Brosset
Christophe Claramunt
Xiang Li
Tianzhen Wang

Organization

Program Committee

Masatoshi Arikawa	University of Tokyo, Japan
Andrea Ballatore	Birkbeck, University of London, UK
Scott Bell	University of Saskatchewan, Canada
Michela Bertolotto	University College Dublin, Ireland
Alain Bouju	University of La Rochelle, France
David Brosset	Naval Academy Research Institute, France
Elena Camossi	CMRE, Italy
James Carswell	Dublin Institute of Technology, Ireland
Christophe Claramunt	Naval Academy Research Institute, France
Maria Luisa Damiani	University of Milan, Italy
Mahmoud Reza Delavar	University of Tehran, Iran
Thomas Devogele	University of Tours, France
Sergio di Martino	University of Naples, Italy
Matt Duckham	RMIT University, Australia
Zhixiang Fang	Wuhan University, China
Filomena Ferrucci	University of Salerno, Italy
Ali Frihida	ENIT, Tunisia
Jérome Gensel	University of Grenoble, France
Ralf Güting	Fernuniversität Hagen, Germany
Bo Huang	Chinese University of Hong Kong, SAR China
Haosheng Huang	University of Zurich, Switzerland
Yoshiharu Ishikawa	University of Nagoya, Japan
Christian Jensen	Aalborg University, Denmark
Farid Karimipour	University of Tehran, Iran
Ki-Joune Li	Pusan National University, South Korea
Songnian Li	Ryerson University, Canada
Xiang Li	East China Normal University, China
Steve Liang	University of Calgary, Canada
Hui Lin	Chinese University of Hong Kong, SAR China
Yu Liu	Peking University, China
Miguel Luaces	University of A Coruña, Spain
Felix Mata	National Polytechnic Institute, Mexico
Gavin McArdle	University College Dublin, Ireland
Sebastien Mustiere	IGN, France
Kostas Patroumpas	Athena Research Centre, Greece
Dieter Pfoser	George Mason University, USA
Martin Raubal	ETHZ, Switzerland
Cyril Ray	Naval Academy Research Institute, France

Kai-Florian Richter	University of Umea, Sweden
Anne Ruas	IFSTTAR, France
Markus Schneider	University of Florida, USA
Kazutoshi Sumiya	Kwansei University, Japan
Taro Tazuka	Tsukuba University, Japan
Yannis Theodoridis	University of Piraeus, Greece
Martin Tomko	University of Melbourne, Australia
Christelle Vangenot	University of Geneva, Switzerland
Marlene Villanova-Oliver	University of Grenoble, France
Agnes Voisard	Fraunhofer ISST and FU Berlin, Germany
Xin Wang	University of Calgary, Canada
Robert Weibel	University of Zurich, Switzerland
Stephan Winter	University of Melbourne, Australia
Alexander Zipf	University of Heidelberg, Germany

Additional Reviewers

Karagiorgou, Sophia
Saeedi, Sara

Contents

Web Technologies and Technics

Automatic Tag Enrichment for Points-of-Interest in Open Street Map

Stefan Funke[1]([⊠]) and Sabine Storandt[2]

[1] University of Stuttgart, Stuttgart, Germany
funke@fmi.uni-stuttgart.de
[2] JMU Würzburg, Würzburg, Germany
storandt@informatik.uni-wuerzburg.de

Abstract. The user experience of geo-search engines and map services heavily depends on the quality of the underlying data. This is especially an issue for crowd-sourced data as e.g., collected and offered by the Open Street Map (OSM) project. In this paper we are focusing on points-of-interests (POIs), such as restaurants, shops, hotels and leisure facilities. Many of those are incompletely tagged in OSM (missing e.g., the *amenity* tag), which leads to such POIs not showing up in respective search queries or not being displayed correctly on the map. We develop methods that can automatically infer tags characterizing POIs solely based on the POI names. The idea being that many POI names already contain sufficient information for tagging. For example, 'Pizzeria Bella Italia' and 'Chau's Wok' most certainly refer to restaurants, whereas 'Cut & Color' is likely a hairdresser. We employ machine learning techniques to extrapolate such additional tag information; our approach yields an accuracy of more than 85% for the considered tags. Moreover, for restaurants, we aimed for extrapolation of the respective cuisine tag (*italian*, *sushi*, etc.). For more than 19.000 out of 28.000 restaurants in Germany lacking the *cuisine* tag, our approach assigned a cuisine. In a random sample of those assignments 98% of these appeared to be true.

1 Introduction

In the context of crowd-sourced data gathering efforts like Open Street Map (OSM), the issue of data quality and completeness is of utmost importance. Competing commercial offerings will always claim an alleged superior data quality to justify their business. Sometimes, their typically more centralized approach of data maintenance and collection indeed allows for an easier monitoring of quality issues; for crowed-based approaches this is much harder to achieve.

In the concrete case of OSM, data quality is very much dependent on the contributors' tagging discipline. While there are well thought out guidelines how to tag mapped elements, in principle every contributor can tag at his/her discretion. This freedom undisputedly has its advantages in terms of flexibility, it also creates some consistency problems, though. For example, when querying a location-based service or a geo-search engine for points-of-interest (POIs) in a certain

© Springer International Publishing AG 2017
D. Brosset et al. (Eds.): W2GIS 2017, LNCS 10181, pp. 3–18, 2017.
DOI: 10.1007/978-3-319-55998-8_1

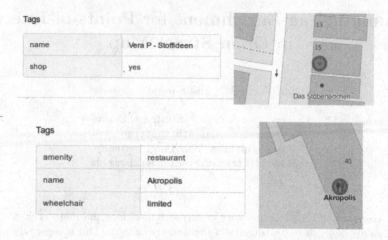

Fig. 1. Missing tag information in OSM. In the upper example, there is a *shop* tag, but it is only set to *yes*. As the POI is indeed a drapery, the *shop* tag should be set to *fabric* instead. In the lower example, most likely a Greek restaurant is depicted (considering its name). But there is no *cuisine* tag, so a search for 'Greek restaurants' will not include this POI.

region or next to the current user location, one often asks for classes ('hotels New York', 'supermarkets Berlin', 'Italian restaurants London') rather than single points ('Hotel Belvedere New York'). In OpenStreetMap (OSM), one can specify the basic class along with every POI e.g., via the *tourism* tag (*tourism=hotel*), the *shop* tag (*shop=supermarket*), the *amenity* tag (*amenity=restaurant*), or several other specialized tags as the *cuisine* tag (*cuisine=italian*) for restaurants. Not providing the appropriate tags when mapping the respective element typically leads to omission of these elements in the result list for a class-based query. These tags are also useful to categorize search results. For example, when searching for 'Venice beach' the user should be informed that there are beaches, hotels, fitness studios and clothing stores with that name. See Fig. 1 for two examples of missing or wrong tags.

In OSM, there are plenty of POIs where important tags are not provided. Many of those POIs exhibit a *name* tag (as e.g. 'Sunset Hotel', 'Walmart', 'Thai Bistro'), though, which already contains some information. In this paper, we investigate methods for automatic extrapolation of tags based on POI names. Using machine learning tools we extract typical words and phrases that occur in *name* tags and learn respective POI classifiers.

As a result we can augment the existing OSM data by inferred tags and improve the data quality. This can be done either fully autonomously or with humans in the loop who verify the augmentations suggested by our algorithms – again, a community-based approval mechanism for such changes might be an interesting option. There are several tools out there for detecting data inconsistencies and missing data (e.g. Keep Right[1]) to make them visible to the

---

[1] http://wiki.openstreetmap.org/wiki/Keep_Right.

community and spur corrections. Such services could also feature our suggestions for tag enrichment. But ideally, mapping and tagging tools for OSM would already provide automatic suggestions as soon as a POI name was typed in (see Fig. 2 for examples). In that way the user is encouraged to enter more information, and with already listing the best options for doing so, it is just a matter of one click.

```
<node>
<tag k="name" v="Walmart"\>
<\node>

Would you like to add a shop=supermarket tag?

<node>
<tag k="name" v="Walmart"\>
<tag k="shop" v="supermarket"\>
<\node>
```

```
<node>
<tag k="name" v="sakura sushi"\>
<tag k="amenity" v="restaurant"\>
<\node>

Would you like to add cuisine=sushi?

Would you like to add cuisine=  japanese
                                asian

<node>
<tag k="name" v="sakura sushi"\>
<tag k="amenity" v="restaurant"\>
<tag k="cuisine" v="sushi; japanese"\>
<\node>
```

Fig. 2. Dialog system that encourages users to provide more information during tagging by making specific suggestions based on learned name classifiers.

1.1 Related Work

Numerous papers use machine learning (ML) techniques to work on/for OSM data. Basically, ML can be employed either on the application level – leaving the underlying data pool untouched – or to verify and even augment the underlying data pool. For the former, e.g., [7] propose the use of artificial neural networks and genetic algorithms to infer land-use patterns without directly feeding the results back into the OSM data pool. For the latter, e.g., inferring the structure of the road network by analyzing GPS traces using ML techniques was discussed in [4]. There are plenty of other studies on completeness and correctness of the OSM data, see e.g. [6] or [8]. The problem is that there either needs to be a ground truth one can compare to in an automated way (as investigated in [3] for building footprints in Munich), or data has to be manually compared to proprietary data. In both cases, the ground truth sample sizes are typically limited. For our application, though, there is a large pool of correctly and completely tagged POIs from which features can be extracted.

Machine learning was also applied in order to automatically assess the quality of the road network data [10]. Here, characteristics of certain street types (as e.g., motorways) were learned, including features such as total street length, number of dead-ends, number of intersection points and connectivity to other street types. In the quality analysis, feature vectors of streets are compared to the learned feature vector for the respective street type. If they do not resemble each other it is assumed that the data quality of the considered street is poor.

In our scenario of extrapolating POI tags, it is easy to verify that tags are missing. But determining what kind of tags should be extrapolated is challenging.

Preliminary results on automated quality improvement of OSM data were also reported in [9]. Here, Artificial Neural Networks (ANN) are applied to distinguish residential and pedestrian streets; features include node count within a bounding box and betweenness centrality. In [5], also missing street sections as well as street names were automatically extrapolated using ML (based on Random Forests) with an accuracy of over 90%. But in all these cases, the tags that should be learned were predefined (street type expressed as *highway* tag or *street name*), while in our application a variety of tags (e.g. *amenity, shop, tourism*, etc.) might apply, and there are typically hundreds of possible values for each (e.g. *amenity=restaurant, amenity=pub, amenity=kindergarten, amenity=bus_station* and so on). In [11], an automatic recommendation system for OSM tags was discussed, making use of SVMs. The focus there is rather on the geometry of the entities, like number of contained points and area. Names are only used if they contain precomputed indicator words as school or park. With our approach, we can also extrapolate tags for POIs where the name does not explicitly contain the amenity (e.g. *50's diner* is recognized as a burger restaurant).

There are also several approaches for other auto tagging applications, e.g. using deep convolutional neural networks as described in [2] for music classification or for tagging web services [12]. But there, the input differs significantly from the structured OSM data we consider in this paper.

1.2 Contribution

We describe a framework for automatic tag extrapolation based on POI names. We explain in detail how to process the OSM data and how to determine extrapolatable tags. Then we introduce a machine learning approach primarily based on k-grams of POI names. We apply our framework to extrapolate selected *tourism, leisure, amenity, shop* and *cuisine* tags for the dataset of Germany. Our experimental evaluation shows the ability of our framework to enrich the OSM data. For example, for *cuisine*, we can extrapolate more than 70% of missing tags with a precision of 98%.

2 POIs in OSM

We are interested in nodes in the OSM data that potentially are POIs. Nodes in OSM come with a specific ID and geo-coordinates (lat/lon). In addition, tags in form of key-value-pairs (k, v) can be specified, as shown in this example:

```
<node id=''360485476'' visible=''true''
uid=''11374'' lat=''47.9955298'' lon=''7.8447728''>
<tag k=''name'' v=''Backshop''/>
<tag k=''shop'' v=''bakery''/>
<tag k=''wheelchair'' v=''yes''/>
</node>
```

In the following, we will list tags that indicate POIs of various kinds (like *shop*) and explain their taxonomy.

2.1   Restaurants, Cafes, Pubs and Fast-Food Facilities

Let us first consider tags associated with going out to eat or drink. We differentiate restaurants, cafes, pubs and fast-food facilities in accordance with the OSM Wiki[2]. The *amenity=restaurant* tag is by far the most frequent *amenity* tag. As specified in the Wiki, *amenity=restaurant* should be used 'for a generally formal place with sit-down facilities selling full meals served by waiters and often licensed (where allowed) to sell alcoholic drinks'. The cuisine tag can be used in addition to further refine what kind of restaurant it is. A cuisine can refer to the ethnicity of the food (*cuisine=chinese*), to the way of food preparation (*cuisine=wok* or *cuisine=grill*), to the food itself (*cuisine=pasta*) or to other classifications (*cuisine=fine_dining*).

Instead of *amenity=restaurant*, one should use the tag *amenity=fast_food* for 'a place concentrating on very fast counter-only service and take-away food'. The *cuisine* tag is used in this context as well (e.g. *cuisine=burger*). Nevertheless, also *amenity=restaurant* and *cuisine=fast_food* or *cuisine=burger* are commonly used. The tag *amenity=cafe* should be used for 'a generally informal place with sit-down facilities selling beverages and light meals and/or snacks', including coffee-shops, tea shops and bistros. Again, combinations like *amenity=restaurant* and *cuisine=coffee_shop* are often used instead.

For drinking, the tags *amenity=pub, amenity=biergarten* and *amenity=bar* are intended. All are used for establishments that sell 'alcoholic drinks to be consumed on the premises'. Hereby, a pub should indicate a facility where you can sit down, food is available and the atmosphere is rather relaxed. In contrast, a bar is assumed to be more noisy, with music and no meal-like food. A biergarten is like a pub, but outdoors. Also combinations like *amenity=pub* and *biergarten=yes* are possible. Other *amenity* tags associated with eating and drinking are *bbq, drinking_water, food_court* and *ice_cream*.

Note, that there is overlap between all mentioned amenities, and tags are combined in various ways to classify places. Therefore we consider all of them together in our learning approach.

2.2   Shops, Services and Entertainment

Besides restaurants, cafes, pubs and similar facilities, there exists a large variety of other amenities that mark POIs. For example, places for entertainment as *cinema, theatre, casino* or *nightclub* fall into that category. But also *parking, post_office, post_box, fuel* (for gas stations), *public toilets, library, dentist* and other facilities that are public or provide some kind of (health) service are valid *amenity* tags. Usually, they are more easily to classify than facilities associated with eating and drinking. But there is some overlap with another important tag,

---

[2] https://wiki.openstreetmap.org/wiki/Main_Page.

namely the shop tag. It should be used for all kind of facilities where products are sold, as e.g. supermarkets, kiosks, bakeries, clothing stores, furniture stores, and many more. There are also nodes tagged with *amenity=shop, amenity=shopping* or variants thereof. For those the OSM Wiki encourages to check whether a shop tag can be used instead.

2.3   Hotels, Tourism Spots and Leisure Facilities

The *tourism* tag is used to describe possibilities for paid lodging as *hotel, hostel, motel, camp_site* and so on. But also in the context of sights and attractions the *tourism* tag should be used, including *zoo, museum* or *theme_park*. There is also an attraction tag for specification, e.g. *attraction=big_wheel*. Alternatively, one can tag a sight primarily according to its type, e.g. *waterway=waterfall* and then add *tourism=yes*. The *leisure* tag applies to all kind of facilities where people can spend their spare time. Most prominent representatives are *playground* and *sports_centre*. When it comes to e.g. parks and gardens there is some overlap with the *tourism* tag, though.

3   Extrapolation Framework

To be able to extrapolate missing tag information our overall plan is to identify characteristic properties (also called features) of the name tag value that are 'typical' for a certain *amenity, cuisine, shop*, etc. tag. For those OSM nodes which should bear a respective tag, (e.g. *shop=hairdresser*) but do not because either the information was not provided or added in a non-conformal way (e.g. as part of the informal description tag), we hope to infer the missing tag by examining its name tag for characteristic features typical for nodes actually bearing this tag. This section gives an overview of the necessary steps for this task.

3.1   Data Extraction and Processing

We only consider named nodes in the OSM data, i.e. the tag k = 'name' is required. Most named OSM nodes refer to streets or parts of the public transport system (as e.g. *amenity=bus_station, name=Norris_Street*). Such nodes are not POIs according to our definition. They are excluded by checking for presence of *highway* and *public_transport* tags. Moreover, we pruned nodes tagged with *cemetery, power, fire_hydrant, historic, natural* and *man_made*. In order to learn the correlation between names and certain tags, we need to have POIs with complete information, that is, a name and the tags we are interested in. These POIs will serve as training data in our machine learning approach. For extrapolation, we consider the POIs that potentially miss tags of a certain kind.

3.2 Selection of Extrapolatable Tags

Not all tags are suitable for extrapolation. First, there need to be sufficiently many POIs which exhibit a certain tag to allow the machine learning approach to work. There are plenty of tags in the OSM data which occur only once or very few times, either because they are over-specified (e.g. *cuisine=asian;curry;noodle*), too specific (e.g. *cuisine=self made cake*), home-brewed (e.g. *cuisine=german-bohemian*), exhibit spelling errors (e.g. *cuisine=chineese*), are not in English (e.g. *cuisine=bürgerliche_küche*), simply used wrong (e.g. *cuisine=music*) or indeed rare (e.g. *cuisine=israelian*). Therefore, we count how often a certain tag or a combination of tags occurs and only further consider tags whose respective count exceeds 200. Second, there are tags which subsume each other or overlap in terms of their semantics. For example, *cuisine=asian* is used but also *cuisine=japanese, chinese, vietnamese, thai* amongst others. To accommodate for such dependencies, we first group tags and specify their relations manually. If we consider two tags to be interchangeable like *cuisine=steakhouse* and *cuisine=steak*, we merge them into one. For a class subsuming several others, we check whether the subclasses are large on their own. If that is the case, we try to learn the more specific group. Otherwise, we cumulate the names of all subgroups and try to learn the more general group.

3.3 Feature Extraction

Once we fixed the set of classes/tags, we need to specify suitable features (characteristic properties of the name tag) that allow to learn the correlation between names and tags. We want to identify words and phrases that are typical for certain classes. Consider for example this list of names of hairdressers of a city in Germany:

Claudia's Frisierstube, Cut & Color, Der Goldene Schnitt, emporio, Freiseur Ryf, Frerich, Friseur Ganter, Friseur Roth, Friseur Ryf, Friseur Salon H.Jonas, Frisör Charisma, Frisörsalon Annette, Frisuren-Atelier, Gutjahr Hairlounge, Haar-WG, HaarBalance, HaarBar, Haarstudio Burger, Haarstudio Marina Lindle, Haarstudio Marita, Hair Body Soul, Hair Saloon, hairkiller, HairSpeed, Helbling, Horst Fischer Friseursalon, Nölle, Power Hair Styling, Salon Carmen, Salon Haargenau, Toni & Guy, Via Style

We observe that e.g. 'fris', 'seur', 'haar' (the German word for hair), 'hair', 'styl', 'salo' and 'studio' appear multiple times and therefore might be good indicators for *shop=hairdresser*. Determining indicator phrases manually for thousands of POIs in hundreds of classes is impractical, though. To automatize the process, we proceed as follows. Let N be the list of names associated with a certain tag (e.g., *shop=hairdresser*). For each name in N we construct all k-grams for k between 3 and 10. A k-gram of a string/word is a consecutive substring of length k. For example, all 4-grams for 'Hair Styling' would be 'Hair', 'air', ir S', 'r St', ' Sty', 'Styl', 'tyli', 'ylin', 'ling'. We count for each k-gram how often it occurs in N. We consider a k-gram to be significant when at least two percent of names in N share this k-gram. If a significant k-gram is a substring of another significant k-gram with a similar count (e.g. considering *cuisine=burger*, 'onald' and 'McDonald's' both appear 753 times), we prune the smaller k-gram as we assume it has no significance on its own. As a counter-example, 'burger' appears more often in the list than 'Burger King', therefore both k-grams are kept. After this pruning step, we have for each class a final list of indicator phrases (k-grams) at hand, each with a percentage specifying the fraction of nodes of this class exhibiting the respective k-gram. Then we construct for each name a so-called feature vector. A feature vector of a name is a vector with as many real-valued entries as there are class/significant k-gram combinations. The entry corresponding to a certain indicator phrase and class is set to the length of the phrase multiplied by the percentage of nodes in the class containing this k-gram. Here the intuition is that long shared sequences between the name and the names in N, as well as a shared sequence with many names in N indicate a high correlation with the class. Standard machine learning can then be applied to the derived feature vectors of the names.

3.4 Machine Learning

We use the Random Forest [1] approach for learning the classifier, as it allows to take care of dependencies between the feature vector entries. We expect to learn a classifier for POI names that can decide which tag (from a given set) should be assigned. As it might very well be the case that no tag is suitable, we have to accommodate for that. Therefore, we not only aim for the classification itself but rather for a probability distribution over the classes. So for each name to classify, we derive a probability for every class denoting how likely it is that the name belongs to this class. The sum over all class probabilities for a name always equals 1. If no class has a significantly higher probability than the others, it can be assumed that none of the classes fit.

3.5 Evaluation

In order to check whether the selected features allow for an accurate classification, we first perform a 5-fold cross validation. Here the training data (the set of POIs with known tags) is split into five equal sized parts P1, P2, P3, P4, P5. Then for each part Pi, we train on the other four parts and classify the feature vectors in Pi on that basis. So we train on P2, P3, P4, P5 and check whether the resulting classifier works as intended for set P1 (for which we know the correct classification), and repeat for P2 vs P1, P3, P4, P5, as well as P3 vs P1, P2, P4, P5, etc. As a quality measure we compute the following statistical standard machine learning quantities (averaged over the 5 experiments):

Recall: for a specific category as e.g. *amenity=hair_dresser*, we consider the ratio (#items correctly classified by our algorithm)/(#items that really have *amenity=hair_dresser* items)

Precision: for a specific category we consider the ratio (#items correctly classified by our algorithm)/(#total number of items that are classified as *amenity=hair_dresser* by our algorithm)

A perfect precision score of 1.0 (or 100%) means that every item classified as having *amenity=hair_dresser* by our algorithm is indeed a hairdresser (but does not imply that every hairdresser was found). On the other hand, a perfect recall score of 1.0 means that all hairdressers were actually classified as having *amenity=hair_dresser* by our algorithm. Note that for tag enrichment, the quality measures precision and accuracy are more important than recall – because adding a wrong tag to a POI is problematic and should be avoided by all means, while not being able to add extra tags to all POIs is not as severe and partially unavoidable (e.g. if the POI name does not contain any useful information at all).

4   Experimental Results

We implemented the described framework using C++ for the feature extraction and Python for machin learning. In particular, we relied on the scikit-learn package [13] there, also using the predefined standard parameters. Our experiments were conducted on a single core of an Intel i5-4300U CPU with 1.90 GHz and 12 GB RAM. The Germany data set extracted from OSM as basis for all our experiments contains 771,325 named nodes. Among those, we identified 84,618 with insufficient tagging (about 12,000 contained only the name tag, the others only non-classifying additional tags as e.g. *wheelchair=yes/no*, *opening_hours*, website or Wikipedia references and address information).

4.1   Amenity and Cuisine Tags for Eating and Drinking

Restaurants, Fast Food Facilities, Cafes, Pubs, Bars and Biergartens. Filtering our data set for eating and drinking related amenities, the following distribution was observed: 60,819 POIs with *amenity=restaurant*, 18,823 with *amenity=cafe*, 18,701 with *amenity=fast_food*, 14,484 with *amenity=pub*, 3,862 with *amenity=bar*, 2,078 with *amenity=biergarten*, 786 with *amenity=ice_cream*, 746 with *amenity=drinking_water*, 391 with *amenity=bbq*.

Conducting a cross-validation on this data, we observed that pub, bar and biergarten are not sufficiently separable with our basic approach as many bars and biergartens are indeed tagged with *amenity=pub*. Also *pub* and *restaurant* were confused frequently. Therefore, we inserted an additional step: We first learned a classifier for *bar* and *biergarten* and applied it to all POIs with *amenity=pub*. Then we excluded those classified as *biergarten* or *bar* from the training data for *pub* and re-ran the experiment. The precision increases from 68% to 82%. Moreover, we used the classifiers for *pub*, *bar* and *biergarten* to prune the training data for *restaurant* and the *ice_cream classifier* to prune *cafe* names. Based on the remaining training data, we learned the final classifier. In the cross-validation, the overall accuracy was 76%.

Next, we applied the learned classifier to data with missing tags. We only assigned a tag automatically when the classification probability was 100%. In that way, we created 461 new tags. For 100 of these, we manually checked the correctness by using the OSM search engine and Google on the name (and possibly further associated tags). In 85% of the instances, the assigned tag was valid. Examples for misclassification are e.g. 'kaffeemaschinenservice kafas' classified as *cafe* (but should be a *shop*), 'uh80 ga weingarten' classified as *biergarten* but really is a *fire_hydrant*, and 'lind haustechnik' classified as *restaurant* (because 'haus' as part of 'gasthaus' occurs quite frequent in German restaurant names) but is a building service.

Cuisine Tags. In total, about 1500 different *cuisine* tags among POIs with *amenity=restaurant* were contained in the data set. Many of those occurred only once or very few times. The most frequent ones are listed in Table 1. They all either indicate ethnicity or type of food. If a *cuisine* tag contained multiple entries (as *cuisine=pizza;kebab*), we counted the POI in both categories.

Table 1. Overview of cuisines.

Ethnicty	Frequency	Type of food	Frequency
Italian	7,365	Pizza	3,275
German	6,753	Kebab	2,926
Regional	6,673	Ice_cream	1,921
Greek	3,002	Burger	1,491
Chinese	1,847	Coffee_shop	723
Asian	1,808	Sandwich	568
Turkish	1,299	Steak_house	310
International	787	Sushi	305
Indian	661	Fish	244
Thai	582	Chicken	125
Bavarian	532	Seafood	116
Mexican	394	Vegetarian	108
Spanish	369		
Japanese	281		
Vietnamese	281		
French	240		
American	163		
Croatian	108		

We performed the following modifications manually to increase the performance and meaningfulness of our approach. We merged *regional* and *german* into one group as they are both too diverse to easily tell them apart. Also *bavarian* was integrated into this group. In contrast, *japanese, chinese, thai* and *vietnamese* were considered each on their own and not accumulated into the *asian* group.

Targets \ Predictions	pizza	sandwich	burger	kebab	ice	coffee	seafood	steak	sushi	
pizza	2572 / 21.7%	18 / 0.2%	29 / 0.2%	442 / 3.7%	121 / 1.0%	28 / 0.2%	29 / 0.2%	26 / 0.2%	10 / 0.1%	78.53% (correct)
sandwich	20 / 0.2%	449 / 3.8%	13 / 0.1%	45 / 0.4%	13 / 0.1%	22 / 0.2%	4 / 0.0%	2 / 0.0%	0 / 0.0%	79.05% (correct)
burger	34 / 0.3%	7 / 0.1%	1241 / 10.4%	151 / 1.3%	22 / 0.2%	16 / 0.1%	7 / 0.1%	9 / 0.1%	4 / 0.0%	83.23% (correct)
kebab	272 / 2.3%	14 / 0.1%	54 / 0.5%	2469 / 20.8%	46 / 0.4%	25 / 0.2%	13 / 0.1%	25 / 0.2%	8 / 0.1%	84.38% (correct)
ice	145 / 1.2%	10 / 0.1%	13 / 0.1%	124 / 1.0%	1527 / 12.9%	74 / 0.6%	12 / 0.1%	11 / 0.1%	5 / 0.0%	79.49% (correct)
coffee	65 / 0.5%	19 / 0.2%	16 / 0.1%	77 / 0.6%	93 / 0.8%	430 / 3.6%	14 / 0.1%	6 / 0.1%	3 / 0.0%	59.47% (correct)
seafood	44 / 0.4%	3 / 0.0%	8 / 0.1%	43 / 0.4%	15 / 0.1%	6 / 0.1%	235 / 2.0%	5 / 0.0%	1 / 0.0%	65.28% (correct)
steak	42 / 0.4%	1 / 0.0%	10 / 0.1%	61 / 0.5%	11 / 0.1%	10 / 0.1%	7 / 0.1%	167 / 1.4%	1 / 0.0%	53.87% (correct)
sushi	7 / 0.1%	0 / 0.0%	0 / 0.0%	59 / 0.5%	6 / 0.1%	2 / 0.0%	3 / 0.0%	3 / 0.0%	225 / 1.9%	73.77% (correct)
	80.35% (correct)	86.18% (correct)	89.67% (correct)	71.13% (correct)	82.36% (correct)	70.15% (correct)	72.53% (correct)	65.75% (correct)	87.55% (correct)	78.42% (correct)

Fig. 3. Precision, recall and accuracy of the learned food type classifier in a cross-validation.

We excluded *international* as we do not expect to identify consistent phrases and words that indicate this cuisine. Regarding type of food, we merged *fish* and *sea-food* into *sea_food* as they were used synonymously and the OSM Wiki recommends to use *sea_food* for both. Furthermore, we excluded *vegetarian*, as it should not be a *cuisine* tag but a *diet* tag instead. The *croatian, american* and *chicken* groups do not contain enough POIs for consideration. So in total, we distinguish 12 ethnicity cuisines and 9 cuisines related to food type.

We first performed a cross-validation, subdivided by ethnicity and food type. For food type the results are presented in Fig. 3.

The overall accuracy is about 78%. We observe, that the accuracy is worse for groups with a small number of representatives as *coffee, seafood, steak* and *sushi*. In addition, there are some natural mix-ups as *pizza* and *kebab*, or *ice* and *coffee* which often occurred together in *cuisine* tags of our input data. For ethnicity, we achieved an overall accuracy of about 81%. For *cuisine=german*, the precision was even above 91% and the recall about 94%. Again, for smaller groups the results were worse. The largest number of mix-ups occurred for *german/italian, mexican/spanish, thai/chinese* and *greek/turkish*.

For our evaluation on unclassified data, we considered 28,218 POIs tagged with *amenity=restaurant* but without a *cuisine tag*. We tried to classify those POIs by food type and ethnicity. We only assigned an ethnicity tag when the probability for a certain class exceeded 75%, and a food type when the classifier was 100% sure. The reason for the different percentages being that we expect most POIs to belong to none of the food types in question. But the classifier creates a probability distribution over the classes with the probabilities summing up to 1. With only nine classes to consider, the chance of a false classification would be too high otherwise. In contrast, for ethnicity, we expect most POIs indeed to belong to one of the classes we consider. For 19,671 out of the 28,128 restaurants, our approach assigned an ethnicity cuisine with a sufficient probability, and for 1,460 a food type was matched. Some POIs received both an ethnicity and a food type cuisine, with the most popular combinations being *pizza;italian*, *kebab;turkish*, *ice_cream;italian* and *sushi;japanese*.

We manually checked 250 extrapolated cuisines for ethnicity and 250 for food type (by having a look at the restaurant's website). We first selected 10 examples for each considered class randomly (if possible). The remaining samples were selected completely randomly among all classified POIs. Table 2 shows an excerpt of 30 samples for ethnicity and food type cuisines assigned by our framework. For food type, two examples for misclassification can be seen: 'rosenburger hof' and 'speisekammer' both serve German food. But as those names contain 'burger' and 'eis' (the German word for ice) respectively, they get assigned *cuisine = burger* and *cuisine=ice_cream* with high confidence. Nevertheless, for the 500 samples in total, the classification accuracy was 98%. As observable in the tables, even spelling errors as 'kebap' could be taken care of with our k-gram based approach, as well as names borrowed from places or persons as 'delphi', 'dschingis khan' and 'cafe mallorca'. The reason for the better precision on real data than in the cross-validation is due to only assigning a class to a POI with unknown cuisine when the probability for that class is high enough. In the cross-validation, every POI gets assigned the class with the highest probability automatically.

4.2   Other Amenity and Shop Tags

In total, the data set contained 938 different *amenity* and 1,853 *shop* tags. The five most frequent *amenity* tags not related to eating and drinking are *bank* (18,765 times), *pharmacy* (16,256), *place_of_worship* (14,309), *parking* (10,853) and *kindergarten* (10,174). The most prominent *shop* tags are in order of frequency *bakery* (22,634 times), *supermarket* (17,655), *clothes* (14,440), *hairdresser* (13,310) and *butcher* (6,862). Overall, we identified 67 reasonable *amenity* and 73 reasonable *shop* classes. The cross-validation revealed a classification accuracy of 84%. Applied to real data, we got 4,212 new tags for previously unclassified POIs. We manually checked for each of the 140 considered classes two extrapolated POIs with that class for correctness. The accuracy was about 76%. Considering only the ten most frequent classes listed above, and 10 examples each, the accuracy was 88%, though.

Table 2. Result excerpts for cuisine classification according to food type and ethnicity. Red entries indicate misclassification.

food type		ethnicity	
pizzahaus	pizza	zum neuen schwanen	german
fischerklause	seafood	sausalitos	mexican
la stella	pizza	my thai	thai
pizzeria capriccio	pizza	mr. kebab	turkish
eiscafe rialto	ice_cream	dschingis khan	chinese
pizzeria italia	pizza	el paso	mexican
pizzeria venezia	pizza	cafe mallorca	spanish
50's diner	burger	mykonos	greek
block house	steak_house	zum bembelsche	german
fischhaus	seafood	delphi	greek
calimero	ice_cream	deutscher hof	german
ristorante pizzeria isola d'ischia	pizza	rhodos	greek
nordsee	seafood	il capriccio	italian
pizzeria marino	pizza	sushi for friends	japanese
rosenburger hof	burger	schusterstübchen	german
nazar kebap stube	kebab	winzerhof weinstuben	german
chilli peppers rock cafe	coffee_shop	brauhaus am schlössle	german
eis-cafe da vinci	ice_cream	gasthof pension drexler	german
steakhouse cheyenne	steak_house	einkehr	german
eiscafe dolce vita	ice_cream	pizzeria venezia	italian
fischkombüse	seafood	kartoffelhaus	german
baguetterie filou	sandwich	zur feurigen bratwurst	german
classic western steakhouse	steak_house	pizzeria italia	italian
shaki sushi	sushi	taverna ilios	greek
cafe kamps	coffee_shop	gameiro pizza-express	italian
trattoria la grappa	pizza	bauernstübchen	german
sakura sushi & grill	sushi	pizzeria capriccio	italian
speisekammer	ice_cream	china imbiss drache	chinese
piccola italia	pizza	ginnheimer wirtshaus	german
döner haus	kebab	schwaben-bräu	german

Table 3. K-grams and their percentage of occurrence for selected shops.

Bakery	Supermarket	Clothes	Hairdresser	Butcher
38.75 bäcker	12.01 edeka	10.87 mode	25.45 fris	54.84 erei
38.71 rei	11.72 netto	7.94 haus	19.91 friseur	51.62 erei
33.27 bäckerei	11.42 markt	7.13 kik	15.91 haar	42.67 ger
11.36 back	10.67 rewe	5.61 textil	15.10 salon	35.08 metzger
11.20 sch	10.03 aldi	4.41 family	13.84 hair	34.99 metzgerei
5.62 ste	6.69 lidl	2.91 s.oliver	8.96 studio	24.50 fleisch
4.60 mann	6.51 penny	2.85 jeans	8.20 friseur	16.13 fleischere
2.80 konditorei	5.72 kauf	2.31 peek	5.00 haarstudio	16.13 leischerei
2.13 backstube	3.81 norma	2.20 kleid	4.62 cut	4.83 land

Table 3 lists the most frequent k-grams for the main *shop* tags. Reconsidering our example *shop=haidresser*, the main k-grams extracted by our program are close to what one would select manually. Interestingly, for *supermarket*, the k-grams almost exclusively are names of supermarket chains. We observed a similar result for gas station chains. Nevertheless, for almost all classes we identified k-grams that occurred in over ten percent of the respective class names. This fact, and the overall good classification accuracy, shows that indeed many names contain classification information.

4.3   Tourism and Leisure Tags

We identified 168 different *tourism* tags of which 16 occurred more than 200 times. *information* (45,879), *hotel* (12,228) and *attraction* (9,404) had the highest counts. The other popular ones are *viewpoint, artwork, hostel, museum, alpine_hut, picnic_site, camp_site, guest_house, caravan_site, chalet, theme_park, apartment,* and *zoo*. For *leisure*, 153 different tags were contained in the data. Only 9 of them exhibit a high frequency: *sports_centre* (4,622), *playground* (3,108), *marina* (1,734), as well as *park, water_park, pitch, stadium, slipway* and *nature_reserve*. We excluded *artwork*, as due to its nature where is little hope for consistent indicator phrases. Furthermore, we excluded *attraction* as this class is too diverse and the extracted k-grams were too general. The remaining 23 classes were fed in our classifier. The first cross-validation indicated too much mix-up between *information* and *hotel*. Therefore, we first created a *hotel* classifier in order to prune the *information* data. After this step, the overall accuracy improved from 62% to 73%.

For the real data, we newly augmented 3,452 POIs with a *tourism* or *leisure* tag. Computing the precision by manually looking up samples was not so easy in this case, as entities tagged with *information* are often simply signs next to hiking trails. Moreover, most classes were not assigned at all. Therefore, we restricted ourselves in the precision calculation to *hotel, playground, marina,* and *sports_centre*. We checked 50 examples for each class. The overall accuracy was 92%. For *sports_centre*, we even achieved 98% (e.g. 'tennishalle görner', 'willy-lemkens-sportpark', 'eissporthalle', 'the strike bowlingcenter', 'tanzsportzen-trum', 'turnhalle herringhausen' are correct examples).

4.4   Discussion

We also tried other machine learning approaches as logistic regression but got comparable (or slightly worse) results. Analyzing the not correctly extrapolated tags in our cross-validation, we observed three main sources of error: (1) POI names without any amenity, shop or cuisine information, (2) same/very similar POI names but different amenity or cuisine etc., (3) mixed or misleading POI names, as e.g. the example in Fig. 4 shows. In all three cases, also a human reading the POI name is unlikely to come up with a correct extrapolated tag. Therefore, we conclude that only tuning the machine learning part cannot lead to drastic quality improvements.

Fig. 4. Extrapolating from the POI name *Chico's mexican restaurant* that pizza is served there is very unlikely for any reasonable classifier.

5   Conclusions and Future Work

We showed the potential of OSM name tags to serve as basis for extrapolating tags that indicate the class of a POI. Our machine learning approach for automatic tag extrapolation was proven to work well on real data. The accuracy was significantly over 80% for most considered tags. And in particular for *cuisine*, a significant fraction of missing tags was correctly inserted with our approach.

In future work, other tags beside the *name* tags could be considered to improve the results further. For example, the *opening_hour* tag could help to distinguish between restaurants and pubs. The *brand* tag could be helpful when it comes to supermarkets, gas stations, dealerships, clothing stores and so on. Also the free text tags *note* and *description* could be parsed for that purpose. Furthermore, other countries apart from Germany should be investigated. Some tags only occur in certain parts of the world, and the indicator phrases as well as their frequencies for certain tags are expected to change significantly for other countries.

As indicated in the introduction, there are different approaches for integrating the outcome of automatic tag-inference tools into the Open Street Map data pool. In spite of the high precision of our approach, the outcomes should possibly not be automatically fed into OSM without human verification and possible intervention. Mapping and tagging tools like OSMtracker[3] might incorporate the classifiers developed using our approach. By suggesting suitable tags once the user has specified the name of the new POI, the tagging process, which is often experienced as tedious and annoying (manifested in many nonsense tags), could be greatly improved, both in terms of usability for the mapper as well as the resulting data quality. As our classifiers, once learned, can make new reasonable tag suggestion for a POI in milliseconds, it would be feasible to use it a real-time dialog system.

---

[3] http://wiki.openstreetmap.org/wiki/OSMtracker.

References

1. Breiman, L.: Random forests. Mach. Learn. **45**(1), 5–32 (2001)
2. Choi, K., Fazekas, G., Sandler, M.B.: Automatic tagging using deep convolutional neural networks. In: Proceedings of the 17th International Society for Music Information Retrieval Conference, ISMIR, New York City, United States, 7–11 August, pp. 805–811 (2016)
3. Fan, H., Zipf, A., Fu, Q., Neis, P.: Quality assessment for building footprints data on openstreetmap. Int. J. Geogr. Inf. Sci. **28**(4), 700–719 (2014)
4. Fathi, A., Krumm, J.: Detecting road intersections from GPS traces. In: Fabrikant, S.I., Reichenbacher, T., Kreveld, M., Schlieder, C. (eds.) GIScience 2010. LNCS, vol. 6292, pp. 56–69. Springer, Heidelberg (2010). doi:10.1007/978-3-642-15300-6_5
5. Funke, S., Schirrmeister, R., Storandt, S.: Automatic extrapolation of missing road network data in OpenStreetMap. In: Proceedings of the 2nd International Workshop on Mining Urban Data Co-located with 32nd International Conference on Machine Learning (ICML), Lille, France, 11th July, pp. 27–35 (2015)
6. Girres, J.-F., Touya, G.: Quality assessment of the French OpenStreetMap dataset. Trans. GIS **14**(4), 435–459 (2010)
7. Hagenauer, J., Helbich, M.: Mining Urban land-use patterns from volunteered geographic information by means of genetic algorithms and artificial neural networks. Int. J. Geogr. Inf. Sci. **26**(6), 963–982 (2012)
8. Haklay, M.: How good is volunteered geographical information? A comparative study of OpenStreetMap and ordnance survey datasets. Environ. Plan. B Plan. Des. **37**, 682–703 (2010)
9. Jilani, M., Corcoran, P., Bertolotto, M.: Automated quality improvement of road network in OpenStreetMap. In: Agile Workshop (Action and Interaction in Volunteered Geographic Information) (2013)
10. Jilani, M., Corcoran, P., Bertolotto, M.: Multi-granular street network representation towards quality assessment of OpenStreetMap data. In: Proceedings of the Sixth ACM SIGSPATIAL International Workshop on Computational Transportation Science, IWCTS 2013, pp. 19:19–19:24. ACM (2013)
11. Karagiannakis, N., Giannopoulos, G., Skoutas, D., Athanasiou, S.: OSMRec tool for automatic recommendation of categories on spatial entities in OpenStreetMap. In: Proceedings of the 9th ACM Conference on Recommender Systems, pp. 337–338. ACM (2015)
12. Lin, M., Cheung, D.W.: An automatic approach for tagging web services using machine learning techniques. Web Intel. **14**(2), 99–118 (2016)
13. Pedregosa, F., Varoquaux, G., Gramfort, A., Michel, V., Thirion, B., Grisel, O., Blondel, M., Prettenhofer, P., Weiss, R., Dubourg, V., Vanderplas, J., Passos, A., Cournapeau, D., Brucher, M., Perrot, M., Duchesnay, E.: Scikit-learn: machine learning in Python. J. Mach. Learn. Res. **12**, 2825–2830 (2011)

Creating Web-Based GIS Applications Using Automatic Code Generation Techniques

Nieves R. Brisaboa, Alejandro Cortiñas, Miguel R. Luaces[✉],
and Oscar Pedreira

Laboratorio de Bases de Datos, Universidade da Coruña, A Coruña, Spain
{brisaboa,alejandro.cortinas,luaces,oscar.pedreira}@udc.es

Abstract. Geographic Information Systems (GIS) have increased its popularity for some time now, specially in the context of mobile devices. There are many disciplines and companies improving their workflow by using GIS on devices with geolocation features. To satisfy the emergent demand, lots of web-based GIS applications are being developed. These applications diverge in their target and context, but they all share a common set of the features. For some time an effort has been carried out to define standards in GIS, and currently the level of interoperability between GIS software assets is the highest ever. Given that there is a need to create web-based GIS applications sharing a set of features and that, thanks to the standards, GIS technologies are interoperable, it is not only possible but desirable to apply strategies of reuse, mass-customization and software generation to develop web-based GIS applications.

This work summarizes the design of a tool, GISBuilder, for the semi-automatic generation of web-based GIS applications. GISBuilder is a Software Product Line (SPL) with enhanced capabilities through the usage of a *scaffolding*-based transformation engine, which is able not only to assemble static software assets but to generate product-specific code.

Keywords: Web-based geographic information systems · Software product lines · Model-driven engineering · Scaffolding

1 Introduction

The technologies used to implement Geographic Information Systems (GIS) [10,11,19] used to follow different and incompatible conceptual, logical and physical data models. For example, a simple concept like the data type *polygon* had inconsistent definitions between GIS technologies, making interoperability almost impossible. The standardization process carried out by the Open Geospatial Consortium (OGC) and International Organization for Standardization (ISO) in the last years has helped to solve this problem defining a set of

Funded by MINECO (PGE & FEDER) [TIN2016-78011-C4-1-R, TIN2016-77158-C4-3-R, TIN2015-69951-R, TIN2013-46238-C4-3-R, TIN2013-46801-C4-3-R]; CDTI and MINECO [Ref. IDI-20141259, Ref. ITC-20151305, Ref. ITC-20151247]; and FPI Program [Ref. BES-2014-068178].

D. Brosset et al. (Eds.): W2GIS 2017, LNCS 10181, pp. 19–34, 2017.
DOI: 10.1007/978-3-319-55998-8_2

standards for GIS that are currently followed by most software libraries. Nowadays, web-based GIS applications are very similar to each other, and they share not only functional features but also most of the technologies. For example, there are two major open source alternatives to implement a web map viewer, OpenLayers or Leaflet, and almost all the web map viewers are implemented with one of them. The repetitive appearance of the same features in every web-based GIS, the existence of many software artefacts following international standards that implement these features, and the fact that most web-based applications also share the same technologies make suitable the application of techniques for the automatic generation of this kind of products, web-based GIS.

Software engineering has put much effort on facilitating and improving software reuse. The research field of Software Product Lines (SPL) focuses on reusing the same software artefacts on different products that share features: each feature is implemented once, and the resultant software component is shared between all the products with the feature [7,16]. However, the actual implantation of SPL in industry is very low [3] and focused mainly in embedded systems [18]. Similarly, the research field of Model Driven Engineering (MDE) applies the advantages of modelling to software engineering activities [3]. The main concepts in MDE are models, which are simplified representations of the reality focused on a concrete domain, and transformations, which are manipulative operations over these models. Even though direct application of MDE in the industry is low, there are frameworks like Ruby on Rails or Grails based on the *scaffolding* technique that is used frequently in the software industry to speed up software development by generating code from its specification. Therefore, *scaffolding* is somehow an informal application of some MDE principles.

We have used a hybrid approach, based on SPL and on MDE, to design a tool, named GISBuilder, for the semi-automatic generation of web-based geographic information systems. In order to apply both approaches simultaneously, we have created a SPL engine based on *scaffolding* that generates the source code of a web-based GIS dynamically. As far as we know, this is the first attempt to do such two things. The remainder of this paper is organized as follows. Section 2 explains background concepts of the techniques used in GISBuilder, some previous work and motivation. Section 3 describes the products we aim to build. Section 4 details the architecture of our tool, which is complemented by Sect. 5, focused on the transformation engine, and by Sect. 6, which presents a use case. Finally, conclusions and future work are explained in Sect. 7.

2   Related Work

The evolution of the software development industry has been directed primarily to increment the layers of abstraction between the pure machine-code and the way a developer must describe the desired behaviour for a software asset. Assembly languages were followed by high-level procedural languages like Fortran, Lisp, Cobol or C. Then, new paradigms like Object Oriented Programming followed with languages such as C++ or Java. Nowadays, software frameworks like the

Spring framework provide for higher levels of abstraction using techniques such as inversion of control, dependency injection, or aspect-oriented programming to save the programmer thousands of lines.

One of the latest concepts in this direction is *scaffolding*, which is a popular technique in many trending software development frameworks, starting with Ruby on Rails in 2005. A *scaffolding* engine generates code from an specification or model created by a developer and a set of pre-defined templates. This way, most of the repetitive and generic code of the applications is automatically written, and the developer can start its work from a mid-stage or half-built architecture. *Scaffolding* is not limited to any context, and it can be used to generate any kind of code, from the user interface of an application to the documentation.

We can see *scaffolding* as an informal application of Model-Driven Engineering. MDE combines domain-specific modelling languages, which formalize the application structure, behaviour, and requirements within particular domains, with transformation engines and generators that analyse certain aspects of models and then synthesize various types of artefacts [17]. This is, from a set of models defined for an application, and through a series of transformations, some code is generated specifically for the product. However, this code is usually not replicated in any other product unless the models are the same. Therefore, MDE is useful to reduce the cost of developing a single product, but it is not as useful in the case of families of similar products.

The field of Software Product Lines [1] is specialized in sets of products sharing some common assets and features. In SPL, the features of a product family are modelled using a *feature model*, which represents the variability of the platform [8], and implemented in components or software assets. To build a new product, an analyst selects the features desired and the components related to them are assembled together. So, instead of strictly generating code, a SPL only handles inclusion or rejection of code blocks.

In [5], we identified the features and components of a generic web-based GIS product, and we designed a SPL to generate these products. We also concluded that the data model of each product has to be specified by the analyst because each application requires different data. Furthermore, all the source code related to the data schema must be automatically generated during the assembling process, even the creation of the database tables. However, current SPL implementation techniques, most of them shown on [1,14], are not suitable for dynamic code generation from the specifications of the products. Even though MDE and scaffolding are appropriate for this task, as far as we know, these techniques have not been used to implement SPLs so far.

3   Product Architecture

In this section we describe the products our tool is able to produce. We have identified the functional and non-functional features for a generic web-based GIS after analysing existing GIS applications with different scopes and features, such as [4,6,12,13,15]. We have also determined which software assets are required to provide all the features identified, and which product architecture is the adequate. The products of our platform have three main characteristics:

- Each product is based in a **complex data model** that is specifically designed for the product. The data model is composed by a set of entities, with their own properties and relationships among them. The different entities are used in the web application as the basis for listings, reports, creation and modification forms, and map layers.
- The products share a set of **common elements to any web-based application**: hierarchical menus to structure the contents, static HTML pages to display information that is not included in the data model, dynamic pages displaying listings and forms of entities from the data model, and private sections and functionalities available only to authenticated users with specific roles.
- Some pages of the product **display geographic information using a map viewer**. Each product may define its own collections of map layers, visualization styles, and maps. Furthermore, each product may define one or more map viewers, each one with its own configuration that includes the visualization type (e.g., the map viewer may be embedded in some other content, it may be shown in full-page mode, or the map viewer panning bounds may be limited) or the selection of the different tools that can be enabled (e.g., zooming and panning the map, showing a form for the selected map element, etc.)

Figure 1 shows the functional architecture of our products. It uses the classical three-layer architecture pattern composed of a *user interface*, responsible for the interaction with the user; a *processing layer* which contains all the functionality defined for the GIS; and a *model management* layer, responsible for physical data storage and data management. We use three shades of grey in the figure to classify the different modules according to how much they change for each product. The darker ones are *reusable software assets* that can be used in any product without any change in their code because they are not designed for a specific product but instead they can be used by any of them. Modules filled with white must be generated specifically for each product (e.g., menu structure or data model). Finally, those with a medium shade of grey are external software assets connected to the products through some API, so they are totally independent of each product (e.g., the database management system). The different modules are described next.

Reusable Software Assets. The reusable software assets of the products are the following:

- **Data Importer.** Even though the products provide a way for the final user to input data directly into the different entities using web forms, in many cases this is not enough because there are applications with lots of data in which using the manual way is not acceptable. Focusing on GIS, manually loading the data is simply not doable because this would mean that the final user has to draw the geographic objects manually. Therefore, our products can include a component for loading files directly in the applications. The files supported

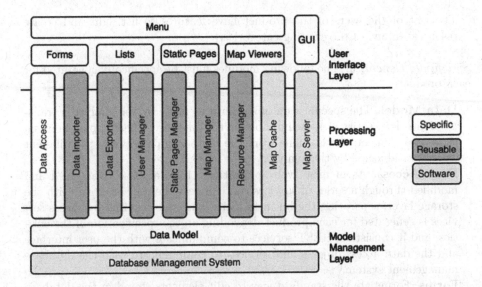

Fig. 1. Functional architecture of the products

are the most common: *comma-separated values* (CSV), *Excel and LibreOffice spreadsheets*, *shapefiles*, and *raster* file formats. The component also allows the user to map the data from the files into the different properties and entities of the data model (i.e., the attribute names do not have to be the same).

– **Data Exporter.** Exporting listings into CSV files or spreadsheets and the current map visualization into a downloadable image or *shapefile* is a common feature in information systems. This component provides this feature.

– **User Manager.** Most web-applications handle different types of users, providing different functionalities depending on the role of the connected user. They also allow the user to sign up, and there is an administrator who can list and edit the existing set of users. This component provides for all these features.

– **Static Pages Manager.** Even though many content pages in web applications are static in the sense that they do not change during the lifetime of the application, some other content in the pages must be editable. This component provides this functionally, and it can also used by an administrator user to create or delete content pages.

– **Map Manager.** Geographic data, maps, layers and styles, can be specified by the analyst when the product is generated. When this is not enough for the requirements of a product, this component lets the administrator user change the different maps, layouts and styles used by the application on runtime. The changes are applied to the different map viewers existing in the product.

– **Resource Manager.** Most web applications have to deal with multimedia resources, whether they are *pdf* files, *images*, *music* files or *videos*. This component offers the administrator user an interface to define new categories of resources, and to define the attributes for the resources of each category.

The rest of the users of the product have features to list, edit and create resources in any of the existing categories.

Specifically Generated. The following modules must be specifically generated for each product:

- **Data Model.** The specification of the entities made by the analyst is translated into Java entity classes and tables in the database. The mapping between these two elements is also done from the relationships between the different entities established by the analyst.
- **Data Access.** As in most web applications, the database is accessed and modified through a series of services that connect the user interface with the storage layer, separating the business logic. The code required by theses services is generated for each product depending on the specification of the entities, and it consists of REST services to communicate with the user interface and the data access objects and services to communicate with the database management system.
- **Forms.** Forms are the standard way to edit elements stored in the database and to create new ones. The forms are created from the entities choosing which properties can be edited in each form.
- **Lists.** Lists are created in a similar way to forms, that is, by selecting which properties of each entity should be shown in the listing. There are certain additional options for the lists, such as sorting, filtering or searching over the elements listed.
- **Static Pages.** The analyst can create a set of *static pages* using a WYSIWYG (*What You See Is What You Get*) editor. These pages can be accessed by the final user through the menus, and one of them can be chosen as the welcome page.
- **Menu.** Most of the features of any software are accessed trough a menu. The different components and modules provide a set of views that allow the user to access their features. Some of the views are the *authentication page*, the *csv import page*, any of the *lists* dynamically generated, or any of the resources created in the resource manager. The analyst defines the menu structure combining three types of menu elements: a link to a view provided by any of the modules, an external link to any web page or a sub-menu element that groups another set of elements.
- **Map Viewers.** All the entities which have a geographic property can be visualized using a map viewer in the final application. To do that, the analyst must define those viewers and choose the options that the user will have over each entity. For example, a link to edit an element in the map can be set to go to one of the *forms* defined before.
- **Graphical User Interface** (GUI). Our tool generates not only the visual theme of the application but also lets the analyst decide about the position and number of menus of the application, and the position of the widgets provided by other components.

External Software Assets. The following modules are considered external to the product and deployed without modification:

- **Database Management System.** The storage layer of our products must be provided by an external component. Nowadays, most web applications store their data in a relational database. In our case, since we are managing data of geographical nature, we need to use a database management system with geographic capabilities such as PostGIS, Oracle Spatial or MySQL.
- **Map Server.** If the volume of data is not really high, a web-based GIS can be built without a map server drawing all geographic information on the client-side (and possibly fetching base layers from public services like OpenStreetMap or similar ones). However, in cases where the amount of data is high, or if we need to customize the styles of the layers, our product needs a map server connecting the database data with the map viewers.
- **Map Cache.** Rendering each layer every time a user accesses a map viewer can be very costly, specially with large sets of geographic data. With a map server cache the layers remain rendered for some time, so the processing and bandwidth cost are reduced.

In Fig. 2 we show the technological architecture of the products generated by GISBuilder. All the technologies involved are commonly used nowadays by web developers. The web client is implemented using an open-source web application framework called Angular. It presents a modular design and takes advantages of patterns like inversion of control, which allows us to easily create variants of the

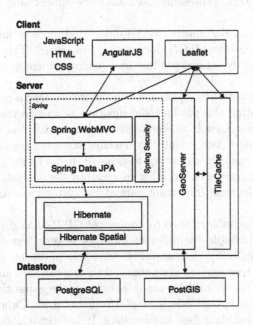

Fig. 2. Technological architecture of the products

products using different software artifacts. The map viewing technology chosen is Leaflet because it is lightweight, mobile-oriented and flexible, and it supports additional functionality by plugins. The server-side is based on Spring MVC: we implement the REST services with Spring controllers and the services that provide communication with the database are built using the dependency injection pattern of Spring. We also use Spring Security to support user authentication and access-control. The geographic information is served to the client by an internal map server (GeoServer) and a map cache (TileCache), even though external map services may also be used. Finally, Spring JPA and Hibernate are used as the data access technology and PostgreSQL (and PostGIS) is our alternative as database management system.

4   GISBuilder

The GISBuilder architecture is shown in Fig. 3, and it is consists of the *specification interface*, the *project repository*, the *transformation engine*, and the *component repository*.

The *specification interface* allows an *analyst* to define different products using two strategies: on the one hand, he or she can select the features included in the product as in any other SPL; on the other hand, the interface provides tools for the analyst to define the data model, the menu structure, and the lists, forms or map viewers that are included in the final product. Behind the scenes, the interface builds the product specification, an instance of the GISBuilder Domain Specific Language (DSL) represented as a JSON document, and validates it using JSON Schema.

The *project repository*, another GISBuilder module, is a database where all the product specifications (JSON documents) are stored. This way, an analyst can restore a previously defined product and generate it again, refine it, or create a new version of it.

When the analyst decides to generate the source code of a project, the JSON document representing the product specification is sent to the *transformation engine*. Then the *transformation engine* assembles the different components and generates the required code, using the reusable software assets and code templates from the *component repository* to achieve this. The output of the engine would be the source code of the product specified by the analyst. Being the *transformation engine* the most important part of our system, we carefully explain it in Sect. 5.

In terms of the technology used to implement GISBuilder, using a framework that allows us to decouple the different modules is very beneficial. Also, there is more need for flexibility than stability, since our platform is an evolving set of artefacts whose components are supposed to grow in size and quantity, and it is not expected to be used by many people at the same time. That is the reason to implement it on Node.js, a platform build on Chrome's JavaScript runtime for easily building fast applications. It is lightweight, independent of operating systems and IDEs and currently one of the most important platforms,

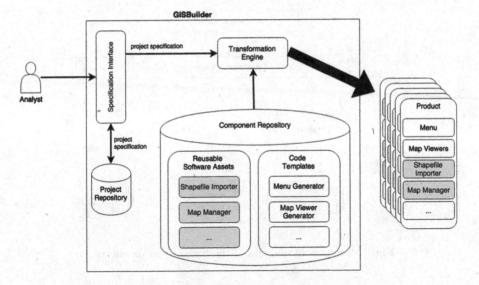

Fig. 3. Functional architecture of GISBuilder

with growing popularity. Node.js provides for a huge flexibility that facilitates the integration of its libraries and applications.

In SPL it is common that the specification interface is simple or almost non-existent, since it is only used to select which features are included in the product. However, due to the complexity of our products and their definition, GISBuilders *specification interface* is a web application implemented with Angular that communicates with a Node.js server via REST. This server handles the interaction with the *project repository* and with the *transformation engine*. Since the project specification is represented with a JSON document, the technology chosen to store these specifications is MongoDB, a document oriented database that handles the data precisely in this format. The *transformation engine* is also a Node.js tool, so the integration is straightforward using an API provided by the engine. Lastly, the *components repository* is nothing more than a directory with files of the code of every asset and template, which are accessed directly by the *transformation engine*.

5 Transformation Engine

Figure 4 shows the structure of our transformation engine, which consists of three different components: the *feature model manager*, the *file manager*, and the *template engine*. The *transformation engine* defines an API used by the *specification interface* to generate the different products. It also provides a small command line utility so the engine can be used independently of the tool, which specially useful when developing or debugging the platform.

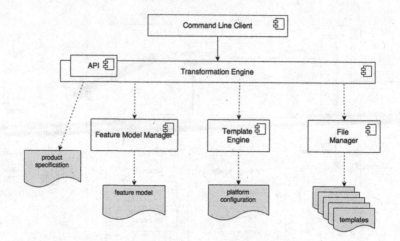

Fig. 4. Component diagram of the transformation engine

The **feature model manager** main purpose is to manage the feature model of the platform and to check whether the selection made by the analyst is correct. This is performed using the well-known operation *Valid Product* of SPL [2]. It also provides some of the other analysis features to improve the maintainability of the platform and the products, like finding features used in the code templates that are not defined in the feature model.

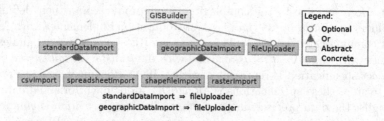

Fig. 5. Excerpt of the GISBuilder feature model

The feature model is represented following the specification of Feature IDE [9], and it can be loaded from a file in three different formats: XML, JSON or YAML. It can also be created programmatically, a feature expected to be used in the future to allow changing the feature model graphically from the *specification interface*. In addition to features, the feature model also allows to define constraints defined with logical operators. In Fig. 5 a excerpt of our feature model is shown.

The **file manager** handles all task related to the access to the templates. For example, it allows the *transformation engine* to walk through every template of a directory recursively and apply changes to them. It also detects when a binary file is found in order to skip processing it and just copy it to the output.

The latest and more important part of the *transformation engine* is the **template engine**. In a SPL, there is usually a derivation engine handling the process of assembling the product from a set of features using the reusable components. In MDE, transformations are applied to models to generate new models in different levels of the architecture, until one of these transformations generates source code. Our **template engine** is able to handle these two kinds of operations, being able to generate products from:

- **SPL-like assemblable components:** for each product, it can be specified a set of features to be included in it, like in a classic SPL. Our engine takes the components implementing these features and assembles them into the final product. The set of components corresponds the *reusable software assets* from Sect. 3.
- **MDE-like model transformations:** a set of models are used to generate each product. These models specify the data model, layers and maps of each product, as well as many other generic parameters like graphical interface options. Our engine transforms these models into specific modules included in the final product. These are the specifically generated modules from Sect. 3.

In order to handle this duality, we have designed the *template engine* to be based on the *scaffolding* technique. It treats every module as a set of templates, no matter whether the module is a reusable component that needs just to be assembled or whether its code must be specifically generated from the application models. Thus, the *component repository* described in Sect. 4 is nothing but the templates of every module, including the code for the *reusable software assets* and the *code templates* that are used to transform the modules into product specific code.

In Fig. 6 a excerpt of the Java code for the data importer is shown. In the *static* block we can see some variation of the code to produce depending on the selected features. Template annotations are defined as comments of the programming language in which the template is written and its content can be any JavaScript code. Thus, they do not interfere with the compiler, IDE or validation tool used by the developer of the platform code.

Besides annotations related to which code blocks are included in the product, our template engine allows using variables and complex control sequences in the code. Moreover, the developer of the platform can even create JavaScript functions to use within the annotations, or use temporal variables to store data used more than once. In the Fig. 7 a simplified template to generate entities of a product is shown. The template specifies how to create Java classes for each entity defined by the analyst. Inside the class, the code for each property of the entity is created depending on its specification. The latter is an example of a *code template* generating product specific code, whereas the former example is just a *reusable software asset* with an small variation depending on the sub-features selected. Even with the latter template simplified, we can see the difference of complexity between the two types of templates.

```
 1  private static final Set<String> validExtensions = new HashSet<String>();
 2
 3  static {
 4      /*% if (feature.shapefileImport) { %*/
 5      validExtensions.add("shp")
 6      /*% } %*/
 7      /*% if (feature.csvImport) { %*/
 8      validExtensions.add("csv")
 9      /*% } %*/
10      /*% if (feature.spreadsheetImport) { %*/
11      validExtensions.add("xls")
12      /*% } %*/
13  }
14
15  @Component
16  public class DataImporter() {
17      // ...
18  }
```

Fig. 6. Annotated Java class

```
 1  /*%@ return entities.map(function(en) {
 2      return {
 3          fileName: en.name + '.java',
 4          context: en
 5      };
 6  }) %*/
 7  package es.udc.lbd.gisbuilder.model.domain;
 8
 9  @Entity
10  @Table(name = "t_/*%= context.name.toLowerCase() %*/")
11  public class /*%= context.name %*/ {
12      /*% context.properties.forEach(function(prop) {
13              var propertyClass = prop.class;
14              var validGeomTypes = ['Point', 'MultiLineString', 'MultiPolygon'];
15
16              if (validGeomTypes.find(propertyClass) != null) { %*/
17      @JsonSerialize(using = CustomGeometrySerializer.class)
18      @JsonDeserialize(using = Custom/*%= propertyClass %*/Deserializer.class)
19      @Column(columnDefinition="geometry(/*%= propertyClass %*/, 4326)")
20          /*% } %*/
21      private /*%= propertyClass %*/ /*%= normalize(prop.name) %*/;
22      /*% }); %*/
23  }
```

Fig. 7. Simplified excerpt of model transformation template

6   Use Case

In this section we describe the process an analyst follows to specify and create a
product. The current implemented version is still a prototype, but it is already
able to generate production-ready products with menus, static pages, forms,
lists, simple maps and a small set of components, including the *data importer*
and the *resource manager*.

When the analyst starts defining a new product, the first step is to define
some general information about the product, such as the name and the version

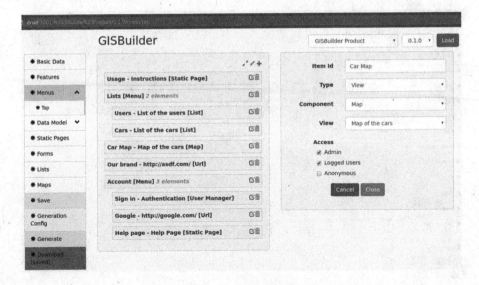

Fig. 8. Menu structure design page

(because our tool supports different versions of the same product). The analyst must also choice which component and view will be the welcome page, and the set of languages in which the application will be available. The next step is to decide which *reusable components*, from the ones shown in Sect. 3, must be included in the product. Some of the components have their functionality split between a set of subcomponents which can be selected independently. That is, if the product only needs the feature to import CSV, there is no need to include the rest of the features of the *data importer* component. However, there are some components depending on others, and the application checks that the required ones are selected.

The menu structure is designed using the interface shown on Fig. 8 where we can see a list of elements and some of them grouped in sub-menus. The analyst can restrict the visibility of any element by choosing which kind of role must the logged user have. The different static pages required by the product can be defined during the specification stage, or once the application is running (if the *static pages manager* is included).

One of the most important elements the analyst must specify is the data model. Each entity existing in the application is defined using the interface shown in Fig. 9. The properties of every element are detailed, indicating their names, types and some extra typical options such as if a concrete property is required or optional. If an entity has a relationship with another entity, the property determining this relation is also defined.

From the set of entities defined in the specification of the data model, the analyst can create forms, lists and maps. The analyst decides which properties of the entities can be edited in forms and which are shown in lists and maps.

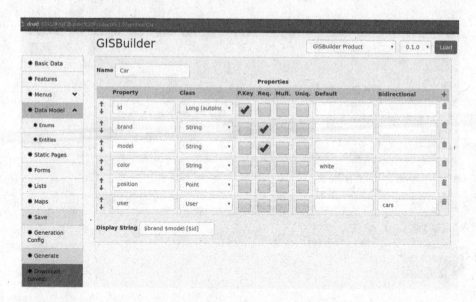

Fig. 9. Entity definition page

Both list and maps can be customized with static filters, and the functionality of dynamic filters can be enabled over some maps, so the user can apply its own filters. In the case of the maps, there are also options regarding the layers to be shown on the map.

7 Conclusions and Future Work

In this paper we have presented a functional tool called GISBuilder able to generate semi-automatically production-ready web-based geographic information systems. To design the tool, we have reviewed the current state of art of GIS, we have identified the functional and non-functional requirements of a web-based GIS product, we have designed an up-to-date architecture for web-based GIS and we have implemented a transformation engine following the *scaffolding* technique that allows us to mix SPL and MDE concepts in the generation of our products.

As future work, we are designing and implementing the rest of the components required by our products and designing a methodology to confront the evolution of the products and the platform code supported by *git*, a Version Control System.

References

1. Apel, S., Batory, D., Kästner, C., Saake, G.: Feature-Oriented Software Product Lines. Springer, Heidelberg (2013)
2. Benavides, D., Segura, S., Ruiz-Corts, A.: Automated analysis of feature models 20 years later: a literature review. Inf. Syst. **35**(6), 615–636 (2010)
3. Brambilla, M., Cabot, J., Wimmer, M.: Model-Driven Software Engineering in Practice, vol. 1. Morgan & Claypool Publishers, San Rafael (2012)
4. Brisaboa, N.R., Cotelo-Lema, J.A., Fariña, A., Luaces, M.R., Parama, J.R., Viqueira, J.R.R.: Collecting and publishing large multiscale geographic datasets. Softw.-Pract. Exp. **37**(12), 1319–1348 (2007). http://onlinelibrary.wiley.com/doi/10.1002/spe.807/abstract
5. Brisaboa, N.R., Cortiñas, A., Luaces, M.R., Pol'la, M.: A reusable software architecture for geographic information systems based on software product line engineering. In: Bellatreche, L., Manolopoulos, Y. (eds.) MEDI 2015. LNCS, vol. 9344, pp. 320–331. Springer, Heidelberg (2015). doi:10.1007/978-3-319-23781-7_26
6. Brisaboa, N.R., Luaces, M.R., Places, Á.S., Seco, D.: Exploiting geographic references of documents in a geographical information retrieval system using an ontology-based index. GeoInformatica **14**(3), 307–331 (2010). http://link.springer.com/article/10.1007/s10707-010-0106-3
7. Clements, P., Northrop, L.: Software Product Lines: Practices and Patterns. Addison-Wesley, Boston (2002)
8. Kang, K.C., Cohen, S.G., Hess, J.A., Novak, W.E., Peterson, A.S.: Feature-Oriented Domain Analysis (FODA) feasibility study. Distribution **17**(November), 161 (1990). http://www.sei.cmu.edu/reports/90tr021.pdf
9. Kästner, C., Thum, T., Saake, G., Feigenspan, J., Leich, T., Wielgorz, F., Apel, S.: FeatureIDE: a tool framework for feature-oriented software development. In: 2009 IEEE 31st International Conference on Software Engineering, pp. 611–614. IEEE (2009). http://ieeexplore.ieee.org/lpdocs/epic03/wrapper.htm?arnumber=5070568
10. Laurini, R., Thompson, D.: Fundamentals of Spatial Information Systems, 1st edn. Academic Press, London (1992)
11. Longley, P.A., Goodchild, M.F., Maguire, D.J.: Geographic Information Science and Systems, edicin: revised edn. Blackwell Publication, Hoboken (2015)
12. Luaces, M.R., Brisaboa, N.R., Paramá, J.R., Viqueira, J.R.: A generic framework for GIS applications. In: Kwon, Y.-J., Bouju, A., Claramunt, C. (eds.) W2GIS 2004. LNCS, vol. 3428, pp. 94–109. Springer, Heidelberg (2005). doi:10.1007/11427865_8. http://link.springer.com/chapter/10.1007/11427865_8
13. Luaces, M.R., Pérez, D.T., Fonte, J.I.L., Cerdeira-Pena, A.: An urban planning web viewer based on AJAX. In: Vossen, G., Long, D.D.E., Yu, J.X. (eds.) WISE 2009. LNCS, vol. 5802, pp. 443–453. Springer, Heidelberg (2009). doi:10.1007/978-3-642-04409-0_43. http://link.springer.com/chapter/10.1007/978-3-642-04409-0_43
14. Meinicke, J., Thüm, T., Schröter, R., Benduhn, F., Saake, G.: An overview on analysis tools for software product lines. In: Proceedings of the 18th International Software Product Line Conference on Companion Volume for Workshops, Demonstrations and Tools - SPLC 2014, pp. 94–101. ACM Press, New York, September 2014. http://dl.acm.org/citation.cfm?id=2647908.2655972
15. Places, Á.S., Brisaboa, N.R., Fariña, A., Luaces, M.R., Paramá, J.R., Penabad, M.R.: The Galician virtual library. Online Inf. Rev. **31**(3), 333–352 (2007). http://www.emeraldinsight.com/doi/full/10.1108/14684520710764104

16. Pohl, K., Böckle, G., Linden, F.V.D.: Software Product Line Engineering, vol. 49. Springer-Verlag New York, Inc., New York (2005). http://www.springerlink.com/index/10.1007/3-540-28901-1

17. Schmidt, D.C.: Guest editor's introduction: model-driven engineering. Computer **39**(2), 25–31 (2006). http://dx.doi.org/10.1109/MC.2006.58

18. Weiss, D.M., Clements, P.C., Krueger, C.W.: Software product line Hall of Fame. In: SPLC 2006: Proceedings of the 10th International Software Product Line Conference, pp. 237–237 (2006). http://ieeexplore.ieee.org/lpdocs/epic03/wrapper.htm?arnumber=1691614

19. Worboys, M.F., Duckham, M.: GIS: A Computing Perspective, 2nd edn. CRC Press, Boca Raton (2004)

Heterogeneous Data Integration Using Web of Data Technologies

Danielle Ziébelin[1(✉)], Kim Hobus[2], Philippe Genoud[1], and Sylvain Bouveret[1]

[1] Université Grenoble-Alpes CNRS LIG, IMAG building - 700 avenue Centrale,
Domaine Universitaire, 38401 Grenoble St Martin d'Hères, France
`{Danielle.Ziebelin,Philippe.Genoud,Sylvain.Bouveret}@imag.fr`
[2] Yukon Water Board, Suite 106, 419 Range Road, Whitehorse, YT Y1A 3V1, Canada
`Kim.Hobus@gov.yk.ca`
`http://www.liglab.fr/fr/presentation/equipes/steamer`,
`http://www.yukonwaterboard.ca`

Abstract. The Coordinated Online Information Network (COIN) is a spatial data infrastructure (SDI) which provides an online network of resources to share, use and integrate information of geographic locations in North Canada. COIN incorporates semantic web technology that integrates, publishes and visualizes time series water data allowing users to access a multitude of datasets in order to compare the data and draw conclusions. COIN utilizes a number of standards from OGC (Open Geospatial Consortium) and W3C (Resource Description Framework, RDF, Web Ontology Language OWL, SPARQL query language for RDF) and GeoSPARQL for geospatial query). COIN benefits from generic ontologies transforming data into semantics, enriching data sets and making the data available and interoperable via WFS and WMS standards. These principles facilitate publication and exchange of data across the web, increasing transparency and interpretability. Through modernized data submission and retrieval we hope to break down the silos of data, allowing users to visualize time series water quality and hydrometric data from multiple sources to increase knowledge in relationship to impacts on Yukon water.

1 Introduction

In the domain of the environment, the study of the evolution of observation data is a central task; it is essential for researchers to review and compare other data. However, the heterogeneity of models, data, metadata and formats and their change over time, remains a major difficulty in integrating different sources. Currently, after the tremendous growth of Web 2.0, we are witnessing an evolution of the World Wide Web to what the W3C refers to as web data: a model for simple, flexible and powerful data. The Resource Description Framework (RDF) [1], is based on web infrastructure and facilitates publication and exchange of data across the web. The representation models and the ontologies, expressed in RDFS (RDF Schema) [2] and OWL [3], give a semantics to data. In this paper, we present how data sources could be integrated in a RDF graph,

© Springer International Publishing AG 2017
D. Brosset et al. (Eds.): W2GIS 2017, LNCS 10181, pp. 35–47, 2017.
DOI: 10.1007/978-3-319-55998-8_3

visually presented in a time series format, and processed by associating a semantic model from ontologies, enriched by linking to other data sets.

Advanced hydrological science suggested new data networks, spatial and temporal heterogeneity in hydrologic processes, field observations and experiments with complex model www.cuahsi.org, http://cleaner.ncsa.uiuc.edu, www.watersnet.org. Comprehensive infrastructures are used to capitalize on advances in information technology, data networks, digital sensors, software and middleware services and tools https://www.nsf.gov/pubs/2007/nsf0728/index.jsp

COIN was developed in order to help Yukon Water Board officials in their evaluation of water license applications. Officials need to synthesize multiple information concerning a particular area and the immediate surrounding area. COIN utilizes different technologies necessary for its implementation and according to the OGC and W3C web services description and orchestration recommendations, COIN uses: XML, HTTP, WFS (web feature service), WCS (Web Coverage Service), WMS (Web Map Service), and CSW (Catalog *Service* for the Web). For observations and measurements: SensorML, O&M ISO 19156 were studied. For the exchange of hydrological time-series, as we did in COIN, WaterML 2.0 is the standard exchange format that we used. Our case study focused on the Yukon ecosystems, biological, chemical and physical data come either from water monitoring stations or sampling results. The purpose of these data sets is to help researchers to answer questions about water regulation, water quality, water management, and identify changes in the Yukon environment. Over the years a number of datasets have been collected, sometimes different types and forms, stored in various file formats. For easy operation, we propose a semantic web architecture that follows the Semantic Web stack [4], implements processing functionalities in our application with queries, ontologies, inference rules and analysis services based on an RDF format and then links them to other external data sources. COIN was financed by Natural Resource Canada (NRCAN) and with the help of Gubala Consulting.

2   Architecture of COIN

Data web sites and services are developed in a complex context of natural resources such as environmental and water resources, other resources such as energy, fiscal, foreign, development, security, spatial planning, water resources, investment, and regulations at national and international levels. In Yukon these applications cover several fields of knowledge including natural and technical sciences, social sciences, political sciences, legal studies, and information technologies (Yukon Water Board (YWB), Geomatics Yukon Oil and Gas board). The challenge of this project is that user questions, however simple they may appear, will mostly require elements and expertise from these different fields to be properly answered. The COIN project brings together experts from a wide range of disciplines in order to ensure that data web sites and services are collected, stored and made accessible in the most useful way in order to correspond to user needs. The goal of COIN is to provide users the best possible information, in a simple and flexible way using an ontology-based platform. To accomplish this goal, COIN will assess sources of data and information and conduct analyses of appropriate methods and services in order to provide data information and analysis. The COIN project is built upon the concepts of data description and methods description. These concepts of data and methods and process description are integrated into the global spatial data infrastructure (Fig. 2). COIN project has strong links to the efforts of the current Yukon Water Board, Yukon Geomatics, Oil and Gas department projects where publishing data platforms are being developed.

Thus the main objectives of COIN can be summarized as follows:

- Identification and definition of user groups and their requirements;
- Consolidation of relevant data on existing data bases;
- Determination of appropriate methods, tools and services to satisfy user requirements;
- Development of knowledge-based platforms integrating information on data and methods/tools/services with a user interface capable of answering questions. This paper deals in particular with the architecture and the web of data technology used to develop COIN's knowledge based platform.

The basic idea of open and shared data is to establish a way to create an open and extendable infrastructure, which gives free access to information, its use and re-use. That means nonproprietary formats with low barriers and an open data license to ensure the possible re-use by anyone. It is crucial to link information and data with their context as it creates new knowledge. Tim Berners-Lee in 2010 [5] presented his 5* model to explain the cost and the benefit of such architecture:

'*' Information is available on the Web (any format) under an open license
'**' Information is available as structured data (e.g. Excel instead of an image scan of a table)
'***' Non-proprietary formats are used (e.g. CSV instead of Excel)
'****' URI identification is used so that people can point at individual data
'*****' Data is linked to other data to provide context

In the W3C linked Data Cookbook [6] W3C recommend the following steps to publish data: (1) Identify, (2) Model, (3) Name, (4) Describe, (5) Convert, (6) Publish, and (7) Maintain.

To meet these objectives, we chose to build a triple store web application, as a web of data approach. According to the W3C, web services are self-contained and self-described application components using XML and HTTP for communication with other applications by using open protocols [7]. To be OGC compliant the web services need to be developed in the following way:

- for spatial data WFS for vector and discrete data,
- WMS for image and maps,
- CSW for catalogue service and metadata
- WCS for continuous and raster data access.

Web services are essential in the orchestration of internet-based workflows. Currently, two main architectural styles are most commonly used: SOA and REST. SOA services use remote procedure calls to invoke functions on remote systems. REST, or

Representational State Transfer, is an alternative architectural model where each resource has a URI. We have developed the following features:

- Interactive map of Yukon
- Display hydrometric data in a graph as well as allow for downloading data
- Display water quality data in a table or graph
- Search water quality data by chemical as well as by geographic area
- Set data submission standards for water quality data
- Filter map layers to anything within a geographic area
- Display and search Yukon Water Board (YWB) water license information
- Display water flow direction
- Link to Wikipedia for information regarding chemistry
- Tool to determine water allocated within a watershed.

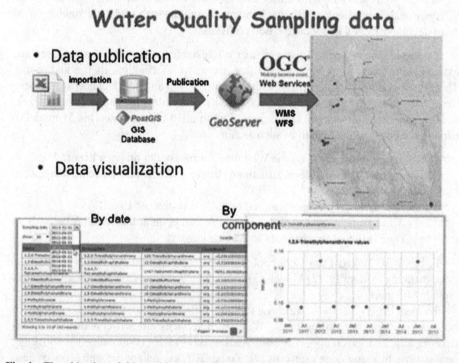

Fig. 1. The objective of this tool is to help the public, government, First Nation governments, and licensing officers to answer questions about water quality, water management and water allocations. To reach this objective we created an online information network with an ontology-based interface to visualize data and information source content

Figure 2 represents the components typically used in a Semantic Web infra-structure. A survey of Semantic Web applications described in the literature and their components is presented in W3C site, our architecture follows those principles: to publish heterogeneous data sources, RDF graph dereferences content, URIs serve as unique identifiers and are used to identify the resources. W3C developed specifications for standardized

RDF model, but, there are several implementations of triplestores and APIs for RDF, and processing SPARQL queries. Ontology languages such as OWL give semantics to RDF data, reasoners process domain ontologies and make inferences similar to rule engines. The user interface enables users to interact with Semantic Web data.

3 COIN Data

Numerous datasets are available from different sources in different formats i.e. database, excel, and pdf. Figure 1 presents an example of sampling stations: a set of measures at different dates, in different locations and with different technology. The COIN application can then make this data accessible to users in an easy way with a graphical web user interface using maps. According to the OGC and W3C web services description and orchestration recommendations, COIN uses: XML, HTTP, WFS, WCS, WMS, and CSW as mentioned above. For observations and measurements: SWE [8] and SOS [9], SensorML [10], O&M ISO 19156 [11] and for exchange hydrological time-series, WaterML 2.0 [12] is the standard exchange format. GeoSciML [13] is a standard of data format. These are the principles that we applied to environmental data on water quality in northern Canada and which were used to study the impact on water in the Yukon Territory [14].

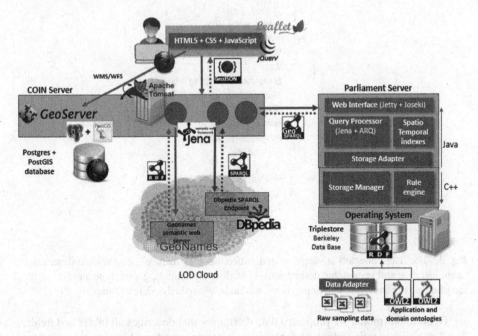

Fig. 2. The architecture shows how the different elements are organized. The RDF triple store for storing and integrating spatiotemporal datasets and the use of the web services provide access to the map and visualization interfaces though GIS layers. The RDF representation with the ontology is connected though data on the web.

The objective is to store different and heterogeneous types of observations collected by different structures: hydrometric stations, water license applications, water quality analysis etc.). These data structures which store selected fields, values and tables are the key elements of the data model. To build our system and make these heterogeneous format interoperable, we propose a data model that describes all tables and fields. The data series identify which variables have been measured at which locations and for what time stamps or periods. The data series are sets of observation values with specific properties (continuous or discontinuous measurements, unit). These data series illustrate the dataflow. Derivations and estimations are inferred by processing these data values. An appropriate method allows to obtain computed data values, provide logical grouping of data and make explicit the relationship between different monitoring and observation sites. It is critical that the different data sources are carefully documented and annotated with an adequate metadata structure. This structure will be used by different actors to collect data sets, this practice will document an easy access to the information (Fig. 3).

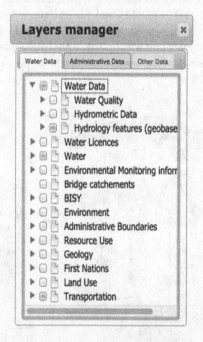

Fig. 3. The data collected at sampling and collecting sites include: geographical description (administrative and geographic description), of station, of monitoring sites, type and size of the sampling area (ponds, lakes, springs, rivers, wetlands, watersheds), date of sampling.

To build our model we propose a data dictionary that describes all tables and fields. The data series identify which variables have been measured at which locations and for what time stamps or periods. The data series are sets of observation values with specific properties (data values could be continuous or discontinuous, measurements, unit). These data series illustrate the dataflow. Derivations and estimations are inferred associated to these data values. It is critical that the different data sources are carefully documented and annotated with an adequate metadata structure. This structure will be used by different actors to collect data sets, this practice will document an easy access to the information.

The aim of open and linked data is to make accessible the datasets on a website but also to connect them to other scientific, economic, social and possibly political data sources in relationships with these elements. COIN's datasets provide different representation of sites: raw data, water quality, water microbiological information, environmental status of the site, information about agricultural and mining waste etc. from different land and territory status. In order to ensure that these data sets are available to be reused and correlated to other data sets, they must be available as open and linked data. The initiative of open and linked data (Linked Open Data) [15] follows this line, whose principles were set out by Tim Berners-Lee [16]:

(1) use of URIs (Uniform Resource Identifiers) to name (identify) things,
(2) use of HTTP URIs to consult these addresses,
(3) when a URI is accessed, provision of useful information using open standards (RDF, SPARQL, …), and
(4) inclusion of links to other URIs in order to discover more linked data.

4   Ontologies and Models

To model data in the form of an RDF graph, an OWL ontology has been specifically defined for this application. This ontology includes a number of classes and properties for representing observational data. To represent spatial information (coordinates of sampling sites, geometry regions) we relied on the GeoSPARQL standard proposed by OGC [17, 18]. Figure 4 shows in the form of a UML diagram the various classes and relationships (owl: ObjectProperties) defined for our application. The standards used in

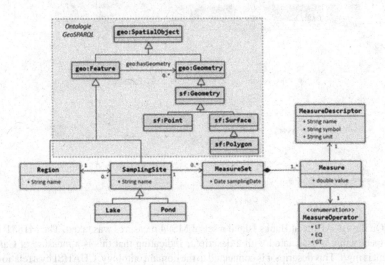

Fig. 4. The ontology of the application and its links with GeoSPARQL ontology.

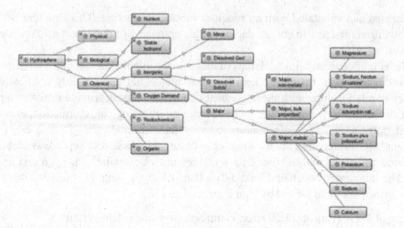

Fig. 5. An extract of the ontology of the CUAHSI hydrosphere. Only the classes corresponding to the major metal concepts are developed in this hierarchy.

the Semantic Web are RDF Schema, the ontology language, OWL a selection of ontology constructs are explained based on our example {namely rdfs:subClassOf, owl:sameAs and property chains. The rdfs:subClassOf construct can be used to model class hierarchies, the rdfs:subClassOf property. Another construct is that of owl:sameAs which can be used to specify that two resources are identical. OWL enables complex modelling constructs, such as cardinality restrictions, disjoint classes, constraint validation, so reasoners are able with a knowledge base to check the consistency of the knowledge base and to infer new statements based on existing ones.

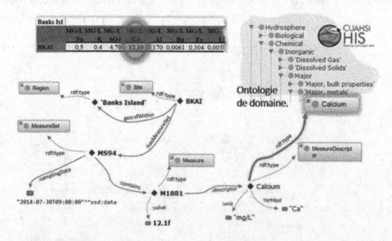

Fig. 6. On the BKAI site at Banks Island a set of MS94 measures was taken. The M1881 12.10 measurement value is associated with a descriptor indicating that this is a measure of Calcium and its unit is mg/l. This descriptor is connected to the domain ontology. CUAHSI by a relationship rdf:type.

We have extended our application ontology with a general ontology from hydrology used by the Consortium of Universities for the Advancement of Hydrologic Science (CUAHSI) [19].

This ontology defines a taxonomy that can structure hierarchically more than 4,000 words describing physical, chemical and biological measures related to water. It is used by the System Information CUAHSI (CUAHSI-HIS Hydrologic Information System) and consists of a set of servers and databases connected to client applications such as web services to facilitate the discovery of time series data collected at a given point. We have taken this ontology, defined in tabular form, to translate it as an OWL class hierarchy (Fig. 5). The use of this ontology in our model is made by combining corresponding measures in the terminology of CUAHSI with the descriptor measures identified during sampling (Fig. 6).

5   Exploring and Analysing Data

To publish data and to use Linked Data principles, the system provides a query language SPARQL [20] and a web service for executing queries over the Linked Data sets or resources. This service is called a SPARQL endpoint; it supports the query language SPARQL and accesses resources by using the corresponding SPARQL protocol.

5.1   Sparql Queries

We follow the official W3C specification to use SPARQL [21]. SPARQL is based on an evaluation function that maps a SPARQL expression and a set of RDF triples to obtain a set of valuations. Our formalization includes query language and query semantics in order to:

1. integrate different hydrometric datasets from different hydrometric stations;
2. filter different data from different water uses and licenses (agricultural, industrial, mining etc.) and
3. combine spatial queries in order, for example, to find the watersheds from a water license and calculate the amount of water allocated for that watershed (by using web service).

5.2   Linked Data Queries

Queries through the web by using linked data are specific because they allow for infinitely large sets of RDF triples and in consequence the resulting sets of valuations may be too many for the user to check, rank and evaluate. The results need to be synthesized and to be presented in a compact format. Using semantic annotations could be helpful and user-friendly. Federated query processing approaches expand SPARQL endpoint and build data workflows from different open data sources in order to make specific queries manageable and relevant. We did some experiments with the framework SILK [22] to link the different data sources that we found. SILK allows combinations of concepts in a global model, combining them in a relevant way.

5.3   GeoSPARQL

To explore and analyze the observational data thus represented, we used a web mapping interface for data queries through SPARQL and its spatial extension GeoSPARQL.

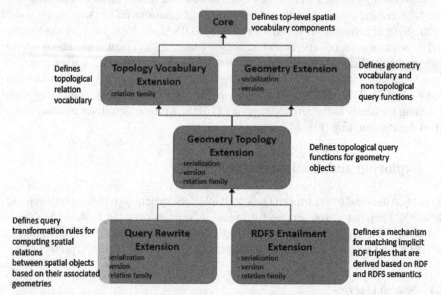

Our sampling results, stored in excel, were converted to RDF and stored in a specially designed database for storage and data recovery, called triplestore. Although published in 2012, few triplestores currently support the standards GeoSPARQL [23], Strabon [24], USeekM [25] and Parliament [26]. Our choice of triplestore architecture fell on Parliament, which has a relatively good balance between ease of installation and use, supports GeoSPARQL and has acceptable performance (although far from the performance offered by the spatial databases [27]).

On the Parliament server, an RDF graph is created in which are loaded:

- Ontologies used: the domain ontology (prefix cuahsionto :), the application ontology (ccionto :) prefix;
- Observational data from Excel files and converted into RDF using vocabularies defined by previous ontology and GeoSPARQL vocabulary for their spatial dimension.

When loading, Parliament automatically performs a number of inferences: RDFS inference over a number of OWL inferences (equivalent classes or properties; inverse properties: symmetrical, transitive or functional). Once loaded, the data can be queried via GeoSPARQL requests transmitted (via http) to the access point of the Parliament server (Jetty server + Joseki).

The interface of the COIN application allows the user to visualize the different sampling sites on an interactive map. The selection of a sampling site on the map provides access to the various comments made at each site. In the dialog box that appears the user has three tabs (Fig. 7) that allow the user:

- To filter the measures to display. Filtering is achieved through the hierarchy of concepts of the domain ontology. The RDFS inferences made in loading data help to automatically add a link ("rdfs:subClassOf") between each superclass of the Cuashi ontology to the descriptors measures. Only comments with a measurement concept as a descriptor are displayed, with a subclass descriptor of the selected concepts.
- To view all the comments for a given date.
- To view all the comments for a given measurement (time series).

```
PREFIX rdfs: <http://www.w3.org/2000/01/rdf-schema#>
PREFIX geo: <http://www.opengis.net/ont/geosparql#>
PREFIX geof: <http://www.opengis.net/def/function/geosparql/>
PREFIX coin: <http://coin.yukonwaterboard.ca/ont/coinOnto#>
PREFIX cuahsiOnto: <http://coin.yukonwaterboard.ca/ont/cuashiOnto#>
SELECT ?s, ?name
WHERE {
    ?s a coin:WaterQualityStation;
       rdfs:label ?l ;
       geo:hasGeometry [
           geo:asWKT ?ptWKT
       ].
    ?ws a coin:WaterShed;
        rdfs:label "Takhini";
        geo:hasGeometry [
            geo:asWKT ?rGeom
        ].
    FILTER (geof:sfWithin(?ptWKT,?rWKT))

}
```

```
?s coin:hasMeasureSet ?ms.
?ms coin:hasMeasure ?m.
?m coin:mDescriptor ?md.
?md rdf:type cuahsiOnto:MinornonMetal.
?m coin:mValue ?val.

FILTER (?val >=10.0)
```

Fig. 7. Filtering observations using the domain concepts of hierarchy are displayed as comments regarding Minor non metals.

A second enrichment of the initial data that allows their representation in the form of an RDF graph allows the ability to link with other external data sets published, respecting the principles of open and linked data. To demonstrate the potential of such enrichment we linked our data represented using our domain ontology with data from DBpedia [28]. With the links to DBpedia, the user can access additional information that the application will look for dynamically in the web data. The DBpedia link allows for a given observation in Wikipedia to provide a description of the item measured.

Furthermore, the use of GeoSPARQL allows for queries combining both a spatial component and a semantic component. For example, the following query "find the water quality stations in a Takhini watershed that have a value for a heavy metal whose value is greater than 10.0 mg/l and that are less than 10 km from a First nation feature" can be expressed using a GeoSPARQL query (Fig. 8):

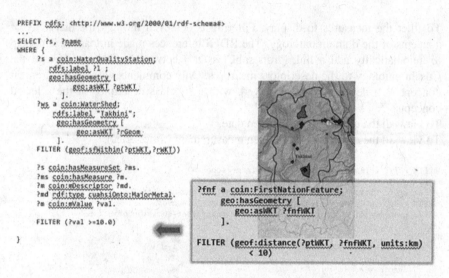

```
PREFIX rdfs: <http://www.w3.org/2000/01/rdf-schema#>
...
SELECT ?s, ?name
WHERE {
    ?s a coin:WaterQualityStation;
        rdfs:label ?l ;
        geo:hasGeometry [
            geo:asWKT ?ptWKT
        ].
    ?ws a coin:WaterShed;
        rdfs:label "Takhini";
        geo:hasGeometry [
            geo:asWKT ?rGeom
        ].
    FILTER (geof:sfWithin(?ptWKT,?rWKT))

    ?s coin:hasMeasureSet ?ms.
    ?ms coin:hasMeasure ?m.
    ?m coin:mDescriptor ?md.
    ?md rdf:type cuahsiOnto:MajorMetal.
    ?m coin:mValue ?val.

    FILTER (?val >=10.0)

}
```

```
?fnf a coin:FirstNationFeature;
    geo:hasGeometry [
        geo:asWKT ?fnfWKT
    ].

FILTER (geof:distance(?ptWKT, ?fnfWKT, units:km)
        < 10)
```

Fig. 8. An additional spatial query has been added to the query in Fig. 7.

6   Conclusion

The application described in this article provides a means to analyze and publish hydrologic and environmental observation data. The results of COIN's analysis enable us to understand better how the water constituents move through the watersheds. COIN software shows how semantic heterogeneity in heterogeneous data can be easily accessed and interpreted by using the web of data techniques. Beyond the analyses and the computing of data time series the system allows the user's questions to be answered by using ontologies and spatial relations. Additional linked data extend COIN's analysis to quantify human modification and land use effects on hydrologic and hydrochemical water information. The additional information included by linking data techniques increases the ability of the system to answer these types of question and greatly facilitates extensive analysis.

References

1. Cyganiak, B., Wood, D., Lanthaler, M.: RDF 1.1 Concepts and Abstract Syntax. W3C Recommendation (2014). http://www.w3.org/tr/rdf11-concepts/. Accessed 25 Feb 2014
2. Brickley, D., Guha, R.V.: RDF vocabulary description language 1.0: RDF Schema. W3C Recommendation (2004). http://www.w3.org/tr/rdf-schema/. Accessed 10 Feb 2004
3. Hitzler, P., Krötzsch, M., Parsia, B., Patel-Schneider, P.F., Rudolph, S.: OWL 2 Web Ontology Language Primer (2nd edn.). W3C Recommendation (2012). http://www.w3.org/tr/owl2-primer/. Accessed 11 Dec 2012
4. W3C 2005, Semantic Web Stack. https://www.w3.org/Consortium/techstack-desc.html
5. http://5stardata.info/en/
6. W3C linked Data Cookbook

7. Bizer, C., Heath, T., Berners-Lee, T.: Linked data – the story so far. Int. J. Semant. Web Inf. Syst. **5**(3), 1–22 (2009)
8. OGC Standard: New generation sensor web enablement. Sensors **11**(3), 2652–2699 (2011)
9. OGC Standard. Sensor Observation Service (2008). Accessed 29 Oct 2008
10. www.opengeospatial.org/standards/sensorml
11. http://www.opengeospatial.org/standards/om
12. www.opengeospatial.org/standards/waterml
13. www.geosciml.org/
14. Lim, D., Smol, J., Douglas, M.: Recent environmental changes on Banks Island (N.W.T., Canadian Arctic) quantified using fossil diatom assemblages. J. Paleolimnol. **40**(1), 385–398 (2008)
15. Bizer, C., Heath, T., Berners-Lee, T.: Linked data - the story so far. Int. J. Semant. Web Inf. Syst. **5**(3), 1–22 (2009)
16. Berners-Lee, T.: Linked data – design issues (2006). http://www.w3.org/DesignIssues/ LinkedData.html. Revised 2009
17. Open Geospatial Consortium. OGC GeoSPARQL - A Geographic Query Language for RDF Data (2012). https://portal.opengeospatial.org/files/?artifact_id=47664
18. Battle, R., Kolas, D.: GeoSPARQL: enabling a geospatial semantic web with parliament and GeoSPARQL. Semant. Web J. **3**(4), 355–370 (2012)
19. Couch, A., Hooper, R., Pollak, J., Martin, M., Seul, M.: Enabling water science at the CUAHSI water data center. In: 7th International Congress on Environmental Modelling and Software, San Diego, California, USA (2014)
20. https://www.w3.org/TR/rdf-sparql-query/
21. W3C Recommendation. http://www.w3.org/TR/sparql11-query/. Accessed Mar 2013
22. http://silk-framework.com/
23. Athanasiou, S., Bezati, L., Giannopoulos, G., Patroumpas, K., Skoutas, D.: Market and Research Overview. GeoKnow Deliverable 2.1.1 (2013)
24. Kyzirakos, K., Karpathiotakis, M., Koubarakis, M.: Strabon: a semantic geospatial DBMS. In: Cudré-Mauroux, P., et al. (eds.) ISWC 2012. LNCS, vol. 7649, pp. 295–311. Springer, Heidelberg (2012). doi:10.1007/978-3-642-35176-1_19
25. https://www.w3.org/2001/sw/wiki/USeekM
26. https://www.w3.org/2001/sw/wiki/Parliament
27. Patroumpas, K., Giannopoulos, G., Athanasiou, S.: Towards GeoSpatial semantic data management: strengths, weaknesses, and challenges ahead. In: Proceedings of the 22nd ACM SIGSPATIAL International Conference on Advances in Geographic Information Systems, Dallas, Texas, USA (2014)
28. Lehmann, J., Isele, R., Jakob, M., Jentzsch, A., Kontokostas, D., Mendes, P.N., Hellmann, S., Morsey, M., van Kleef, P., Auer, S., Bizer, C.: DBpedia – a large-scale, multilingual knowledge base extracted from Wikipedia. Semant. Web J. **6**(2), 167–195 (2015)

Paths and Navigation

Design Patterns for Modelling Life Trajectories in the Semantic Web

David Noël[1(✉)], Marlène Villanova-Oliver[1], Jérôme Gensel[1], and Pierre Le Quéau[2]

[1] LIG, University of Grenoble Alpes, 38000 Grenoble, France
{david.noel,marlene.villanova-oliver,jerome.gensel}@imag.fr
[2] PACTE, University of Grenoble Alpes, 38000 Grenoble, France
pierre.le-queau@univ-grenoble-alpes.fr

Abstract. Most of the existing approaches for trajectory modelling propose to enrich structured spatiotemporal trajectories with semantics. In social sciences, the term of "trajectory" is often used to describe some evolution that is not necessarily related to some geographical movement. In this paper, we propose ontological design patterns that (i) allow modelling multiple spatial or aspatial trajectories and (ii) include explanatory factors for a better understanding of trajectory events. Algorithms for the exploitation of our patterns are also presented. As a case study, we model the multiple trajectories that compose a life trajectory having in mind to focus on and study residential choices. This is an important issue for decision makers and urban planning experts in metropolitan areas who need to better understand choices citizens make. We show how our trajectory model, once instantiated, can be exploited using temporal, spatial and thematic dimensions.

Keywords: Trajectory modelling · Life trajectory · Metaphorical trajectories · Design patterns · Semantic web · Residential choices

1 Introduction

Urban planning experts and decision makers face many challenges related to residential choices made by inhabitants of metropolitan areas. These choices are strongly influenced by the various phases individuals go through in their personal lives. As an example, in general and in Europe, couples with children prefer to live far from the metropolitan centers [5]. This exodus of working couples with (young) children towards peri-urban areas is one of the causes of important problems major cities have to solve in the field of urban planning. For instance, it leads satellite cities in the periphery of such metropolitan areas to provide different kinds of amenities (for instance, nurseries and schools) with adapted opening hours, but it also increases the time workers need to commute from home to work, which generates pollution and traffic congestion.

Reasons for residential choices can be better understood through a comprehensive approach for life trajectories of individuals that takes into account many decisive aspects of citizens' lives: familial, professional, etc. Then, in order to study the residential trajectory of an individual (the succession of its residential choices in time and space),

© Springer International Publishing AG 2017
D. Brosset et al. (Eds.): W2GIS 2017, LNCS 10181, pp. 51–65, 2017.
DOI: 10.1007/978-3-319-55998-8_4

such a trajectory should be considered as an integrated part of a broader vision of her/his life trajectory [19]. The life trajectory of an individual is thus composed of multiple semantic trajectories, each depending on a particular thematic point of view (residential, professional, familial…). The term "trajectory" obviously evokes a spatial dimension. If, most of the time, the spatiality of a trajectory relates to a geographical reference system, it sometimes refers to more abstract spaces, like trajectories studied in sociology and, more widely, in social sciences. For instance the notion of *career* defined by Howard Becker [4], "refers to the sequence of movements from one position to another". If the analogy with a geographical space is strong, we nevertheless consider that some trajectories are "ageographical", meaning that they cannot be exactly considered as geographical ones. A second point is that such a professional trajectory includes "both objective facts of social structure and changes in the viewpoints, motivations, and desires of the individual". Thus for Grafmeyer and Authier [6], a residential trajectory "tends to suggest that successive positions in a given set is not simply by chance, but rather are linked together by an intelligible order". Part of our objective is to elicit the explanatory factors or combinations of factors that have shaped a given life trajectory.

In the case of residential trajectories, we want to bring to light the underlying reasons why individuals move to a given place, at a specific moment of their lives. *External factors* can be found in the context surrounding the life trajectory (the evolution of the housing market or some changes in the surroundings of the housing, etc.). *Internal factors* are related to life circumstances of the individual: they are directly linked to the specific characteristics of one or more points of view in her/his life trajectory. For instance, one may observe that a family moves for a new apartment with an additional room because of a birth to come. Here, a *residential event* (the move) is – partly – explained by an *event* belonging to the family point of view. In this context, our work focuses specifically on highlighting cause and effect relationships between events that arise in the life of individuals.

One of our objectives is first to integrate in the same representation the multiple thematic points of view that belong to a single life trajectory, whether they are spatial or aspatial. Further, we plan to analyse and to compare parts of trajectories, whether they belong to the same or to different persons (*e.g.* compare someone's residential and professional trajectories, or compare residential trajectories of two individuals). To easily combine (parts of) trajectories, we need to represent them using the same concepts to structure information and, as far as possible, well-known frames of reference to characterize it. This latter point in particular encompasses time and space representation. We thus propose an approach based on ontology design patterns (ODP[1]) compatible with Semantic Web initiatives such as Timeline Ontology [14] or GeoSPARQL [13]. One of these ODP allows modelling both spatial and aspatial specific trajectories (*i.e.* a residential trajectory, a professional trajectory, etc.) as parts of one life trajectory ontology. A second ODP is dedicated to the representation of explanatory factors. Gathering these design patterns together and applying them as many times as needed in a design process leads to the production of an ontological representation of the different points of view

---

[1] http://ontologydesignpatterns.org/.

of people's life trajectory, including explanation about choices they made. Once filled, such an ontology can be used to explore, analyse and compare life trajectories.

This paper is organized as follows. In Sect. 2, we present related works that laid the foundation of our work. In Sect. 3, we describe the ontological design patterns (in RDF) we propose to build ontological models of trajectories composed of multiple thematic points of view, and that include explanatory factors for a better understanding of trajectory events. In Sect. 4, we present a set of algorithms that define how to produce a model (i.e. an RDF ontology) from our patterns. We show in Sect. 5 how the obtained ontology can be exploited (i.e. fulfilled and queried), before we conclude.

2 Related Work

2.1 Semantic Trajectory Modelling

Many semantic trajectory models have been proposed in the recent years, offering different solutions to enrich space-time trajectories of mobile objects[2]. Most of these models are based on a spatiotemporal segmentation of trajectories. For example, in one of the major works in the field [17], that follow Hägerstraand [7] and the "time-geography", these trajectories are structured through the concept of *stop*, which characterizes a part of a spatiotemporal trajectory where the object's position stays fixed, and the concept of *move* where, contrariwise, its position changes in time. Information about the trajectory is then added to these structures, such as the nature of the moving object, the mode of transportation during a *move*, or the visited places at a *stop*. This model is particularly adapted for characterizing a semantic evolution that is related to movements in a geographical space. Other researchers have modelled spatio-temporal trajectories through periods of trips and periods of activities [20].

Other design patterns, connected to the Semantic Web, have also been proposed. For example, [8] present a geo-ontology design pattern that allows describing a semantic trajectory as a sequence of spatiotemporal points, and which makes use of widely known upper level ontologies. In this pattern, the concept of *segment* is used to represent a portion of trajectory that gathers *fixes* together. A *fix* here is given as a spatiotemporal point indicating the position of a moving object at one instant in time. Krisnadhi et al. [10] propose a generalization[3] of this pattern by employing the notion of *place*, instead of *location/geo-coordinate*, to represent the location associated with a fix (this confirms the position defended in [8] that no granularity is imposed for the location associated with a fix). Compared to [17], at a conceptual level, a *segment* can cover the meaning of both *stop* and *move* concepts (considering that, at the logical level, the spatiotemporal information is not associated with the segment itself but rather with the fixes).

All these works propose a generic, high-level representation of trajectories. They mainly address the description of trajectories that have a strong spatiotemporal dimension, with an anchoring in a geographical space, and in which both the periods of stability

---

[2] Mobile objects can be of different sorts including people.

[3] http://ontologydesignpatterns.org/wiki/Submissions:Trajectory.

and of movement can be represented. It has to be noted that semantics is added using attributes attached to the main concepts of the trajectory (stop, move, segment, fix, etc.).

In [17], the authors also point out that: *"the term trajectory is sometimes used in a metaphorical sense to describe an evolution, although the evolution at hand is not related to physical movement"*. They call this kind of trajectories *metaphorical trajectories* in reference to *"the idea of an object (e.g. the person) moving in an abstract space"* and give the example of *a* career trajectory to illustrate it. Then they propose to simply model such a *metaphorical trajectory* using the conceptual model based on *stop* and *move,* transposing these two notions in the so-called *abstract space*. In this case, a given position in the abstract space is characterized by a *stop* in the trajectory. However, although the authors say nothing about it, it seems to us that the concept *move* has here a limited meaning in such metaphorical trajectories: the movement characterized by a *move* is difficult to translate in the abstract space (*e.g.* what does moving from one job position to another means from a spatial and temporal points of view?). In [16], Raubal also propose an approach based on time geography that allow to characterize an evolution of semantic over time in an abstract space. The proposed approach rest on an algebraic model and is not a design pattern using semantic web technology.

The other works we cite in Sect. 2.1 do not concretely address this issue of so-called *metaphorical trajectories* that are important in our context. In [8], the authors mention that social sciences fields (psychologists, anthropologists, geographers, traffic planners) have investigated human trajectories to better understand human behaviour. Nevertheless, the example of a human trajectory they give, based on their pattern, deals with a daily individual's trajectory data recorded by a handheld GPS receiver (*i.e.* is not a metaphorical trajectory and not a life-long trajectory).

The issues we address in this paper are closely related to previous approaches on life trajectory modelling, which refine and adapt the notion of trajectory to a specific context. In particular, the work conducted by Thériault *et al.* is a reference in this field. The space-time model for the analysis of life trajectories [18] is based on three different trajectories - residential, family and professional. Each of these trajectories is conceptually modelled by *episodes* – corresponding to stable statutes during a time interval - and *events* which alter one or more of these statutes. The conceptual model is based on a relational approach. Later, the model has been modified in order to determine the likelihood of an event occurring under certain conditions in a life trajectory [19]. These models are centred on the temporal aspect of residential choices: the focus is more on *when* people have moved at some place (depending on some life circumstances) than on the reasons *why they have chosen* the place where they have moved to.

Regarding our objective, these works show to have some limitations. First, in [18, 19], the support to the representation of integrated multiple trajectories is limited to three predefined points of view. If one could imagine that some other dimension could be added, the authors do not provide any methodological guidelines and support that help to perform it in an easy way. We aim at a more generic modelling approach able to support any relevant point of view that makes sense for studying life trajectory. Second, the works [8, 17] do not handle clearly the ageographical (i.e. non geographic) dimension of some trajectories and make therefore no recommendation for mixing and integrating such trajectories with geographical ones in the same model. For these reasons, these models and ontological design patterns are not fully adapted to our problematic.

Furthermore the different concepts used to segment a trajectory in these approaches (stop, move, segment, fix, etc.) do not exactly carry the meaning we need to study: the multiple thematic points of view that belong to the same life trajectory. Our problematic requires representing the *states* of the individuals, according to the different points of view, but also providing a representation of the *events* between these *states*. This event representation allows characterizing the transitions between states. Further, we claim that some influences exist between states and events of a trajectory that led to the appearance of new events. Such influences are *explanatory factors* that can make a trajectory more understandable. This leads us to consider works dealing with event and explanatory factors representation.

2.2   Modelling Events and Explanatory Factors

Beyond the description of the different states that compose a trajectory, there is a need for representing the events that have conducted to a change of state. In [10] the ODP Event Core[4] is proposed as a core, minimalistic, and generic pattern for representing any event. Basically, an event here occurs at a Place and Time, has participants, and is associated with other "non-essential information" such as names, URIs, textual descriptions, *etc.* Illustrations that are given mainly relate to some cultural or sports events. The meaning given here to an event does not exactly correspond to what we need to represent in our approach. We use the term *event* in the sense of life events, such as a move, a promotion, a new job, a birth, etc. Thus, what we call *Event* is to be understood as a transition between two states.

The Event Ontology[5] (EO) is an upper level ontology used to describe events at a generic level similarly to [15]. An interesting point is that it includes a property *factor* that "relates an event to a passive factor" (in this ontology a *factor* is considered as passive since it is not an *agent* that takes part in the event). Conversely, the property called *product* relates an event with anything that could be considered as a consequence of this event. These properties, which are used to represent cause and effect, are very high-level properties: they have no range. It means they relate an event to any class as a factor. In the case study we have chosen, for a better understanding of the trajectory itself and an elicitation of the motivations that have led to a residential move, we propose to structure what can be explanatory factors of events. We claim that specific classes and properties could be defined in order to characterize different kinds of influence events may have in the life trajectory: the birth of a child (i.e. an event) has probably influenced the move (i.e. another event) of the family. This leads us to consider and differentiate whether the cause of an event is internal to the individual's trajectory, or external (it is exogenous) or related to her/his social network (i.e. depending on the trajectory of some other individuals she/he is strongly related with). Such a typology for

---

[4] http://ontologydesignpatterns.org/wiki/Community:EventCore.
[5] http://motools.sourceforge.net/event/event.html.

representing cause of events intends to facilitate the analysis and the comparison of trajectories and their associated elements of explanation.

3 Design Patterns for Explainable Multiple Trajectories

3.1 The Ontology Design Pattern Trajectories

The Ontology Design Pattern Trajectories we propose is presented on Fig. 2. The main concepts that compose the trajectory are *episode* and *event*. An **episode** is a stable state seen from a thematic point of view during a time interval. A state is considered as stable when the values of all its descriptive attributes remain unchanged[6]. An **event** characterizes a transition between two stable states. Classes and relationships that compose the pattern are described below.

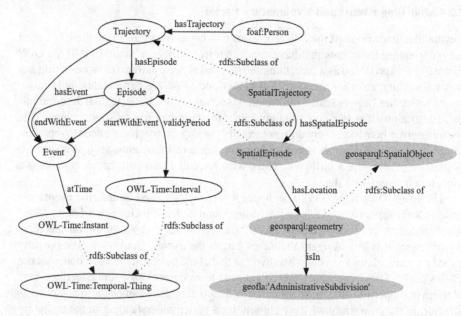

Fig. 1. The ontology design pattern for semantic trajectories

`Trajectory`. This class characterizes the trajectory of a given thematic point of view. It is linked to a `foaf:person` class through a property `hasTrajectory`. The use of the well-known friend of a friend[7] (foaf) ontology allows to link individuals with the proposed property. The use of this ontology is also a way to foster interoperability

---

[6] This modelling choice requires to choose carefully the information to represent (i.e. the relevant attributes), but also to determine the relevant degrees of precision. For instance, in our application case, regarding the rent of some accommodation, the precise amount might be less relevant than a range of values.

[7] http://xmlns.com/foaf/spec/.

between our model and social networks. The trajectory is related to the episodes and events that compose it through the property hasEpisode and hasEvent.

Episode. This class describes an episode of the trajectory. The property validityPeriod represents the episode duration that corresponds to a time interval between two instants t_s and t_e (as $t_s < t_e$). Each of these two instants corresponds to an event in the trajectory: an episode starts and ends with an event (startWith and EndWith *properties*). A non-strict order relation can be established between episodes using the algebra of Allen [1].

Event. This class characterizes an event of the trajectory. The property atTime associates an event with a chronon [1] relevant for the observed phenomenon (allowing to localize the event in time).

The temporal dimension of episodes and events is characterized using the OWL-Time ontology[8].

If the trajectory to model is a spatial trajectory, a more specific class characterizing episodes has to be used, the class SpatialEpisode.

SpatialEpisode. This class is a specialization of the Episode class. Since it carries the spatial component of the trajectory, the spatial episode is connected to the geosparql:geometry class of the geosparql ontology[9].

Finally, the location is related to the geofla ontology[10] of the French National Geographic Institute that describes the French administrative subdivisions. The use of this ontology is optional and obviously only relevant for case studies located in France.

This design pattern has been implemented in RDF/Turtle.

3.2   Explanatory Factors of Events

The second design pattern that we propose allows modelling explanatory factors of events. In our approach, we consider that life events can be explained either:

- by other life events: for instance, because Thomas had a promotion (event), he moved for a bigger apartment (event), or
- by the characteristics of an episode: for instance, because Thomas' apartment was too small (surface = 35 m^2, episode's characteristics), he moved to a bigger one (event). Combinations of such explanations are obviously possible: for instance, because *(i)* Thomas had a promotion (event), *(ii)* he had a baby (event) and *(iii)* his apartment was too small (surface = 35 m^2 and numberOfRoom = 1, episode's characteristics), then he moved to a bigger apartment (event).

Our design pattern is presented in Fig. 3. The classes and properties of this design pattern are described below. In this representation the class Event corresponds to the event to be explained.

Factor is a general class that characterizes an explanatory factor for an event. A factor is related to an event through a property hasFactor. The data property

---

[8] https://www.w3.org/TR/owl-time/.

[9] http://schemas.opengis.net/geosparql/.

[10] http://data.ign.fr/def/geofla/20140822.en.htm.

`Explanation` relates a `Factor` to a `String` that provides additional explanation about this particular factor, if needed. The data property `Weight` associates a `Factor` with an `Integer` that allows to express the weight of this particular factor on the explained event. When several explanatory factors exist for the same event, this is useful for a finer understanding of the influence of each.

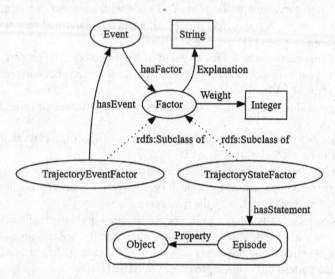

Fig. 2. Design pattern for explanatory factors of trajectory events

The class `Factor` is subsumed by two classes: `TrajectoryEventFactor` and `TrajectoryStateFactor`.

`TrajectoryEventFactor` characterizes an explanatory factor that has an explaining event. This explaining event belongs to the trajectory of any individual. For instance, Thomas' move (the explained event) could be explained by his promotion at work (a factor – explaining event – from his professional trajectory) or by his wife's promotion at work (a factor – explaining event – from his wife's professional trajectory). A `TrajectoryEventFactor` is therefore related to an *explaining* event through a relationship `hasEvent`. This class has two sub-classes (not presented on the figure): `InternalEventFactor` and `NetworkEventFactor` for supporting the examples given above.

`InternalEventFactor` is related to an explaining event that belongs to the trajectory of the same individual. In the previous example, the promotion of Thomas is therefore characterized by the `InternalEventFactor` Class.

`NetworkEventFactor` is related to an explaining event that belongs to the trajectory of another individual. In the previous example, the promotion of Thomas' wife is characterized by the `NetworkEventFactor` Class. The two (possibly indirectly) related individuals form consequently (a part of) a network. When possible, such relationships are expressed using the `foaf` ontology.

`TrajectoryStateFactor` characterizes an explanatory factor that has an explaining *statement* that describes a state in the trajectory of the individual. In our model, statements describing states are related to episodes. For instance, a residential move (the resulting event) is explained by some characteristics of the previous residential episode such as a too small number of rooms (the explaining statement). `Trajec-toryStateFactor` is therefore related to an *explaining* statement through a relationship `hasStatement`. This property uses RDF reification, a mechanism that allows making a statement about another statement (i.e. triple *subject-predicate-object* altogether is assigned a URI and treated as a resource about which additional statements can be made).

4 Exploitation of the Design Patterns

In this section, we show how our design patterns can be exploited to create a life trajectory model that supports the representation of both multiple thematic component trajectories and explanatory factors.

4.1 Modelling a First Trajectory

We present a simplified version of the algorithm that allows applying the proposed design pattern to create the first thematic trajectory of the model. The algorithm *InitializeModelTrajectory* creates a trajectory model (see Fig. 3) for a given point of view and according to its nature (spatial or not). The Boolean `isSpatial` is true if the trajectory is spatial, otherwise false. The String `viewStamp` is a relevant string for describing the point of view used to stamp the trajectory. For instance, we use the stamp "Residential" for the residential spatial trajectory.

The `HashTable EpisodeAttributes` is a `<<String,String>>` HashTable that stores each attribute (`AttName`) and its associated type (`AttType`). These couples of information characterize the episode of the thematic trajectory. For example, for the residential point of view, relevant attributes could be *HousingType (a string) and the NumberOfRooms* (an integer).

```
1. Boolean isSpatial
2. String viewStamp
3. HashTable<<String AttName, String AttType>> EpisodeAttributes

4. Algorithm InitializeModelTrajectory (viewStamp, isSpatial)
5.    Initialize (foaf:Person)
6.    CreateRelevantClassesAndRelations(isSpatial, viewStamp)
7.    Connect (foaf:Person, Trajectory, viewStamp)
8.    CharacterizeEpisodes (EpisodeAttributes)
9. End Algorithm
```

Algorithm 1 . InitializeModelTrajectory

The method `Initialize(foaf:Person)` (line 5) creates the foaf prefix in the ontology and initialize the foaf:Person class.

The method `CreateRelevantClassesAndRelations(isSpatial, viewStamp)` (line 6) creates the classes and relationships using the relevant part of the pattern according to the value of the Boolean `isSpatial`. If the Boolean valuates to false, the created classes are `Trajectory`, `Episode` and `Event` and the created relationships are `hasTrajectory`, `hasEpisode`, `hasEvent`, `endWith`, `startWith`. If the Boolean `isSpatial` is true, the classes `SpatialTrajectory` and `SpatialEpisode` are created instead of the aspatial version. In both cases, each class and relationship of the pattern is renamed at its creation time by prefixing its name with the String `viewStamp`.

The method `Connect (foaf:Person, Trajectory, viewStamp)` (line 7) creates a relationship between the `foaf:Person` class and the (just stamped) Trajectory class.

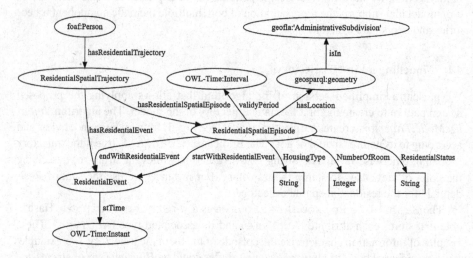

Fig. 3. The residential trajectory

The method `CharacterizeEpisodes(EpisodeAttributes)` (line 8) creates, for each pair of the HashTable `EpisodeAttributes`, the relevant predicate whose domain is the stamped `Episode` (or `SpatialEpisode`) class. This method creates a data property. For instance, for the pair <<*NumberOfRoom, Integer*>> the data property *NumberOfRoom* whose range is an *Integer* and whose domain is `ResidentialSpatialEpisode`, is created (see Fig. 3).

4.2   Modelling Multiple Trajectories

To build a more complex model that integrates the multiple points of view of a life trajectory, we propose a second algorithm. It works in the same way as for Algorithm 1, except that it does not create a new instance of a `foaf:Person` but associates this new trajectory with the existing class. Thus, in addition to the variables used in the previous algorithm, this one is using a String `PersonUri` that is the URI of a previously created `foaf:Person` class.

```
1. Boolean isSpatial
2. String viewStamp
3. HashTable<<String AttName,String AttType>> EpisodeAttributes
4. String PersonURI
5.
6. Algorithm AddTrajectory (viewStamp, isSpatial, PersonURI)
7.    CreateRelevantClassesAndRelations(isSpatial, viewStamp)
8.    Connect (PersonURI, Trajectory, viewStamp)
9.    CharacterizeEpisode (EpisodeAttributes)
10.   End Algorithm
```

Algorithm 2 . AddTrajectory

Figure 4 illustrates how two thematic trajectories, respectively stamped with A and B, are finally linked into the same model corresponding to the life trajectory of an individual. The class property *hasFactor* (see Sect. 3.2) that relates an *Event* to a *Factor* can then be used for each stamped Event class.

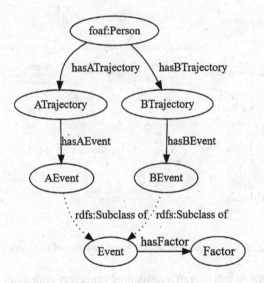

Fig. 4. Modeling of two thematic point of view

In the next section, we show through a case study how such an ontology, produced using our patterns, can be exploited.

5 Exploitation of the Ontology

5.1 Application to Residential Trajectory Data

The life trajectory model obtained using the design pattern was tested to store life trajectory data related to the residential choices and their explanation. Data were collected during a survey among 30 individuals in the French city of Grenoble metropolitan area. A semi-directed interview was conducted with each individual. During the interview, people were asked to explain their own trajectory as precisely as possible in a chronological way. The interviewer followed survey guidelines that help to collect useful data. Collected data were then used to fulfil an ontology model built from our design patterns. Our objective was to test the validity of the produced ontology and its expressiveness.

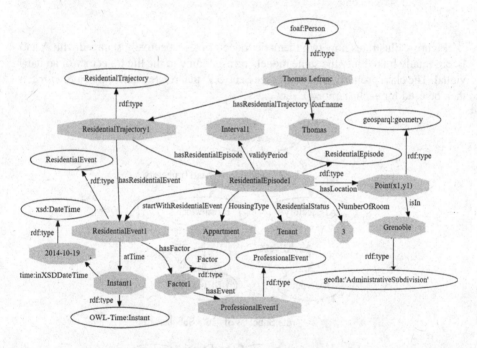

Fig. 5. An example of annotated instance of the model

Figure 5 presents an instance of a residential trajectory compliant with the ontology shown in Fig. 3. This is an excerpt of Thomas' residential trajectory (*ResidentialTrajectory1*) that includes a residential episode (*ResidentialEpisode1*) that started with Thomas' move (*ResidentialEvent1*) on 2014-10-19. During this residential episode, Thomas was a tenant of a three-room apartment. We know the location of the housing (*hasLocation*) that is in the Grenoble administrative division, in France. The model also tells us that the *ResidentialEpisode1* started with (*startwith*) the *ResidentialEvent1* whose one of the *factors* is a professional event (*ProfessionalEvent1*, a promotion, not shown here).

5.2   Querying Residential Trajectory Model

Once filled, the ontology can be exploited to query the multiple trajectories.

The multiple semantic points of view that compose the whole trajectory can be queried together. With respect to our case study, we give some queries example. The life trajectory model has been implemented in the parliament triple store[11] and the queries have been tested using the provided SPARQL endpoint. The prefix LTO (Life Trajectory Ontology) was used for this example. These queries allow to access the relevant resource(s) which are identified with an URI.

Q1: What are the explanatory factors of the residential event ResidentialEvent1 and what is the explanation associated with these factors?

```
1.  SELECT ?Factor ?Explanation
2.  WHERE {
3.  LTO:ResidentialEvent1  LTO:hasFactor  ?Factor .
4.  ?Factor  LTO:hasExplanation ?Explanation . }
```

This query returns the URI that corresponds to Factor1 and the associate explanation (see Fig. 1). From Factor1, one could navigate to the associated event (here ProfessionalEvent1).

Q2: Which residential events were influenced by a professional event?

```
1.  SELECT ?ResidentialEvent
1.  WHERE {
2.  ? ResidentialEvent LTO:hasFactor  ?Factor .
3.  ?Factor  LTO: hasEvent ?ProfessionalEvent . }
```

Q3: Which are the residential trajectories that pass through Grenoble?

Such a query illustrates how geographical information is used. The Grenoble entity is an instance of the class *commune* (and an administrative subdivision) in the French *geofla* ontology. The label of the Grenoble entity is *"GRENOBLE"@fr*. The *geofla* ontology and data on the administrative subdivision are available as linked data on the open data portal of the French National Geographic Institute[12] (IGN). The following query uses a SPARQL *service* to request the SPARQL endpoint[13] available on this portal.

```
1.  SELECT ?ResidentialTrajectory
2.  WHERE {
3.  ?ResidentialTrajectory  LTO:hasResidentialEpisode
    ?ResidentialEpisode .
4.  ResidentialEpisode  LTO:hasLocation ?Location .
5.  ?Location LTO:isIn ?commune .
6.  SERVICE <http://data.ign.fr/id/sparql> { ?commune rdfs:label
    "GRENOBLE"@fr . } }
```

Q4: What are the explanatory factors of the residential move to Grenoble after 2014? This spatio-temporal query involves the OWL-Time ontology and a SPARQL *filter*.

---

[11] http://parliament.semwebcentral.org/.

[12] http://data.ign.fr/.

[13] http://data.ign.fr/id/sparql/.

```
1.  SELECT ?Factor
2.  WHERE {
3.  ? ResidentialEvent  LTO:hasFactor ?Factor .
4.  ?ResidentialEisode LTO:startWithResidentialEvent
    ?ResidentialEvent  .
5.  ?ResidentialEvent  LTO:atTime ?Instant .
6.  ?Instant OWL-Time:inXSDDateTime ?date  .
7.  FILTER (?date > "2014"^^xsd:gYear) .
8.  ?ResidentialEpisode  LTO:hasLocation ?Location .
9.  ?Location LTO:isIn ?commune .
10. SERVICE <http://data.ign.fr/id/sparql> { ?commune rdfs:label
    "GRENOBLE"@fr . } }
```

6   Conclusion and Future Work

In this paper, we have proposed two ontological design patterns that allow modelling multiple spatial or aspatial trajectories and that include explanatory factors for a better understanding of trajectory events. The proposed ontological design patterns are related to several upper level ontologies in order to allow interoperability of the produced models with the web of data. We have also provided algorithms that exploit our patterns to build ontologies. As a case study, we have modelled the multiple trajectories that compose a life trajectory having in mind to study residential choices. Finally, we have shown how the trajectory model we get can be exploited using temporal, spatial and thematic dimensions using the SPARQL language.

One possible perspective of our work is to *rebuild* a model from the analysis of existing trajectories. The STEP ontology [12] propose to structure trajectories into spatiotemporal episodes gathering together raw data that share some characteristics. We may not manipulate the same kind of data (they use raw data concerning joggers runnings) but the adaptation of their principles to our context could lead to make some coarser-grain episodes emerge from a life trajectory. To achieve this, we will need to design algorithms exploiting data at multiple granularity levels using the connected upper level ontologies (OWL-Time and geosparl).

Acknowledgment. We would like to thank the Auvergne-Rhône-Alpes Region Council for his support (D. Noël Ph.D. Grant).

References

1. Allen, J.F.: Maintaining knowledge about temporal intervals. Commun. ACM **26**(11), 832–843 (1983). Alvares, L.O., Bogorny, V., Kuijpers, B., de Macelo, J.A.F., Moelans, B., Palma, A.T.: Towards semantic trajectory knowledge discovery. Data Min. Knowl. Discov. (2007)
2. Authier, J.Y., Bidet, J., Collet, A., Gilbert, P., Steinmetz, H.: État des lieux sur les trajectoires résidentielles (2012)
3. Battle, R., Kolas, D.: GeoSPARQL: enabling a geospatial semantic web. Semant. Web J. **3**(4), 355–370 (2011)

4. Becker, H.: Outsiders: studies in the sociology of deviance (1963)
5. Bonvalet, C., Laflamme, V., Arbonville, D.: Family and Housing: Recent Trends in France and Southern Europe. Bardwell Press, Cumnor (2009)
6. Grafmeyer, Y., Authier, J.Y.: Sociologie Urbaine. Armand Colin, Paris (2011)
7. Hägerstraand, T.: What about people in regional science? Pap. Reg. Sci. **24**(1), 7–24 (1970)
8. Hu, Y., et al.: A geo-ontology design pattern for semantic trajectories. In: Tenbrink, T., Stell, J., Galton, A., Wood, Z. (eds.) COSIT 2013. LNCS, vol. 8116, pp. 438–456. Springer, Heidelberg (2013). doi:10.1007/978-3-319-01790-7_24
9. Krisnadhi, A.A.: Ontology pattern-based data integration. Ph.D. thesis, Department of Computer Science and Engineering, Wright State University (2015)
10. Krisnadhi, A.A., Hitzler, P.: A Core Pattern for Events Workshop on Ontology and Semantic Web Patterns, 7th edn. – WOP 2016, Kobe, Japan, 18 October 2016
11. Krisnadhi, A.A., Hitzler, P., Janowicz, K.: A Spatiotemporal Extent Pattern based on Semantic Trajectories, Workshop on Ontology and Semantic Web Patterns, 7th edn. – WOP 2016, Kobe, Japan, 18 October 2016
12. Nogueira, T.P., Martin, H.: Querying semantic trajectory episodes. In: 4th ACM SIGSPATIAL International Workshop on Mobile Geographic Information Systems (MobiGIS 2015) 2015
13. OGC. OGC GeoSPARQL - A Geographic Query Langage for RDF Data (2012)
14. Raimond, Y., Abdallah, S.: The timeline ontology (2007). http://motools.sourceforge.net/timeline/timeline.html
15. Raimond, Y., Abdallah, S.: The event ontology (2007). http://motools.sourceforge.net/event/event.html
16. Raubal, M.: Representing concepts in time. In: Freksa, C., Newcombe, N.S., Gärdenfors, P., Wölfl, S. (eds.) Spatial Cognition 2008. LNCS (LNAI), vol. 5248, pp. 328–343. Springer, Heidelberg (2008). doi:10.1007/978-3-540-87601-4_24
17. Spaccapietra, S., Parent, C., Damiani, M.L., de Macedo, J.A., Porto, F., Vangenot, C.: A conceptual view on trajectories. Data Knowl. Eng. **65**(1), 126–146 (2008)
18. Thériault, M., Claramunt, C., Séguin, A.M., Villeneuve, P.: Temporal GIS and statistical modelling of personal lifelines. In: Richardson, D.E., van Oosterom, P. (eds.) Advances in Spatial Data Handling, pp. 433–449. Springer, Heidelberg (2002). doi:10.1007/978-3-642-56094-1_32
19. Thériault, M., Séguin, A.M., Aubé, Y., Villeneuve, P.Y.: A spatio-temporal data model for analysing personal biographies. In: Proceedings of the Tenth International Workshop on Database and Expert Systems Applications, pp. 410–418. IEEE (1999)
20. Zheni, D., Frihida, A., Ghezala, H.B., Claramunt, C.: A semantic approach for the modeling of trajectories in space and time. In: Heuser, C.A., Pernul, G. (eds.) ER 2009. LNCS, vol. 5833, pp. 347–356. Springer, Heidelberg (2009). doi:10.1007/978-3-642-04947-7_41

URAN: A Unified Data Structure for Rendering and Navigation

Stefan Funke[1]([✉]), Niklas Schnelle[1], and Sabine Storandt[2]

[1] University of Stuttgart, Stuttgart, Germany
funke@fmi.uni-stuttgart.de
[2] JMU Würzburg, Würzburg, Germany
storandt@informatik.uni-wuerzburg.de

Abstract. Current route planning services like Google Maps exhibit a clear-cut separation between the *map rendering* component and the *route planning* engine. While both rely on respective road network data, the route planning task is typically performed using state-of-the art data structures for speeding-up shortest/quickest path queries like Hub Labels, Arc Flags, or Transit Nodes, whereas the map rendering task usually involves a rendering framework like Mapnik or Kartograph. In this paper we show how to augment Contraction Hierarchies – another popular data structure for speeding-up shortest path queries – to also cater for the map rendering task. As a result we get a unified data structure (URAN) which lays the algorithmic foundation for novel map rendering and navigation systems. It also allows for customization of the map rendering, e.g. to accommodate different display devices (with varying resolution and hardware capabilities) or routing scenarios. At the heart of our approach lies a generalized graph simplification scheme derived from Contraction Hierarchies with a very lightweight augmentation for extracting (simplified) subgraphs. In a client-server scenario it additionally has the potential to shift the actual route computation to the client side, both relieving the server infrastructure as well as providing some degree of privacy when planning a route.

1 Introduction

For route planning and navigation, one typically relies on the availability of a map displaying all relevant roads and hence allowing to find shortest paths. Nowadays, mobile devices are often used as navigation systems and for displaying maps. As these devices typically have limited amount of memory, it is most often not desirable to store the complete map data locally but online map services provide the necessary data for the area of interest on demand. Common online map services like Google or Bing Maps explicitly decouple the *map rendering* from the *route planning* engine. Maps are typically provided as pre-rendered tiles or prepackaged tiles of vector graphic data for fixed zoom levels. The route planning engine on the other hand relies on a graph representation of the road network data. For every route planning query, the server computes the optimal

© Springer International Publishing AG 2017
D. Brosset et al. (Eds.): W2GIS 2017, LNCS 10181, pp. 66–82, 2017.
DOI: 10.1007/978-3-319-55998-8_5

route and sends this information to the client. Therefore, if the client loses its active internet connection, new queries cannot be answered – which is somewhat unsatisfying as we could always come up with some route just by visual inspection of the map. This separation of rendering and route planning induces unnecessary redundancy and network traffic. Moreover, current map rendering schemes are too restrictive and static. Tile based systems often allow only a small number of zoom levels (about 20) and only one or few predefined map renderings are available. OpenStreetMap (OSM) [1] offers five different map layers, see Fig. 1. Those maps are typically designed by coming up with handcrafted rules which determine what should be visible at a certain zoom level. For example, for cycle maps, large highways are pruned out early, while for cars large highways are very important and hence are visible also in a zoomed out view. Manually designing new rule sets to get suitable renderings for many possible user demands is impractical.

Fig. 1. Different map renderings of the same map section: "Standard", "Cycle Map", "Transport Map", "Humanitarian", "MapQuest Open".

Furthermore, while some years ago map data was primarily accessed via a web application on a desktop PC, nowadays there is a variety of different smartphones, laptops, tablets, etc. all with *very* different display resolutions (think of Retina displays), computational power and available network bandwidth. Hence dynamic adaptation to hardware capabilities is of utmost importance.

In this paper, we present a new scheme which lays the algorithmic foundations to solve these problems by unifying the rendering and routing aspects. This is conceptually nicer, guarantees consistency of the data, decreases the necessary bandwidth for data transmission in a server/client-architecture, and has the ability to adapt to different user devices, thereby closing the representative gap between the graph used for route planning and the respective visualization.

1.1 Related Work

There exist approaches [9] where part of the route planning task is shifted from the server to the clients. Here, the server transmits a concise and compressed synopsis of the portions of the graph relevant for the actual route query, and the client locally computes the respective route. Surprisingly, this is possible with very little data transfer. Still, this very same data (or an augmentation thereof) should also be instrumentable to produce a rendering of the map on the client side. We are not aware of any online route planner taking this integrated approach. The separate consideration of map rendering and route planning on their own has been the topic of numerous research papers, we will give a brief overview in Sect. 2.

1.2 Our Contribution

We present a Unified Rendering And Navigation data structure (URAN). At the heart of URAN lies a quasi-continuous graph simplification scheme based on Contraction Hierarchies (CH) which allows to render maps for arbitrary regions at any desired level of detail (no fixed zoom levels or tiles) and at the same time serves as speed-up structure for shortest path computations (like CH). For the construction of the simplified graphs, the edge costs are explicitly taken into account. This allows to create simplifications and respective renderings for different routing purposes (bike, slow car, sports car, tall truck, etc.) without the necessity of a manually designed rule set. As part of URAN we propose REAPER, a very lightweight augmentation of Contraction Hierarchies that allows to extract the relevant subgraphs of the road network for a rendering/routing query. We define formal consistency criteria for map rendering and show to what extent previous rendering approaches and URAN meet those criteria.

Our proposed unified route planning and rendering data structure allows for novel client-server based route planning systems which not only can dynamically adapt to the client's capabilities but also shift the actual route computation to the client side, both relieving the server infrastructure as well as providing some degree of privacy when planning a route.

2 Preliminaries

We first discuss commonly used map rendering and route planning methods and explain their advantages and disadvantages for use in a unified system.

Our assumption is that the road network is available as a graph $G(V, E)$ with node set V and edge set E. Additionally, we have edge costs $c : E \to \mathbb{R}^+$ (e.g., travel time for a car) and node coordinates $x, y : V \to \mathbb{R}$ (e.g., latitude and longitude or some projection thereof).

2.1 Map Rendering

In a rendering query, the user specifies a view rectangle $R = [x, x + width] \times [y, y + height]$ and expects as result the visualization of the part of the road network inside the rectangle. An interactive map typically allows for *panning* and *zooming*, where panning simply shifts the view rectangle

$$R \to R' = [x', x' + width] \times [y', y' + height]$$

while zooming changes the size of the rectangle

$$R \to R' = [x, x + width'] \times [y, y + height']$$

Note that zooming can also affect the x and y component when zooming in or out on a certain point in R.

Simply rendering all roads intersecting the view rectangle is problematic, though, due to the abundance of data. Assume we are to render the road network of Germany on a mobile device like a tablet. If we want to get an overview of the whole of Germany on the display, we certainly do not want to have every small dirt road drawn on the screen – we would end up with a mess of pixels – but rather restrict to a subset of the roads, e.g., the major highways (in case we are interested in route planning for a car). But even when restricting the set of roads to draw on screen, in their typical representation (e.g., in OpenStreetMap) a cross-country Autobahn like the A7 consists of several thousands of individual road segments. Rendering all of them is not reasonable. So typically one would simplify road shapes by replacing subsequences of degree-2 nodes by single road segments. Depending on the screen size and resolution, this can be done without affecting the visual quality of the result. So the two main steps in this *classical map simplification* process are:

– **pruning:** excluding subnetworks from rendering
– **line simplification:** replacing sequences of degree-2 nodes by single edges

Line Simplification. For the line simplification problem there are several known algorithms, the most popular being the algorithm by Douglas and Peucker [6] whose goal is to maximize the number of removed degree-2 nodes subject to certain quality constraints such as shape preservation or geometric faithfulness. There are also variants respecting topological constraints (a town should not move from one country to another when simplifying the country boundaries), e.g. [5]. Note, that even the variant originally considered by Douglas and Peucker is NP-hard to approximate better than within a factor of $n^{1/5-\delta}$ if no self-intersections are to be introduced, see [7].

Pruning. Pruning is typically based on an ad hoc rule set and heavily relies on the respective routing scenario. For an ordinary car, one would first prune out dirt roads, followed by county roads, followed by country roads and finally highways with the rationale being the observation that on long trips (which are typically viewed in a rather zoomed-out view) most parts of the route actually follow some highway. On the other hand, for a bicycle routing scenario highways are probably pruned out first followed by country roads and so on. While for these scenarios coming up with a reasonable rule set seems rather obvious, things become more difficult with more involved metrics. Consider the routing scenario for an extra-wide vehicle which cannot pass through too narrow tunnels and road sections. The structure of optimal (and in fact usable) paths for such a vehicle might differ drastically from those of an ordinary car. And it is not only the narrow passages that should be pruned out early on but also all road segments that are only used on routes via the narrow passage. So, as mentioned above, every new metric (aka routing scenario) requires the (manual) design of a new set of pruning rules. Our goal is to automatically derive pruning strategies based on the underlying routing metric.

In [4], the authors formulate the continuous pruning of a graph as an optimization problem. For given edge priorities (in [4] called edge *weights*) the goal is to determine an elimination sequence of the edges such that the graph maintains connectivity throughout the elimination process and the sum of edge priorities weighted by their lifetime in the elimination process is maximized. The authors prove NP hardness of this problem, provide an ILP formulation, several constant factor approximations, and a greedy heuristic. As before, this approach relies on given edge priorities, though, and is only meant for pruning not incorporating simplification or routing aspects.

2.2 Route Planning

In a route planning query, the user specifies start and target vertices $s, t \in V$ and expects as result the shortest path from s to t in G according to the cost function c.

Previous Work. There has been tremendous progress in the field of route planning on road networks in the last few years, see [2] for a recent survey. For continent-sized road networks, state-of-the-art algorithms can answer queries optimally in a few hundred nanoseconds after a modest preprocessing phase (both in terms of time and space consumption). According to [2], these algorithms can be categorized into goal-directed, separator-based, hierarchical, and bounded-hop techniques, or combinations thereof. Hierarchy-based speed-up methods make use of the observation that sufficiently long shortest paths eventually converge to a small arterial network of important roads such as highways. This matches our intuition about what to render in a zoomed out view of the network. Our URAN scheme will be based on *Contraction Hierarchies (CH)* [8], a very simple and elegant speed-up scheme, that allows for query answering about 1000 times faster than plain Dijkstra's algorithm.

Contraction Hierarchies. The basic idea of CH is to span large sections of shortest paths with direct edges, so-called *shortcuts*, which can then be used at query time to skip many edge relaxation operations in a Dijkstra run. What makes CH really interesting for URAN is the way of its construction, which can be interpreted as a step-wise graph simplification. The elementary operation is the so-called node or vertex contraction. Here, a node v as well as its adjacent edges are removed from the graph. In order not to affect shortest path distances between the remaining nodes, shortcut edges are inserted between all neighbors u, w of v, if and only if uvw was a shortest path. The cost of the new shortcut edge (u, w) is set to the summed costs of (u, v) and (v, w). In the preprocessing phase all nodes are contracted one-by-one in some order (yet to be defined). The rank of the node in this contraction order is also called the *level* of the node. Having contracted all but one vertex, a new graph $G^+(V, E^+)$ is constructed, containing all original edges of G as well as all shortcuts that were inserted in the contraction process. An edge $e = (v, w)$ – original or shortcut – is called upwards, if the level of v is smaller than the level of w, and downwards otherwise. By construction, the following property holds: For every pair of nodes $s, t \in V$, there exists a shortest path in G^+, which first only consist of upwards edges, and then exclusively of downwards edges. This property allows to search for the optimal path with a bidirectional Dijkstra only considering upwards edges in the search starting at s, and only downwards edges in the reverse search starting in t. This reduces the number of Dijkstra operations by three orders of magnitude.

The order in which the vertices get contracted is crucial for the final size of G^+ (and hence the query times). In practice, a very effective strategy is to always contract a set of *independent* (non-adjacent) vertices simultaneously, each of which increase the number of edges as little as possible. Vertices contracted at the same time get the same level assigned. A promising choice for the set to be contracted is to choose vertices with small *edge difference (ED)* which is the number of shortcuts to insert when contracting the node minus the number of edges that are deleted during the contraction. The ED value is possibly negative (e.g., for a node v with degree two, the two adjacent edges $\{u, v\}, \{v, w\}$ are deleted and at most one new edge $\{u, w\}$ is inserted, leading to an ED $\leq 1 - 2 = -1$). It turns out that the resulting levels of the nodes very faithfully reflect relevance for shortest paths in the network. In particular, the nodes contracted later (with high level) are typically nodes which appear in the middle of many long shortest paths (according to the cost function c). This hierarchy implicitly exhibited by the CH preprocessing algorithm will be the basis of our map rendering approach. Note, though, that the levels assigned crucially depend on the metric (edge costs) of the graph. While freeway nodes are likely to end up with high levels in a graph with car travel times on the edges, we expect completely different high-level nodes for a graph with bicycle travel times on the edges.

3 Generalized Map Simplification

For a given view rectangle R, the simplification level should be chosen such that the rendered information is sufficient for the user, but at the same time not too many redundant or superfluous items are displayed to allow for fast rendering and visually pleasing results. As we want to be able to adapt to user preferences as well as hardware capabilities of the client device, we aim for a quasi-continuous map simplification scheme. Therefore we would like to differentiate the entities of the graph according to some value of importance. An entity with a high importance should appear in a very zoomed out view, entities with small importance only if the user zooms in closely. Once a valid importance function is defined, a zoom level becomes nothing else than a threshold parameter, which declares the minimum importance value of an entity to be displayed (with the threshold chosen dependent on the device capabilities). Everything else is pruned away. The simplification should assure that optimal paths between important entities are maintained and the overall shape of the map is preserved even for high importance threshold values. In the classical line simplification problem, only nodes with a degree of 2 can be removed, connecting its two neighbors with a direct edge. But this is too limiting for our application. Disallowing the removal of nodes with degree larger than 2 results in too many nodes and edges in a zoomed out view. Therefore, we generalize the idea of map simplification, by also allowing the removal of nodes with a degree 1 or degree larger than 2, subsuming the classical line simplification and pruning process.

In the following we describe a general map simplification technique based on Contraction Hierarchies which enables quasi-continuous map simplification[1] and efficient route planning at the same time. Our approach explicitly takes the structure of shortest paths with respect to the edge costs into account. The costs could e.g., reflect travel time or euclidean distance or some completely different metric. The map is automatically customized for the considered metric.

3.1   Controlling the Level of Detail via REAPER

If we had an importance value for every road segment (and shortcut), an obvious strategy would be to build a query data structure which for a view rectangle and an importance threshold reports all road segments with sufficient importance intersecting the view. Several combinations of standard data structures from computational geometry like range, segment, or interval trees [3] can be instrumented to report all segments intersecting a view in $O(\log^2 n + k)$ time using $O(n \log n)$ space for the data structure (here n is the total number of segments, k the size of the query result). A straightforward extension to take importance values into account increases space consumption by a further $\log n$ factor. There are a few caveats, though: most of these data structures as such only work for non-intersecting segments which is not the case in our scenario (not for G and certainly not for the augmented graph G^+). Also the segments to be queried consist of all edges of G^+.

Our idea is to augment a given Contraction Hierarchy such that we can efficiently identify important nodes in the view rectangle, i.e., the ones with a CH level larger than some priority threshold T. On query time, we first extract these relevant points and then identify the (adjacent) important edges. This of course incurs some new challenges, e.g., lines which intersect the view but have no end point in it have to be taken special care of. But nevertheless searching first for nodes and only then for edges requires significantly less space and enables a higher degree of flexibility. Moreover this approach combines very well with our CH construction as the CH levels directly provide us with an importance value for each node. Nodes contracted late (so nodes with a high level) are more important, as they appear in many shortest paths and are more significant for shape preservation according to our contraction scheme.

REAPER – a CH-based R-Tree-like Heap Structure. We assume the CH is given as a strongly connected graph $G(V, E \cup E_{sc})$ and a function

---

[1] Essentially the number of zoom levels equals the number of levels in the CH.

$level : V \to \mathbb{N}$. Here E_{sc} are the shortcuts added during the construction, and *level* reflects the respective contraction order. Now with every node $v \in V$ we associate an axis-parallel rectangular region $R(v)$. $R(v)$ is to contain the embedding of all nodes (and hence edges) that are reachable on (undirected), strongly monotonously decreasing (with respect to the node levels) paths from v. Clearly, for the highest-level node, its respective rectangle contains a bounding box of the whole graph, for nodes with minimum level 0, the bounding box contains only the node location itself.

For each remaining node $v \in V$ we compute $R(v)$ in increasing node-level order. Assume the rectangular regions have been computed for all nodes with level less than i, we consider a node v at level i and all its neighbors V_{below} with respect to $E \cup E_{sc}$ having smaller level and construct $R(v)$ as the minimum bounding box containing all rectangular regions associated with nodes in V_{below}.

Lemma 1. *For any v, $R(v)$ contains the embeddings of all nodes reachable from v via edges of $E \cup E_{sc}$ on paths with strongly monotonously decreasing node-level.*

Proof. Follows by construction.   □

It is natural to use this structure to answer a query consisting of a rectangular range $R = [x_{min}, x_{max}] \times [y_{min}, y_{max}]$ and a min-priority value p as follows:

```
QREAPER(R,p,v)
  if visited[v] return
  if prio(v)<p return
  if R(v) does not intersect R return
  visited[v]=true
  if v contained in R
    result:={v}
  result+=union of QREAPER(R,p,v') for all children v' below v
```

It is called with the range and priorities of interest and the highest-level node and explores only nodes v with $prio(v) \geq p$ and for which $R(v)$ has non-empty intersection with R. It remains to see that it also returns all nodes with priority at least contained in R.

Lemma 2. *QREAPER(R,p,root) returns exactly the nodes contained in R having priority at least p.*

Proof. Let v be such a node. All nodes on the path from v to the root must contain v in their rectangular region by construction. Hence all these nodes are explored (as they all have priorities at least p in increasing order), in particular v itself. On the other hand, no node is added to the result if it does not meet the containment and minimum priority requirements.   □

We call our data structure REAPER as the query procedure is very similar to that of R-trees, yet it also incorporates the structure of a hEAP.

Edge Selection from Prioritized Nodes. Having extracted all important nodes inside the view rectangle, the next step is to select a suitable set of edges.

As we demand natural interactions with the map like panning and zooming, we have to be careful when locally selecting a set of important edges that this is consistent with respect to the global view. These operations are most often applied in longer sequences progressively exploring a map, so consistency between consecutive steps is needed to avoid distracting and confusing artifacts. We have identified the following consistency properties:

- *Translation Property:* If an edge e is displayed for the current view rectangle R and intersects the panned view rectangle R' it should be displayed for this as well, assuming the threshold T stays constant. This prevents edges from disappearing when panning.
- *Zoom Property:* If an edge e is displayed for the current view rectangle R with threshold T, e or a refinement of e should be displayed for all subrectangles $R' \subseteq R$ containing e and for all thresholds $T' \leq T$.

Moreover, the graph simplification should actually decrease the complexity of the structure to render, while important graph features should be maintained. We express those criteria more formally in two additional properties:

- *Compression Property:* For a given number N, there should exist a T for every possible view rectangle R, such that the number of important edges intersecting R does not exceed N but the rendering is still reasonable. In particular, the result should only be empty if there are no entities in R.
- *Connectivity Property:* If for any two important vertices s, t rendered for a given R, T the shortest path $\pi_{s,t}$ between them in G is inside R, they should be connected through a path $\pi'_{s,t}$ with the same cost as $\pi_{s,t}$ in R.

Classical (tile-based) renderers use edge categories as selection criterion, e.g., foot paths are only included in tiles belonging to a high zoom level, while interstates are always present. Having a total hierarchy on the edge categories and selecting a respective subgraph for every predefined zoom level, the translation property and the zoom property are automatically fulfilled. But the connectivity property often is not met, as the shortest paths between two points might include edges of a lower category which are not displayed at the actual zoom level. Therefore the shortest path is often drawn 'in the dark', see Fig. 2 left. Using the CH-graph, shortest path information between nodes with high priorities is maintained automatically via shortcuts. Therefore, edge selection strategies which meet this property are possible.

Consistent CH-Based Edge Selection. Given the importance threshold T, we declare all edges/shortcuts (v, w) important with $l(v), l(w) \geq T$, i.e., both endpoints of the edge are important. These edges are exactly the upward outgoing edges and downward incoming edges from important nodes. Hence, if the set of important nodes in a view rectangle is known (via REAPER), we can easily extract the set of important edges. Note that some of the important edges

Fig. 2. Left: Google Maps excerpt with a path that includes the usage of non-rendered roads. Right: Same map section and shortest path rendered without simplification (200,000 edges) and simplified with our scheme (43,000 edges).

are shortcuts spanning other important edges, hence should not be rendered to avoid strange visual artifacts and redundancy. Pruning can be performed efficiently, as it boils down to check if the node bridged by the shortcut has an importance value above the threshold. We call the remaining shortcuts *minimal*. To deal with shortcuts with only one or zero endpoints in R but intersecting it, we artificially enlarge R for node/edge extraction. When storing the maximum shortcut length with every possible threshold value T, enlarging R uniformly in all directions by this value suffices.

Note, that this edge selection assures the connectivity property defined above as a direct consequence of the CH construction process. If a node on the shortest path between s and t (with $l(s), l(t) \geq T$) has a label smaller than T, then there has to be a shortcut between important nodes that spans over this shortest path section. Also the translation and the zoom property are fulfilled. For the translation property, observe that the shortcuts we select for a view rectangle to be rendered are exactly the same as rendering the whole map with threshold T and then cutting out R. For the zoom property, note that with decreasing threshold either new shortcuts are added or existing ones get refined (as the unpacked shortcut becomes a sequence of important enough edges). Edges cannot get lost. For the compression property, suitable values of T have to be selected for changing view rectangle sizes (and depending on the used device). Note that the identified edge set allows for efficient route planning between any pair of important nodes.

Edge Unpacking for Visual Quality. Shortcuts – in particular between very high-level nodes – often represent very long shortest paths. Representing these paths as a straight-line edge in a rendering of the map often does not yield nice renderings. Hence, to improve the visual appearance of the rendering, we unpack a short-cut uw by replacing it by the two edges uv and vw it bridges, if the straight-line segment uw does not faithfully represent the shape of the shortest path between u and w. The notion of faithful here depends on the desired visual quality. By storing with every edge uw the maximum distance err_{uw} from the line segment $\overline{uw}$ to a node on the shortest path from u to w, we can decide at query time if $err_{uw} > err$ for a given upper bound err on the desired inaccuracy. Of course, the new shortcuts might also have to be unpacked until the error bound is not exceeded. In the worst case, the unpacking continues until reaching the original edges of the graph which have an error of 0.

4   Experimental Evaluation

We have conducted experiments for two different road networks as extracted from OpenStreetMap, Table 1 lists the respective network characteristics. We have constructed a standard Contraction Hierarchy based on the travel time metric for a regular car (using maximum speeds for respective road categories to derive travel times on the edges). The time to construct the CH ranges from a few minutes for the Germany dataset to around an hour for the large Europe data set with more than 214 Million nodes and 431 Million edges. In both cases, the CH construction roughly doubled the number of edges, in case of Germany, the maximum node level was 210, in case of the whole road network of Europe 360. Note that this is the number of zoom levels available to us. As usual, the resulting CH allows for provably exact route queries in the millisecond range as already shown in [8].

Timings of our C++ implementation were measured on a single core of a 2.2 GHz Intel Xeon E5-2650 machine with 768 GB of RAM. Note, though, that only the large Europe data set requires a machine with that much memory, a typical data set for a single country can easily be processed on Desktop commodity hardware or even a decent laptop.

Table 1. Road network characteristics.

	Germany	Europe
# nodes	24,608,237	214,088,057
# edges	49,791,294	431,194,569
# CH-shortcuts	41,824,799	385,127,944
Max. CH-level	210	360

4.1   REAPER: Construction Time, Space Consumption

Let us first investigate the overhead induced by the augmentation of the CH to also cater for the map rendering purpose. In Table 2 we list memory consumption of the original CH, the additional space overhead for REAPER, and the construction time for REAPER for our data sets.

Table 2. Space and time overhead for REAPER

	Germany	Europe
Space (graph + CH)	4,622 MB	40,941 MB
Space (graph + CH + REAPER)	5,346 MB	47,321 MB
Time REAPER construction	13.4 s	120.1 s

Not surprisingly, the space overhead for the CH augmentation via REAPER is negligible. We only need to store for each node a bounding rectangle of the subgraph below, which boils down to 4 *float* variables (16 Bytes), and a float for each edge representing an upper bound on the error compared to the chain this edge possibly replaces. The construction of the augmentation is so fast that it is not even worth storing it on disk, but rather create it on the fly after reading the CH-structure into main memory.

4.2   Query Analysis: Varying Level of Detail/Cutouts

Let us now see how efficient the prioritized range queries are compared to a naive scan of the nodes. To that end, we varied both the size of the query region as well as the minimum priority for the nodes to be reported. More precisely, we first determined width w and height h of the full data set and then queried a randomly placed rectangle of width $w/2^i$ and height $h/2^i$, $i = 1, \ldots, 6$ with minimum priorities $p = 0, 2, 8, 16, 32$.

The respective results for Germany can be seen in Table 3. Of course, when all nodes have to be reported, our data structure induces a considerable overhead compared to a naive strategy: simply scanning through all nodes is around 27

Table 3. Timings for prioritized Range Queries (Germany dataset, averaged over 100 queries). Number of reported points in parentheses.

	1/1	1/2	1/4	1/8	1/16	1/32	1/64
$p \geq 0$	5,488 ms	1,898 ms	501 ms	129 ms	32 ms	21 ms	12 ms
	(24M)	(8M)	(2M)	(500K)	(82K)	(38K)	(9K)
$p \geq 2$	2,683 ms	787 ms	287 ms	68 ms	27 ms	16 ms	8 ms
	(7M)	(2M)	(550K)	(150K)	(38K)	(15K)	(4K)
$p \geq 8$	233 ms	104 ms	32 ms	16 ms	11 ms	8 ms	7 ms
	(427K)	(167K)	(37K)	(13K)	(6K)	(4K)	(3K)
$p \geq 16$	34 ms	24 ms	14 ms	9 ms	8 ms	8 ms	7 ms
	(46K)	(20K)	(9K)	(4K)	(3K)	(3K)	(3K)
$p \geq 32$	4 ms	4 ms	4 ms	4 ms	3 ms	3 ms	3 ms
	(6K)	(5K)	(4K)	(4K)	(3K)	(3K)	(2K)
Naive	202 ms	202 ms	202 ms	202 ms	202 ms	202 ms	202 ms

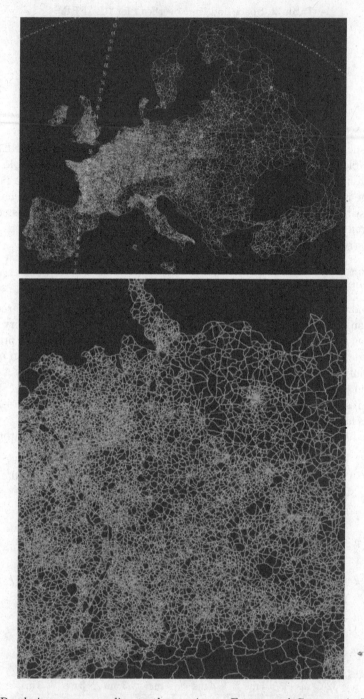

Fig. 3. Renderings corresponding to the queries on Europe and Germany in Table 4. (Color figure online)

times faster. Yet, when the whole of Germany is to be rendered, it does not make sense to draw every detail of the map, so one would resort to higher minimum priorities. Starting from a minimum priority of around 10, range queries covering the whole of Germany are faster using our data structure than the naive approach. For $p \geq 32$ we require only about 1/50th of the time of the naive scan.

Our data structure also becomes faster than the naive approach when querying smaller areas of the map. For example, querying a range of width and height of about 1/16th of the full extent (a box about 50 km by 50 km) can be done in 32 ms, about 6 times faster than the naive scan, even when reporting all nodes in that region. If little detail ($\approx$ higher minimum priority) is desired and the box is small, query times get even down to one-digit milliseconds.

But as explained, rendering a certain range with a certain level of detail not only involves reporting the respective important nodes but also identification of the relevant edges and refinement of the edges for visually pleasing quality. The following analysis was conducted on the full Europe data set, but querying different cutouts at different levels of detail, see Table 4. The respective cutouts are a coarse view on Europe, medium-detail view of Germany, a coarse view of the state of Baden-Württemberg, a detailed view of the state of Baden-Württemberg, and finally a coarse and full detail view of the area around the city of Stuttgart. The respective renderings can be seen in Figs. 3 and 4.

By the renderings we see that our data structure is able to prune out and select a suitable subset of the road network (note that we did not manually select the blue highways/interstates to be drawn, they automatically end up with high levels in the respective CH). In fact, for the Europe and Germany example, we would typically draw even less roads (and then the query time would be even faster). As an example, for the coarse rendering of the state of Baden-Württemberg we selected a minimum priority of 60, and triggered recursive unpacking of an edge if the path exhibits an error of more than 0.005. The time to query the 7,620 nodes within the region and priority at least 60 was 19 ms,

Table 4. Detailed analysis of the rendering process (queries on the Europe data set).

	Europe (coarse)	Germany (medium)	BaWü (coarse)	BaWü (detailed)	Stuttgart (coarse)	Stuttgart (full detail)
Minpriority	60	40	60	20	20	0
Unpack error	0.005	0.001	0.005	0.002	0.0005	0.0005
Node query time	21 ms	39 ms	19 ms	67 ms	51 ms	231 ms
# nodes reported	9,468	17,193	7,620	24,331	12,005	586,989
Edge query time	42 ms	75 ms	34 ms	81 ms	57 ms	151 ms
# edges reported	451,100	235,953	19,069	119,867	8,220	1,108,672
Edge unpacking time	63 ms	72 ms	10 ms	64 ms	6 ms	0 ms
# unpacked edges	327,569	303,827	49,180	328,294	33,334	1,108,672
Total query time	126 ms	186 ms	63 ms	212 ms	114 ms	382 ms

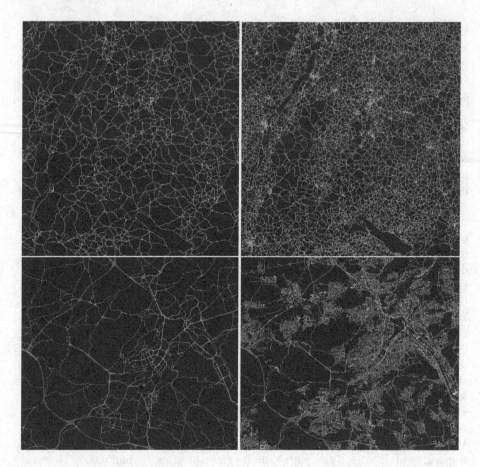

Fig. 4. Renderings corresponding to the queries in Table 4 for Baden-Württemberg and Stuttgart. (Color figure online)

identification of the 19,069 edges took 34 ms, unpacking them to finally 49,180 edges took 10 ms, totaling to 63 ms for the whole process (excluding time for the actual rendering via OpenGL). The effort for the full detail view (including every little dirt road) of the Stuttgart region was highest, which comes as no surprise since more than a million edges are to be reported for the rendering.

One might wonder why the number of unpacked edges for Europe is actually smaller than the number of originally reported important edges. This is due to the fact that a single unpacked edge might be part of many originally reported edges. In particular at higher levels this is quite often the case.

5   Conclusions and Outlook

In this paper we have presented a very light-weight augmentation to the very popular Contraction Hierarchy data structure which allows to deduce visually pleasing renderings of varying level of detail of a map. Without any manual intervention, this approach leads to natural prunings of the map based on the hierarchy induced by the respective shortest path metric. To our knowledge, this is the first instrumentation of Contraction Hierarchies for map rendering.

Conceptually, this approach unifies the route planning and map rendering processes. Our developed data structure has the potential to be the foundation of novel web services where the user can specify very precisely the level of detail of the map rendering (e.g., based on the device and network capabilities) and even use the very same information to perform route planning on the local device.

In future work we plan to fine-tune our data structure further; reducing the overhead of REAPER to almost zero should be possible, e.g., by omitting bounding boxes for low-level single nodes. A more challenging avenue is to externalize the data structure such that it can also be accessed from secondary memory (SSD) in case RAM does not suffice to hold the whole graph (in particular for continent-size networks like the one of Europe). From a user's perspective it is also of interest to be able to generate a single map of varying level of detail, e.g., many details along a given route, but less detail further away from the route. Our approach has the potential to serve that purpose by smoothly varying the minimum priority of nodes to be selected (based on the distance to the route) and the edge selection and unpacking strategies.

Acknowledgements. This work was partially supported by the Deutsche Forschungsgemeinschaft (DFG) under grant FU 700/4-1 as part of the priority program 1894: Volunteered Geographic Information: Interpretation, Visualization and Social Computing.

References

1. The OpenStreetMap Project (2014). http://www.openstreetmap.org/
2. Bast, H., Delling, D., Goldberg, A., Müller-Hannemann, M., Pajor, T., Sanders, P., Wagner, D., Werneck, R.: Route planning in transportation networks. Technical report MSR-TR-2014-4, Microsoft Research, January 2014
3. de Berg, M., Cheong, O., van Kreveld, M., Overmars, M.: Computational Geometry: Algorithms and Applications, 3rd edn. Springer, Heidelberg (2008)
4. Chimani, M., van Dijk, T.C., Haunert, J.-H.: How to eat a graph: computing selection sequences for the continuous generalization of road networks. In: Proceedings of the 22nd ACM SIGSPATIAL International Conference on Advances in Geographic Information Systems, vol. 28, pp. 243–252 (2014)
5. de Berg, M., van Kreveld, M., Schirra, S.: Topologically correct subdivision simplification using the bandwidth criterion. Cartogr. Geogr. Inf. Syst. **25**(4), 243–257 (1998)
6. Douglas, D., Peucker, T.: Algorithms for the reduction of the number of points required to represent a digitized line or its caricature. Can. Cartogr. **10**(2), 112–122 (1973)
7. Estkowski, R., Mitchell, J.S.B.: Simplifying a polygonal subdivision while keeping it simple. In: Proceedings of the 17th Annual Symposium on Computational Geometry, SCG 2001, pp. 40–49. ACM, New York (2001)

8. Geisberger, R., Sanders, P., Schultes, D., Vetter, C.: Exact routing in large road networks using contraction hierarchies. Transp. Sci. **46**(3), 388–404 (2012)
9. Schnelle, N., Funke, S., Storandt, S.: DORC: distributed online route computation - higher throughput, more privacy. In: Proceedings of the IEEE International Conference on Pervasive Computing and Communications Workshops, pp. 344–347 (2013)

A Bayesian Framework for Individual Exposure Estimation on Uncertain Paths

Matthew Horak[1(✉)], Wan D. Bae[1], Shayma Alkobaisi[2], Sehjeong Kim[2], and Wade Meyers[2]

[1] Hanyang University, Seoul, South Korea
{horakmatt,baewd}@hanyang.ac.kr
[2] United Arab Emirates University, Al Ain, United Arab Emirates
{shayma.alkobaisi,sehjung.kim}@uaeu.ac.ae, meyersw3476@gmail.com

Abstract. Current map matching and path reconstruction algorithms exhibit high success rates on dense data. We present a framework for estimating path selection probabilities from extremely sparse GPS data for the purpose of estimating a "measurement of interest" that varies with path and travel time. This work is motivated by limitations involved in applications such as environmental exposure modeling for medical patients. Our contributions are two-fold; first we propose a general Bayesian framework for path selection estimation that is applicable at both population and individual levels, and second, we provide extensive experiments on real and synthetic data that demonstrate the accuracy and robustness of the proposed algorithm and model.

Keywords: Path selection probability · Exposome · Bayesian estimation

1 Introduction

The increasing availability of frequent time stamped GPS data from mobile devices has led to the proliferation of map matching and path detection algorithms for reliably ascertaining the path an individual traversed during a series of readings. This in turn has enabled the development of tracking and monitoring systems for applications as diverse as traffic flow monitoring, health monitoring and wildlife studies. These algorithms perform very well when the frequency of GPS readings is in the order of several seconds.

Sometimes practical considerations such as battery consumption impose significant limitations on the GPS data collection. Additionally, in many situations a model is desired to estimate a measurement of interest that varies with the path taken, such as total exposure to a harmful pollutant that a patient accumulates as he or she travels between two known points via an unknown path. Finally, for applications on the individual level, extensive data on which to train an estimation model are not available so a rapidly training model is required. We formalize these constraints related to path reconstruction as follows.

© Springer International Publishing AG 2017
D. Brosset et al. (Eds.): W2GIS 2017, LNCS 10181, pp. 83–99, 2017.
DOI: 10.1007/978-3-319-55998-8_6

General Problem: An individual routinely travels between locations of interest A and B along one of a finite set of paths, and for each trip travel time is reported but path taken is not reported. With each trip is associated a *measurement of interest*, which depends on path taken and travel time. For each trip we are asked to use the elapsed time to calculate an estimate of the measurement of interest in a way that reduces the error between the estimate and the true measurement as much as possible given knowledge only of travel time.

Although this problem also has clear applications in fields such as military tracking of persons of interest [14] or wildlife studies [9], our primary motivation comes from medical monitoring of patients suffering chronic obstructive pulmonary disease (COPD). Several programs under development aim to help patients manage their conditions by monitoring total exposure to environmental variables known to aggravate their symptoms [2,3,15]. Efficient methods of accurately estimating accumulated exposure based on the exact path taken, elapsed time and reported environmental conditions exist [4], but the power requirement of a GPS device continuously measuring and reporting the location data required for exact path reconstruction is one of the primary obstacles to large scale development and implementation of this program [11]. In similar applications caregivers have expressed the desire for a device to work continuously for 2 weeks or longer without recharging [18]. Our solution to the general problem above allows for users' locations not to be recorded during travels between their known points of interest, and is thus a first step in the solving the continuous monitoring problem faced by caregivers for COPD patients.

We present a general algorithmic framework based on Bayesian analysis for solving this problem that meets the combined challenges of (1) working with location data that is very sparse in time, (2) determining the probability that each of a set of candidate paths was the true path traversed, and (3) limited availability of training data. The Bayesian setting allows for accurate estimates of path selection probabilities and travel times to be built iteratively from previous behavior records of path and travel time probability.

We demonstrate the framework by proposing and testing an algorithm called Exposure Estimation in Bayesian Framework ($E2BF$), which accurately estimates an individual's accumulated exposure to an environmental pollutant during trips between two locations of interest. Based on tests with extensive synthetic data and real data, we find that the algorithm accurately estimates an individual's exposure when we have only reported travel time between two locations. For most levels of variation in environmental levels and personal travel characteristics, our model was able to estimate the accumulated exposure to within 5–7% of the total accumulation with training periods as short as 20 days. Only under extreme environmental variation did the model's error rate exceed 10% of total accumulation.

2   Related Work

Efficient solutions exist for many map matching and path selection problems [20,22] related to ours. At a temporal scale smaller than our problem, high quality *map matching* algorithms exist for detecting the correct road segments on which the person is traveling using high frequency GPS data [17,20,21,24]. A number of recent solutions to the path selection problem perform very well with high frequency GPS data [8] and some perform with up to 70% accuracy for sampling rates as low as 120 s [14], but they require population-level path selection models or extensive training on GPS data for which true paths are known.

When sampling rates are lower, probabilistic frameworks exist to generate a set of potential true paths together with associated likelihood. The authors in [16] proposed an algorithm that uses a Hidden Markov Model (HMM) and Viterbi algorithm that exhibits near-perfect path identification with measurement frequency under 30 s 80% for frequency under 240 s. A similar approach is used by the researchers in [23], which requires extensive population-based data for training.

Another approach to modeling path selection does not rely on accurate GPS data to make predictions once the model parameters are determined with accurate data in a training phase. In [6] population level path selection models are developed that predict average population selection tendencies for travelers on a given path. These models use historical population data to determine the probability of a traveler selecting the next link in a path when the previous links are known.

Work in [5,7] presents a probabilistic method to infer the path of a trip by synthesizing high-frequency smartphone data on many factors (eg., GPS, Bluetooth, and accelerometer). Each measurement provides information to identify the user's upstream trajectory, and the result is a set of candidate multimodal paths, along with a probability for each being the true one. Similarly, work in [13] introduces a method to answer probabilistic path queries while capturing the uncertainty in traffic, which focuses on predicting the best route a user should take in the future to satisfy user-specified probabilistic requirements.

3   General Bayesian Framework

In this section, we prove Lemma 1, which establishes the existence of the theoretically optimal measurement estimate as well as an abstract mathematical form of the optimal estimate. Though this estimate cannot be calculated in practice due to our ignorance of the individual's travel habits, it is an essential component in a general Bayesian framework of later sections.

3.1   Optimal Estimate and Bayesian Framework

Denote by $\mathcal{P}$ and $\mathcal{T}$ the set of candidate paths the individual takes and set of possible times along those paths. For each $(x,t) \in \mathcal{P} \times \mathcal{T}$ resulting from the individual's travels between A and B, we denote the value of the measurement of interest as a function $f(x,t)$ of path and travel time. The individual's travel habits define a probability density function $p_{ind}(x,t)$ on $\mathcal{P} \times \mathcal{T}$.

Let us temporarily drop the requirement that we are able actually to calculate the estimate for $f(x,t)$ in practice and focus on an abstract function $g(t)$, depending only on t, which denotes an estimate of $f(x,t)$. We wish to minimize the Mean Square Error of estimation (MSE) over the course of many trips, which is expressed as an expected value with respect to the probability p_{ind}; $MSE = E((f(x,t) - g(t))^2)$. Each different function $g(t)$ will have a different MSE, and in this section, we find an abstract form for the function, $\tilde{g}(t)$ whose mean square error is smaller than all others' mean square errors.

In practical applications, the function $f(x,t)$ may change periodically, for example as the level of a pollutant fluctuates throughout the day. For each set ϵ of overall "environmental" conditions, we have a function $f_\epsilon(x,t)$ representing the measurement for pair (x,t) during conditions ϵ. In this setting we also use p_{ind} to represent the probability distribution on the set of triples (x,t,ϵ) even though the probability distribution for the ϵ component is the same for all individuals.

If the overall environmental conditions do not change from ϵ_0 and all paths are always traversed in the same constant time t_0 then a standard exercise in statistics verifies that the constant function $\tilde{g}(t,\epsilon) = E(f_{\epsilon_0}(x,t_0))$ minimizes the mean square error, where the expected value are taken over $\mathcal{P}$ with the probability density function equal to the conditional probability $p_{ind}(x \mid t = t_0, \epsilon = \epsilon_0)$. In the case that overall environmental conditions and travel time change, the function $\tilde{g}(t,\epsilon) = E(f_\epsilon(x,t) \mid time = t, environment = \epsilon)$ minimizes the mean squared error for every fixed (t,ϵ), so it minimizes over all (x,t,ϵ). To simplify the formulas, we suppress the notation for ϵ and write

$$\tilde{g}(t) = E(f(x,t) \mid time = t) = \sum_{x_i \in \mathcal{P}} f(x_i,t)p_{ind}(x_i|t) \qquad (1)$$

with the understanding that f is calculated with respect to the currently observed environmental conditions and $p(x_i|t) = p(x_i|t,\epsilon)$. We record these observations as,

Lemma 1. *The theoretically minimal mean square error estimate for $f(x,t)$ given knowledge only of travel time is given by $\tilde{g}(t)$ calculated by Eq. 1, and the theoretically minimal MSE is given by,*

$$MSE_{the} = E((f(x,t) - \tilde{g}(t))^2), \qquad (2)$$

where the expected value is over all (x,t) pairs with respect to $p_{ind}(x,t)$.

Research has shown that individuals do not know their own travel characteristics well. Thus, p_{ind} is not known and the optimal estimator $\tilde{g}(t)$ cannot be calculated in practice. However, the form of $\tilde{g}(t)$ suggests that we approach the problem of determining a calculatable estimate to $f(x,t)$ by determining a calculatable approximation $p_{\mathcal{B}}$ for p_{ind}. We reduce the General Problem of Sect. 1 to the following,

Path Selection Probability Estimation Problem: For a given travel time of an individual between two locations A and B, without knowing the exact path taken or individual probability, we ask for a calculatable approximation, $p_\mathcal{B}(x_i|t)$, for $p_{ind}(x_i|t)$ such that the function,

$$g_\mathcal{B}(t) = E(f(x,t) \mid time = t) = \sum_{x_i \in \mathcal{P}} f(x_i,t)p_\mathcal{B}(x_i|t) \qquad (3)$$

minimizes the expected mean square error in estimation as well as possible given knowledge only over travel time.

3.2 General Bayesian Framework for Path Selection Probabilities

In classical inference, $p_{ind}(x,t)$ would depend on a vector-valued parameter θ and $p_\theta(x,t)$ would denote the probability of observing (x,t) given parameter value θ. A confidence interval for the true value of θ would then be constructed from observed data. Since there is high variability among individuals' travel habits, population-level data cannot be used to estimate an individual's parameters reliably, and we generally do not have enough data from an individual to perform classical inference for $p_{ind}(x,t)$ with a high confidence level.

In Bayesian inference, the focus on the "true" value for θ is replaced by a prior probability distribution π over θ describing the confidence we have that any particular value of θ correctly models the individual. The prior is set according to a collection of rational beliefs. Whenever a set D of data is observed, the prior is updated to the posterior distribution $\pi'(\theta) = \pi(\theta \mid D)$ by Bayes' formula.

In practice, the large number of possible travel times and the high time variability between paths make managing the Bayesian update formulas for π' intractable. To alleviate this difficulty, we adopt a path-based approach that studies travel time distribution on a path-by-path basis. The difficulty with this approach is that "t given x_i" is not a random variable over whose distribution a prior may be placed. However there are only finitely many x_i and for the purposes of setting priors, we interpret $p_\theta(t|x_i)$ as the density function for the distribution of travel times along path x_i. Thus, we impose priors on $p(t|x_i)$ and $p(x)$ to obtain the prior π for $p(x,t)$.

To set the required priors, we assume that mutually disjoint sets of parameters govern $p(x)$ and each $p(t|x_i)$ and express θ as $\theta = (\gamma, \xi_1, \xi_2, \ldots, \xi_k)$ where γ is the vector of parameters for $p(x)$ and ξ_i is the vector of parameters for $p(t|x_i)$. Over each of the ξ_i and over γ, we set priors independently by defining probability densities $\pi_i(\xi_i)$ and $\pi_{k+1}(\gamma)$. Together these determine a prior distribution π on Ω by the formula,

$$\pi(\theta) = \pi_1(\xi_1)\pi_2(\xi_2) \cdots \pi_k(\xi_k)\pi_{k+1}(\gamma). \qquad (4)$$

The posterior $\pi' = \pi'_1\pi'_2 \cdots \pi'_k\pi'_{k+1}$, determines the posterior predictive distribution on $\mathcal{P} \times \mathcal{T}$ as the expected value of $p_\theta(x_i,t)$ with respect to π';

$$p_\mathcal{B}(x_i,t) = E_\Omega(p_\theta(x_i,t)) = \int_\Omega p_\theta(x_i,t)\pi(\theta|D)d\theta. \qquad (5)$$

Another interpretation of the posterior predictive is that it is the marginal distribution of (x_i, t) with θ marginalized out, where the probability density on the random vector (x_i, t, θ) is given by $p(x_i, t, \theta) = p_\theta(x_i, t)\pi'(\theta)$. In other words, the posterior predictive distribution for (x_i, t) gives the probability density function on $\mathcal{P} \times \mathcal{T}$ that is most consistent with the prior beliefs and collected data. Hence, we expect $p_\mathcal{B}(x_i, t)$ to be an essential component in the approximation $p_\mathcal{B}(x_i|t)$.

For approximating $p_{ind}(x_i|t)$, the additional piece of data, $time = t$, allows for one additional improvement given by the following lemma.

Lemma 2. *The probability density minimizing the mean squared estimation error in $g_\mathcal{B}(t)$ from Eq. 3 given the observed data D and the observed time t is,*

$$p_\mathcal{B}(x_i|t) = \frac{p_\mathcal{B}(t|x_i)p_\mathcal{B}(x_i)}{\sum_{j=1}^{k} p_\mathcal{B}(t|x_j)p_\mathcal{B}(x_j)}.$$

Proof. By fixing i and t, view $p_\theta(x_i) = p_\gamma(x_i)$ and $p_\theta(t|x_i) = p_{\xi_i}(t|x_i)$ as functions of the random variable $\theta = (\gamma, \xi)$. Since the priors and posteriors for $p(x_i)$ and $p(t|x_i)$ are all specified independently, $p_\theta(x_i)$ and $p_\theta(t|x_i)$ are independent random variables, as verified by Eq. 4. Therefore, for each i, we have $E_\Omega(p_\theta(x_i)p_\theta(t|x_i)) = E_\Omega(p_\theta(x_i))E_\Omega(p_\theta(t|x_i) = p_\mathcal{B}(x_i)p_\mathcal{B}(t|x_i)$. In integral form,

$$\int_{\theta \in \Omega} p_\theta(t|x_i)p_\theta(x_i)\pi'(\theta)\, d\theta = E_\Omega(p_\theta(x_i)p_\theta(t|x_i)) = p_\mathcal{B}(t|x_i)p_\mathcal{B}(x_i). \qquad (6)$$

Now consider the vector-valued random variable (x_i, t, θ) with probability density given by $p(x_i, t, \theta) = p_\theta(x_i, t)\pi'(\theta)$. Since we have one more piece of observed data, which is travel time, the predictive for $p(x_i|t)$ is the marginal distribution of $p(x_i, \theta|t)$ with θ marginalized out. Thus,

$$p_\mathcal{B}(x_i|t) = \int_{\theta \in \Omega} p(x_i, \theta|t)\, d\theta = \int_{\theta \in \Omega} \frac{p(x_i, t, \theta)}{p(t)}\, d\theta = \frac{\int_{\theta \in \Omega} p_\theta(x_i, t)\pi'(\theta)\, d\theta}{p(t)}$$

$$= \frac{\int_{\theta \in \Omega} p_\theta(t|x_i)p_\theta(x_i)\pi'(\theta)\, d\theta}{\sum_{j=1}^{k} \int_{\theta' \in \Omega} p_{\theta'}(t|x_j)p_{\theta'}(x_j)\pi'(\theta')\, d\theta'} = \frac{p_\mathcal{B}(t|x_i)p_\mathcal{B}(x_i)}{\sum_{j=1}^{k} p_\mathcal{B}(t|x_j)p_\mathcal{B}(x_j)}. \qquad (7)$$

$\square$

4   Exposure Estimation Framework

We now consider the specific problem of estimating the exposure to one single pollutant that an individual accumulates over time as a result of multiple travels along paths in set $\mathcal{P}$. For the calculation of actual exposures for known path and travel time, we use the established *exposome* model detailed in [25].

(a) City of Minneapolis weather stations   (b) Level 1 revision Voronoi diagram

Fig. 1. Cells used in a Level 1 revision Voronoi map data structure

4.1   Exposome Model

Hourly air pollutant data are available in public databases in the USA and many other countries. For storage of this hourly data, our model uses the *Voronoi map* data structure developed in [4]. This data structure begins with the Voronoi diagram determined by the placement of weather stations and performs successive revisions based on centers of triangles in Delaunay triangulations until environmental conditions vary minimally across each cell. Figure 1 shows the locations of weather stations in Minneapolis, Minnesota and the cells used in the Voronoi map data structure given by a Level 1 revision for these weather stations.

Let $G = (V, E)$ be a graph in $\mathbb{R}^2$ representing a road network, where V and E are the set of vertices and edges. A trajectory $traj_{A-B}$ of an individual in road network G is a sequence of $2D$ points (longitude, latitude) with time stamps from point A to point B: $traj_{A-B} = \{(l_1, t_1), (l_2, t_2), \ldots, (l_n, t_n)\}$, where l_m is the sampled point at t_m, for $m = 1, 2, \ldots, n$, and $t_m < t_{m+1}$.

A given $traj_{A-B}$ corresponds to a path x, which is a sequence of road segments (edges in G) that the individual traversed in the road network: $x = \{e_1, e_2, \ldots, e_n\}$. Each road segment has the properties of length of the road segment, average speed and maximum speed. The selected path x is overlaid the Voronoi map to calculate the accumulated exposure to an air pollutant from A to B during the time duration $t = t_n - t_1$. In order to expedite the process of calculating exposures, we pre-compute the points of intersection between a road network and Voronoi cells.

Consider a road network in an area whose Voronoi map contains N cells. Suppose an individual traverses from A to B on this network during time duration t. If the trajectory contains the person's moving data collected every 5–10 s, a path x from A and B can be identified. We overlay the path x on the Voronoi map to find the Voronoi cells that overlap x and calculate the actual accumulated exposure by,

$$f(x_i, t) = \sum_{j=1}^{N} E_j T_{i,j}, \tag{8}$$

where x_i is the path on which the individual traveled, $T_{i,j}$ is the time spent in cell j (which will be 0 if the path x_i does not pass through cell j) and E_j is the pollutant concentration in cell j. By Eq. 8 and Lemma 2, the formula for $g_{\mathcal{B}}(t)$ in Eq. 3 becomes,

$$g_{\mathcal{B}}(t) = \sum_{x_i \in \mathcal{P}} f(x_i, t) p_{\mathcal{B}}(x_i|t) = \sum_{i=1}^{k} \left[\frac{\left(\sum_{j=1}^{N} E_j T_{i,j} \right) p_{\mathcal{B}}(t|x_i) p_{\mathcal{B}}(x_i)}{\sum_{l=1}^{k} p_{\mathcal{B}}(t|x_l) p_{\mathcal{B}}(x_l)} \right]. \tag{9}$$

4.2 Model-Specific Explicit Form for $p_{\mathcal{B}}(x_i|t)$

To make the process of calculating $p_{\mathcal{B}}(x_i|t)$ through Lemma 2 and Eq. 5 computationally tractable, we assume forms for $p(x)$ and $p(t|x_i)$ that are consistent with reasonable beliefs about traffic flow and admit conjugate priors that are similarly consistent with these beliefs. Under these assumptions, updating to posteriors can be performed as an incremental process through rounds of data collection with posteriors for the current round serving as priors for the next round.

For the categorical variable x_i, each possible distribution function $p(x)$ is viewed as a vector of nonnegative numbers $\gamma = (\gamma_1, \gamma_1, \ldots, \gamma_k)$ summing to 1, which are the model parameters for $p(x)$. The conjugate prior we take is the Dirichlet distribution governed by hyperparameters $d_1, d_2, \cdots, d_k$. Given this likelihood-prior pair for $p(x)$, the posterior distribution is also Dirichlet with updated hyperparameters $d_i^* = d_i + c_i$ where c_i is the number of times path i was observed in the training data. The posterior predictive has the straightforward form,

$$p_{\mathcal{B}}(x_i) = \frac{d_i + c_i}{\sum_{j=1}^{k} d_j + c_j}. \tag{10}$$

Next, to set priors for $p(t|x_i)$, we assume that for each fixed i, the distribution of travel time along x_i for the individual is normally distributed with unknown mean μ_i and unknown variance σ_i^2. The σ_i^2 and μ_i are the model parameters for $p(t|x_i)$. For σ_i^2 and μ_i arising in practice, the probability of predicting a negative travel time is negligibly small and this assumption is consistent with current models for path travel time in traffic [12] (Sect. 3.2). The conjugate prior we take for μ_i and σ_i^2 is the "normal-inverse-gamma" distribution governed by hyperparameters V_i, m_i, a_i, b_i. For these pairs, the posteriors are also normal-inverse-gamma with the following updated hyperparameters $V_i^*, m_i^*, a_i^*, b_i^*$:

$$V_i^* = \frac{V_i}{1 + c_i V_i} \tag{11}$$

$$m_i^* = \left(\frac{m_i}{V_i} + c_i \overline{t_i} \right) \frac{V_i}{1 + c_i V_i} \tag{12}$$

$$a_i^* = a_i + \frac{c_i}{2} \tag{13}$$

$$b_i^* = b_i + \frac{1}{2} \left[\frac{m_i^2}{V_i} + \left(\sum_{r=1}^{c_i} t_{i,r}^2 \right) - \frac{m_i^{*2}}{V_i^*} \right] \tag{14}$$

where $t_{i,r}$ is the time observed during the rth occurrence that the individual was observed to traverse path i during the observation period and $\overline{t_i}$ is the average travel time observed for path i (ignoring all other paths) [10].

Minimally informative initial values of hyperparameters may be set following the suggestions in Chap. 3.5 of [10]. We set $d_i = 0, V_i = 1, a_i = 0.01, b_i = 0.01$, and set m_i equal to a reasonable guess for the individual's average travel time on path x_i.

The posterior predictive is given by a Student's distribution,

$$p_{\mathcal{B}}(t|x_i) = t_{2a_i^*}\left(m_i^*, \frac{b_i^*(1+V_i^*)}{a_i^*}\right) = t_{df}(location, scale^2). \qquad (15)$$

5 E2BF: Exposure Estimation Algorithm

We propose an algorithm called Exposure Estimation in Bayesian Framework (*E2BF*) for accurately estimating, after a short training session, the exposure when we have only a reported time of travel between locations of interest. The *E2BF* algorithm, presented in Algorithm 1, consists of the following phases: (1) initialization, (2) training and testing, and (3) model usage.

Initialization. Given two vertices, A and B, in graph G for an individual's traveling between the two vertices, we select k candidate paths (most likely paths) by using average travel time assigned to each edge in $G, \mathcal{P} = x_1, x_2, \ldots, x_k$. For each path x_i in $\mathcal{P}$, we assign a travel time distribution using population-level traffic statistics. The population mean travel time for each path x_i in $\mathcal{P}$ is used to initialize the model's prior hyperparameters according to Sect. 4.2.

To train the model, we collect a set TD of training and testing data consisting of a number of actual path and time (x_i, t) pairs extracted from the observed trajectory dataset $Traj$. We collect time-stamped GPS data at a frequency high enough (5 second sampling rate in our experiments) for an established map-matching algorithm to determine the true path from the dense GPS data.

Training and Testing. A subset TD_{train} is used to learn the person's travel by updating the values of $c_i, \overline{t_i}$, and $\sum t_{i,r}^2$ and thus the predictive distributions according to Eqs. 10 and 15.

Once the model is trained, the estimation quality of the model is analyzed through the testing phase on the remaining data TD_{test} in TD not used for training. For testing the model, $f(x_i, t)$ and $g_{\mathcal{B}}(t)$ are calculated for each $(x_i, t) \in TD_{test}$ according to Eqs. 9, 10 and 15. For each (x_i, t) in the testing phase, we calculate the observed square error $(f(x_i, t) - g_{\mathcal{B}}(t))^2$ and finally average over all test data to determine the empirical MSE, MSE_{emp}, which is used to determine whether or not an additional round of training and testing is required. If more training is needed, the old test data may be regarded as a new training set and hyperparameters are updated. The next round of test is conducted on newly collected data.

Ideally, one would aim to stop training and testing when the empirical MSE, MSE_{emp}, converges closely enough to the theoretically best MSE, MSE_{the}, that additional training will yield insignificant model improvements. Our work with medical doctors [1] indicates that 30 days to 60 days is a reasonable period that can be expected of patients to train the exposure model. However, in practice there are two difficulties to this strategy. First, MSE_{the} cannot be calculated due to our ignorance of the individual's true probability of travel time and path selection. Second, due to natural variation in the data (personal travel times, environmental conditions, etc.), MSE_{emp}, as calculated from a small testing set, may not accurately represent the current state of the model's long term MSE. Hence a heuristic approach for detecting convergence of the empirical mean squared error is required.

In the first approach (described in Algorithm 1), an acceptable MSE error level, MSE_A, may be set and test-train cycles repeated until $MSE_{emp} < MSE_A$ with a certain level of confidence. For this approach, the test data TD_{test} might be considered a random sample of the model's true long-term performance and classical inference performed on the average square error of the observed test round. In the second approach, no a-priori acceptable MSE_A level is set, but MSE_{emp} is obtained through several rounds of training and testing on larger test sets until it appears to stabilize, as guaranteed by the law of large numbers.

Model Usage. In use, only travel time from A to B is collected, and the model g_B is used to estimate the exposure based only on observed travel time t.

6   Experiments

All experiments were implemented in the IPython Notebook environment on an instance of the Amazon server with a 2.4 GHZ 16 Core, 16 GB main memory, and a 32 GB hard disk, running the Linux Redhat 6.0 operating system.

6.1   Experiment Setup

The estimation quality of the model was tested through extensive simulations on: (1) synthetic trajectory data generated on a real road network for 100 individuals and (2) real trajectory data from two individuals' daily commute to work on two different real road networks.

Road Network and k-rank Candidates. For both synthetic data and real data, we took a real map and constructed a graph $G = (V, E)$ representing a road network. For each edge e in G, we initially assigned the Normal distribution on e for the travel time, $N(\mu, \sigma^2)$, where μ is the average travel time and σ^2 is the variance, following the method presented in [13].

In synthetic data simulation, we picked two vertices from G as travel locations, A for departure and B for arrival. We used 3 varied $(A-B)$ travel locations between which the average travel time varies from 15 min to 35 min. In real data

---

Algorithm 1. $E2BF$: Exposure Estimation in Bayesian Framework

---

1: **Input:** $Traj$ {an individual's trajectory data}, MSE_A {acceptable MSE}
        G {a graph of a road network}, Map {a Voronoi map of air pollutants}
2: **Initialization:**
3:    $\mathcal{P} = \{x_1, x_2, .., x_k\}$ ← Compute k candidate paths {k-rank paths from G}
4:    $\mathcal{P}_D = \{(\mu_1, \sigma_1^2), (\mu_2, \sigma_2^2), .., (\mu_k, \sigma_k^2)\}$ ← initialize travel time distributions
5:    H ← initialize hyperparameters d_i, V_i, m_i, a_i, b_i for each path x_i in $\mathcal{P}$
6:    TD ← Extract (x_i, t) pair from each trajectory in $Traj$ $\{1 \leq i \leq k\}$
7:    TD_{train} ← Select a half of (x_i, t) pairs at random from X for training
8:    TD_{test} ← Assign the rest of X for testing
9: **repeat**
10:    **Training:**
11:      c_i ← 0, for each x_i in $\mathcal{P}$ {c_i is the number of occurrences of path x_i}
12:      $\overline{t_i}$ ← 0, for each x_i in $\mathcal{P}$ {average travel time}
13:      $\sum t_i^2$ ← 0, for each x_i in $\mathcal{P}$ {sum of squared travel time}
14:      **for** $s = 1$ to n {for each pair in X_{train}} **do**
15:        c_i ← $c_i + 1$ for the traveled path i {increase the occurrence of path i}
16:        $\overline{t_i}$ ← Update $\overline{t_i}$
17:        $\sum t_i^2$ ← Update $\sum t_i^2$
18:      **end for**
19:      H^* ← Update hyperparameters for each path x_i using $c_i, \overline{t_i}, \sum t_i^2$
20:      MSE_{emp} ← 0
21:    **Testing:**
22:      **for** $s = 1$ to m {for each pair in X_{test}} **do**
23:        E_{act} ← Calculate $f(x_s, t)$ {actual exposure using (x_j, t)} with G, Map
24:        E_{est} ← Calculate $g(t)$ {estimated exposure using t} with G, Map
25:        MSE_{emp} ← MSE_{emp} + newly calculated MSE_{emp}
26:      **end for**
27:      MSE_{emp} ← $\frac{MSE_{emp}}{m}$ {average MSE_{emp}}
28:      **if** $MSE_{emp} > MSE_A$ {more training needed} **then**
29:        TD_{train} ← $\{\}$, TD_{train} ← TD_{test} {use old testing data for a new training}
30:        TD_{test} ← $\{\}$, TD_{test} ← Extract (x_i, t) pair from newly collected data $Traj$
31:      **end if**
32: **until** $MSE_{emp} \leq MSE_A$
33: **Usage:** Start exposure estimation $g(t)$ using a travel time t from A to B

---

analysis, the locations of A and B were captured from individual's trajectory data. For a given $(A - B)$ travel, we calculated the set $\mathcal{P}$, which is the set of k-rank paths based on the travel time distribution assigned on the edges of G. For our simulations, we considered sets of 5 candidate paths for each $(A - B)$ pair. The paths for pair $(A_1 - B_1)$ are shown in Fig. 2.

Individual's Trajectory Datasets. We first set up 100 individuals' profiles and then generated synthetic travel datasets for each individual's travels on three different $(A - B)$ travel locations. For each travel pair $(A - B)$, we generated the data as follows: (1) construct the individual probability functions $p_{ind}(x)$ for the k candidate paths, (2) for each x_i in $\mathcal{P}$, randomly select reasonable μ_i and σ_i and

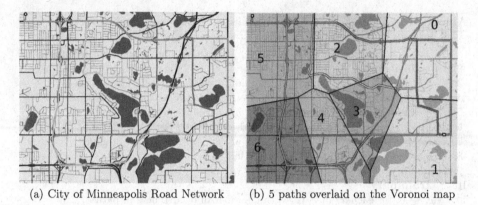

(a) City of Minneapolis Road Network   (b) 5 paths overlaid on the Voronoi map

Fig. 2. 5 paths for travel $(A_1 - B_1)$ overlaid on the Voronoi map of the synthetic tests

set the individual's travel time distribution $p_{ind}(t|x_i)$ to the normal distribution $N_i(\mu_i, \sigma_i^2)$, (3) select a path from $\mathcal{P}$ using the individual's true probability of $p_{ind}(x_i)$, (4) determine a travel time t from A to B using $p_{ind}(t|x_i)$ assigned to each x_i in $\mathcal{P}$, and (5) repeat (1)–(4), create a training and testing set of (x_i, t) pairs of travel data.

Individual path selection and travel time distributions have a significant impact on the model's performance. Each individual's $p_{ind}(x)$ was constructed from the base probability, $p(x)$: $[0.2, 0.4, 0.1, 0.1, 0.2]$ by adding a random number between 0 and 0.5 to each probability and normalizing to get a probability function. Average travel times (in seconds) and standard deviations were constructed similarly with a base of $[960, 900, 1020, 1140, 1050]$ plus/minus 400, $[1380, 1560, 1680, 1440, 1560]$ plus/minus 600 and $[1920, 1980, 2160, 2100, 2100]$ plus/minus 800 respectively for times and $[60, 45, 70, 75, 65]$ plus/minus 40, $[80, 95, 100, 85, 90]$ plus/minus 60 and $[120, 125, 135, 125, 130]$ plus/minus 80 for standard deviations.

Trajectory data from two individuals' daily commute to work on real road networks were also used: 32 days of travel data in the City of Eau Claire Network in the USA, and 48 days of travel data in the City of Al Ain Road Network in the United Arab Emirates.

6.2 Normalized Root-Mean-Square Deviation: $NRMSD$

Synthetic tests were performed to compare the model's long term average square estimation error with the theoretically minimal MSE_{the} of Lemma 1 for each $(A - B)$ pair subject to three different levels of environmental variation. The MSE_{the} depends on the individual's $p_{ind}(x, t)$ as well as the particular layout of the Voronoi map, the environmental variation levels in the Voronoi cells and the layout of the paths in the cells. If the environmental conditions change, the MSE_{the} also depends on the probability of any given set of conditions arising.

Therefore, a different MSE_{the} is achieved for each individual, each of the $(A-B)$ pairs, and for each level of environmental variation.

Since the standard exposome model of environmental exposure described in Sect. 4 relies on the aggregation of weather data into Voronoi cells with similar conditions, the accuracy of any exposure estimate using this definition is susceptible to the *Modifiable Areal Unit Problem* (MAUP), to which scaling of the spatial and temporal dimensions and magnitude of the quantity under investigation are primary contributors [19]. To test our model's robustness against the MAUP, we ensured that the number of Voronoi cells through which the paths used for synthetic data generation passed increased in proportion to their length. We also performed synthetic tests with a range of different variability in the environmental conditions. Specifically, for each pair $(A_i - B_i)$, $i = 1, 2, 3$ the paths overlapped Voronoi maps with $7, 12$ and 18 cells respectively. Environmental conditions were simulated in "high", "medium" and "low" variation. For "high" variation, cell values varied randomly from base values by 75% baseline level, for "medium" variation, fluctuation was 58% of baseline and "low" variation was 40% of baseline.

Since the size of the expected square error grows with the square of the size of the average value of $f(x, t)$, for both MSE_{the} and MSE_{emp} the *Normalized Root-Mean-Square Deviation*, $NRMSD$ was calculated and converted to a percentage value: $Percent\ NRMSD_{emp} = 100 * (\sqrt{MSE_{emp}}/f_{ave})$, and $Percent\ NRMSD_{the} = 100 * (\sqrt{MSE_{the}}/f_{ave})$.

The expected value for the theoretical MSE_{the} in Lemma 1 calls for averaging over all routes and integrating over time and environmental conditions with respect to their densities. Integrals over time were performed with numerical quadrature, but because of the high dimension of the environmental data, integrals over environmental conditions were estimated by drawing a random sample of size 100 from the set of possible environmental conditions and constructing a 99.9% confidence interval. Intervals for percent $NRMSD_{the}$ derived from 99.9% confidence intervals for the MSE_{the} had widths ranging from 0.76 (long paths with low environment change) to 1.89 (short paths with high environment change).

To test the effects of training, 100 synthetic individuals were processed through each $A_i - B_i$ pair and each environmental regime. Hyperparameters were initialized as discussed in Sect. 4.2 with $m_i = 0$ to test a maximally incorrect initial guess on travel time. In practice, initial m_i values closer to the individual's true average travel time would improve the effects of training. Their training duration was varied from 5 to 40 days as shown in Table 1 and the percent $NRMSD_{emp}$ was estimated over 250 days in order to reduce the effect of variation in the daily error and accurately compare the percent $NRMSD_{emp}$ achieved by the model with the theoretical percent $NRMSD_{the}$. As shown in this table, for training cycles as short as 10 or 20 days the model's relative estimation error was under 5% of the average exposure accumulation, and only in highly variable environmental conditions was the estimation error greater than 10% of average accumulation. These results strongly support the model's viability in accurately

Table 1. Comparisons of percent $NRMSD_{emp}$ and percent $NRMSD_{the}$ w/synthetic datasets for varied (training data #, testing data #)

$(A_i - B_i)$	Variance in env.	$NRMSD_{emp}$(%)					$NRMSD_{the}$ (%)
		(5, 250)	(10, 250)	(20, 250)	(30, 250)	(40, 250)	
$(A_1 - B_1)$ $\bar{t} = 898$ sec	High	18.46	15.89	13.52	12.20	11.73	**10.78**
	Medium	7.39	6.02	4.76	4.74	4.47	**4.22**
	Low	5.48	4.68	4.05	3.95	3.65	**3.41**
$(A_2 - B_2)$ $\bar{t} = 1524$ sec	High	8.28	7.39	6.55	6.14	5.85	**5.51**
	Medium	9.77	8.34	7.54	6.91	6.47	**5.94**
	Low	4.06	3.47	2.96	· 2.91	2.60	**2.52**
$(A_3 - B_3)$ $\bar{t} = 2022$ sec	high	7.99	7.14	5.98	5.91	5.51	**4.86**
	Medium	5.36	4.53	3.99	3.83	3.75	**3.41**
	Low	4.53	3.69	3.26	3.05	3.07	**2.60**

Table 2. Comparisons of individuals' percent $NRMSD_{emp}$ and percent $NRMSD_{the}$ w/synthetic datasets for varied (training data #, testing data #)

Ind.	$(A_i - B_i)$	Variance in env.	$NRMSD_{emp}$(%)					$NRMSD_{the}$ (%)
			(5, 250)	(10, 250)	(20, 250)	(30, 250)	(40, 250)	
I_1	$(A_1 - B_1)$	High	19.92	19.42	16.98	13.23	12.74	**11.77**
I_2		Medium	7.17	6.33	5.01	5.55	4.64	**4.80**
I_3		Low	4.19	3.09	3.63	3.84	3.84	**2.61**
I_4	$(A_2 - B_3)$	High	7.68	6.94	6.74	6.46	6.90	**6.43**
I_5		Medium	11.48	9.51	6.95	6.33	6.22	**4.99**
I_6		Low	4.03	3.65	3.70	2.91	2.76	**2.31**
I_7	$(A_3 - B_3)$	High	8.09	6.99	6.61	6.23	5.72	**4.61**
I_8		Medium	7.52	5.35	3.88	3.32	2.73	**2.34**
I_9		Low	4.38	3.17	2.97	3.04	3.42	**2.80**

predicting exposure accumulation. Similar results are illustrated in Table 2 that shows nine synthetic individuals' percent $NRMSD_{emp}$ compared to the percent $NRMSD_{the}$.

The datasets of real individual's travels were of size 32 days and 48 days respectively, so extensive training and testing was not possible. With this data, however, we can observe that with as few as 20 training days, the model's relative percent $NRMSD_{emp}$ appears to be under 10% of the average exposure accumulation for their paths. Table 3 shows results of training and testing for the 2 real data sets for train and test cycles of lengths expected in practice. As can be seen from these tables, while the variability in observed percent $NRMSD_{emp}$ is high, all of the values stay under 10% relative error after training as few as 7 days. As discussed in the next section, daily variability in the estimation error causes difficulties in drawing long-term conclusions from limited testing data.

Table 3. Percent $NRMSD_{emp}$ w/real datasets for (training data #, testing data #) Column 3 gives the range of average travel times and standard devitions for the paths.

Ind	$(A_i - B_i)$	Travel time $p(t\|x_i)$ μ_i, σ_i	Variance in cells in env	$NRMSD_{emp}$(%)		
				(7, 7)	(14, 8)	(22, 10)
I_{r1}	$(A_4 - B_4)$ $\bar{t} = 970$ sec	[827, 1029], [11, 155]	Medium	4.12	5.55	2.71
I_{r2}	$(A_5 - B_5)$ $\bar{t} = 449$ sec	[392, 690], [50, 57]	Medium	8.68	5.20	2.41

6.3   Challenges Due to Variability in $NRMSD_{emp}$

One difficulty we foresee in using the model in practice is the natural high variability of the observed square estimation error for each observed (x_i, t) pair. This unavoidable variation is due to the individual's travel habits, the layout of the Voronoi cells relative to the paths traveled and finally the environmental condition's pattern of change. This causes difficulty for short testing cycles because the observed percent $NRMSD_{emp}$ calculated from a small sample cannot be assumed accurately to represent the model's long term performance under the current training level.

Figure 3 illustrates this phenomenon for two typical synthetic individuals' travels. In that figure, training levels of $5, 10, 20$ and 40 days were compared as testing days varied between 1 and 250 days. As expected, for short testing durations the percent $NRMSD_{emp}$ exhibits high variability, but as the number of testing days grows over 40 or so, the Law of Large Numbers begins to take over and the percent $NRMSD_{emp}$ values begin to approach a limit. This suggests that in practice, a short testing period is unable to accurately measure the model's true training level, and care must be taken in testing and training.

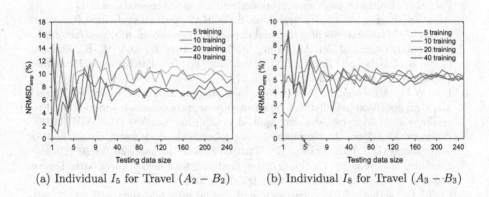

(a) Individual I_5 for Travel $(A_2 - B_2)$ (b) Individual I_8 for Travel $(A_3 - B_3)$

Fig. 3. Convergence in 2 individuals' percent $NRMSD_{emp}$ w/synthetic datasets

7   Conclusions and Future Work

In this paper, we proposed a framework for approximating path selection and travel time probabilities on an individual level for the purpose of estimating accumulated exposure to an environmental factor (e.g., accumulated exposure to the pollutant PM_{10}) an individual accumulated during travels, using only the travel time and locations of the start and end of the path. We further proposed and tested, on real and synthetic data, an exposure estimation algorithm based on this framework. The tests demonstrate that after training on as few as 20 training trajectories, our model is able to accurately estimate accumulated exposure to within about 5 to 7 percent of the total accumulation in conditions as or more varied than expected in practice.

A primary application of our algorithm is to reduce the power requirements involved in monitoring harmful environmental exposure for medical patients by enabling GPS readings to cease during travel between commonly visited points of interest. For full implementation, several further steps are required. First is an analysis of the accuracy of our model extended to multiple points of interest. Second, a method for dealing with trips not originating and terminating at historical points of interest is required, which may involve modifying the current algorithm to work with regularly but extremely sparsely recorded GPS data. A final clear need is a method to predict with confidence when an individual is en route to a location unknown to the model.

Acknowledgments. This material is based upon works supported in part by the Information and Communication Technology Fund of the United Arab Emirates under award number 21T042 and in part by Hanyang University under award number 2016–473.

References

1. Genome research center for allergy and respiratory diseases. Soon Chung Hyang University Hospital, Korea
2. Propeller Health. https://www.propellerhealth.com/. Accessed Jan 2017
3. Alkobaisi, S., Bae, W.D., Narayanappa, S.: SCHAS: a visual evaluation framework for mobile data analysis of individual exposure to environmental risk factors. In: Claramunt, C., Schneider, M., Wong, R.C.-W., Xiong, L., Loh, W.-K., Shahabi, C., Li, K.-J. (eds.) SSTD 2015. LNCS, vol. 9239, pp. 484–490. Springer, Heidelberg (2015). doi:10.1007/978-3-319-22363-6_27
4. Bae, W.D., Alkobaisi, S., Meyers, W., Narayanappa, S., Vojtěchovský, P.: Voronoi maps: an approach to individual-based environmental exposure estimation. In: Proceedings of ACM Symposium on Applied Computing, pp. 596–603. ACM (2016)
5. Bierlaire, M., Chen, J., Newman, J.: A probabilistic map matching method for smartphone GPS data. Transp. Res. Part C: Emerg. Technol. **26**, 78–98 (2013)
6. Bierlaire, M., Frejinger, E.: Route choice modeling with network-free data. Transp. Res. Part C: Emerg. Technol. **16**(2), 187–198 (2008)
7. Chen, J., Bierlaire, M.: Probabilistic multimodal map matching with rich smartphone data. J. Intell. Transp. Syst. **19**(2), 134–148 (2015)
8. Dalumpines, R.: GIS-based episode reconstruction using GPS data for activity analysis and route choice modeling. Ph.D. thesis (2014)

9. Demšar, U., Buchin, K., Cagnacci, F., Safi, K., Speckmann, B., Van de Weghe, N., Weiskopf, D., Weibel, R.: Analysis and visualisation of movement: an interdisciplinary review. Mov. Ecol. **3**(1), 5 (2015)
10. Denison, D.G.: Bayesian Methods for Nonlinear Classification and Regression, vol. 386. Wiley, Hoboken (2002)
11. Fang, S., Zimmermann, R.: EnAcq: energy-efficient GPS trajectory data acquisition based on improved map matching. In: Proceedings of the 19th ACM SIGSPATIAL International Conference on Advances in Geographic Information Systems, pp. 221–230. ACM (2011)
12. He, R.R., Liu, H.X., Kornhauser, A.L., Ran, B.: Temporal and spatial variability of travel time. Institute of Transportation Studies, University of California, Irvine (2002)
13. Hua, M., Pei, J.: Probabilistic path queries in road networks: traffic uncertainty aware path selection. In: Proceedings of the 13th International Conference on Extending Database Technology, pp. 347–358. ACM (2010)
14. Hunter, T., Abbeel, P., Bayen, A.: The path inference filter: model-based low-latency map matching of probe vehicle data. IEEE Trans. Intell. Transp. Syst. **15**(2), 507–529 (2014)
15. Luo, G., Stone, B.L., Fassl, B., Maloney, C.G., Gesteland, P.H., Yerram, S.R., Nkoy, F.L.: Predicting asthma control deterioration in children. BMC Med. Inform. Decis. Making **15**(1), 84 (2015)
16. Newson, P., Krumm, J.: Hidden Markov map matching through noise and sparseness. In: Proceedings of the 17th ACM SIGSPATIAL, pp. 336–343. ACM (2009)
17. Ochieng, W.Y., Quddus, M.A., Noland, R.B.: Map-matching in complex urban road networks. Braz. J. Cartogr. **55**(2), 1–14 (2003)
18. Ouyang, R.W., Wong, A.K.S., Chiang, M., Woo, K.T., Zhang, V.Y., Kim, H., Xiao, X.: Energy efficient assisted GPS measurement and path reconstruction for people tracking. In: 2010 IEEE Global Telecommunications Conference (GLOBECOM 2010), pp. 1–5. IEEE (2010)
19. Paul, T., Stanley, K., Osgood, N., Bell, S., Muhajarine, N.: Scaling behavior of human mobility distributions. In: Miller, J.A., O'Sullivan, D., Wiegand, N. (eds.) GIScience 2016. LNCS, vol. 9927, pp. 145–159. Springer, Heidelberg (2016). doi:10.1007/978-3-319-45738-3_10
20. Quddus, M.A., Ochieng, W.Y., Noland, R.B.: Current map-matching algorithms for transport applications: State-of-the art and future research directions. Transp. Res. Part C: Emerg. Technol. **15**(5), 312–328 (2007)
21. Quddus, M.A., Ochieng, W.Y., Zhao, L., Noland, R.B.: A general map matching algorithm for transport telematics applications. GPS Solutions **7**(3), 157–167 (2003)
22. Shen, L., Stopher, P.R.: Review of GPS travel survey and GPS data-processing methods. Transport Rev. **34**(3), 316–334 (2014)
23. Thiagarajan, A., Ravindranath, L., LaCurts, K., Madden, S., Balakrishnan, H., Toledo, S., Eriksson, J.: VTrack: accurate, energy-aware road traffic delay estimation using mobile phones. In: Proceedings of the 7th ACM Conference on Embedded Networked Sensor Systems, pp. 85–98. ACM (2009)
24. Wang, J.H., Gao, Y.: Identification of GPS positioning solutions deteriorated by signal degradations using a fuzzy inference system. GPS Solutions **8**(4), 245–250 (2004)
25. Wild, C.P.: The exposome: from concept to utility. Int. J. Epidemiol. **41**(1), 24–32 (2012)

Semantic Trajectories in Mobile Workforce Management Applications

Nieves R. Brisaboa, Miguel R. Luaces[✉], Cristina Martínez Pérez,
and Ángeles S. Places

Laboratorio de Bases de Datos, Universidade da Coruña, A Coruña, Spain
{brisaboa,luaces,cristina.martinez,asplaces}@udc.es

Abstract. As a consequence of the competition between different man-
ufacturers, current smartphones improve their features continuously and
they currently include many sensors. *Mobile Workforce Management
(MWM)* is an industrial process that would benefit highly from the
information captured by the sensors of mobile devices. However, there
are some problems that prevent MWM software from using this information: (i) the abstraction level of the activities currently identified is
too low (e.g., *moving* instead of *performing an inspection on a client*, or
stopped instead of *loading a truck in the facility of a client*); (ii) research
work focuses on using geographic information algorithms on GPS data,
or machine learning algorithms on sensor data, but there is little research
on combining both types of data; and (iii) context information extracted
from geographic information providers or MWM software is rarely used.
In this paper, we present a new methodology to turn raw data collected from the sensors of mobile devices into trajectories annotated
with semantic activities of a high level of abstraction. The methodology is based on *activity taxonomies* that can be adapted easily to the
needs of any company. The activity taxonomies describe the expected
values for each of the variables that are collected in the system using
predicates defined in a *pattern specification language*. We also present
the functional architecture of a module that combines context information retrieved from MWM software and geographic information providers
with data from the sensors of the mobile device of the worker to annotate
their trajectories and that can be easily integrated in MWM systems and
in the workflow of any company.

Keywords: Semantic trajectories · Mobile Workforce Management ·
Sensor data · Geographic information systems

1 Background and Motivation

The use of mobile devices has grown incessantly in the last decade and more
than 60% of the people in advanced economies report owning a smartphone [7].

Funded by MINECO (PGE & FEDER) [TIN2013-46238-C4-3-R, TIN2013-46801-
C4-3-R, TIN2013-47090-C3-3-P, TIN2015-69951-R]; CDTI and MINECO [Ref. IDI-
20141259, Ref. ITC-20151305, Ref. ITC-20151247]; Xunta de Galicia (co-funded by
FEDER) [GRC2013/053].

© Springer International Publishing AG 2017
D. Brosset et al. (Eds.): W2GIS 2017, LNCS 10181, pp. 100–115, 2017.
DOI: 10.1007/978-3-319-55998-8_7

Furthermore, the capabilities of mobile devices such as smartphones, tablet computers, and wearable devices have increased continuously. Their computing power is similar to the one of a desktop computer from the last decade, and they include multiple sensors that can be used to measure different variables such as the geographic position using a GPS receiver, the user activity using an accelerometer, or the surrounding environment using a thermometer. An industrial process that would benefit especially from the information collected using mobile devices is *Mobile Workforce Management (MWM)*. MWM systems are used by companies to manage and optimize the task scheduling of their workers (e.g., ensuring that the company has the lowest number of active employees at any time of the day) and to improve the performance of their business processes (e.g., detecting which tasks are costly for the company). As an example, it would be very beneficial for a company that collects waste materials in rural areas to detect if the workers spend a long time in the activity *refueling* to help deciding whether it is good idea to hire someone who does this work at night.

This type of studies are impossible to carry out without the historical movement data of the workers and a procedure to detect and analyze, at a high level of abstraction, the activities they were performing and how much time they required. If the MWM system can detect what has really happened on a working day and compare it to what was scheduled, it can generate useful information to manage the business processes and to detect the critical points. However, current MWM systems are not using the information that can be collected by mobile devices. At most, they are using the location services to record the time when a worker arrived at the client facility, but they do not use the full range of data collected by the sensors of the mobile devices to answer queries such as *was the worker at a traffic jam that made him arrive late?* or *how much time is wasted walking inside a client facility in each visit?* because the data is massive and complex.

The interest in coherently organizing and labeling sequences of spatio-temporal points to handle starts with the seminal works [1,10,11] where the idea of assigning semantic keywords to the raw data obtained from a GPS sensor is presented for the first time. However, these works assume that the semantic keywords are obtained from other sources and not from the GPS data itself. That is, the system analyzes the GPS data sequence and organizes it into coherent sets but, instead of labelling them, it presents them to be annotated by the user. From then on, a new line of research was born in the scientific community dedicated to semantically annotating moving objects, and the center of interest has shifted from raw data obtained from the GPS sensor, to greaters level of abstraction oriented to the needs of concrete applications. There has been lately much research work in the field of *semantic trajectories* addressing the problems of collecting, modeling, storing and analyzing these data. A semantic trajectory is a set of episodes, each one consisting of a start time, an end time, and a semantic keyword. A good summary of the research and the challenges in the field can be found in [6]. However, the research on semantic trajectories is focusing on detecting low-level activities such as *stopped, moving, walking*, or *running* instead of high-level activities such as *stuck in a traffic jam on the way to a client facility*, or *loading the truck in the facility of a client*. The reason of this mismatch in the abstraction level is that research on semantic trajectories is aimed at the general case and there is a limited usage of context information, whereas in a MWM system the context information (e.g., the schedule of the worker) is extremely important.

Some of the techniques proposed in the research field of semantic trajectories have focused on the use of machine learning techniques for the detection of activities [2,8,9]. However, these techniques cannot be applied in MWM systems because they require training data, which is very is expensive to collect. For example, in an MWM system this would mean that employees must annotate for each task they perform during the day the start and end time, which is an expensive and cumbersome process. In addition, there will be a large margin of error because it is very difficult for an employee to perform his work and at the same time to collect the sample data for the training process. The employee will easily forget to tag the start or end of an activity and therefore, the sample data set would be wrong. Finally, this could cause the employees to make mistakes in their real tasks. Hence, the annotation of semantic trajectories using machine learning techniques do seem appropriate.

Other research papers have focused on modeling, representing, processing, querying, and mining object trajectories in their raw state. These lines of research define query languages and model the paths of moving objects so that specific patterns can be extracted later using query languages. In [3] the raw data is divided in *stop* and *move* episodes [10], and relevant geographic information from the application domain is assigned to each episode. Then, the authors define a semantic trajectory data mining query language (ST-DMQL) to extract knowledge (data mining) from the raw data using queries and movement patterns. The authors of [5] propose the idea that a trajectory is formed by segments of different levels of abstraction according to different criteria (e.g., stops and moves versus the transport system used). In [4] the authors define a *symbolic trajectory* as a set of units composed by a time interval plus a value that can be of type *label*, *labels*, *place* or *places*. The authors also define a query language with operators to filter and retrieve those symbolic trajectories. Even though all these approaches can be used to efficiently query trajectory data, they are all techniques of a low level of abstraction and they are hardly integrable in an MWM system because it would require an untrained company manager to write complex queries.

Finally, in addition to the problems mentioned above, all the solutions are generic and do not assume any additional knowledge beyond the data of the trajectory. However, in the case of the integration with an MWM system, it is necessary to keep in mind that additional information is known and must be taken into account.

In this paper, we present the functional architecture of a module for MWM systems that can be used to collect the information captured by the sensors of the mobile devices, to analyze and annotate the trajectory with high-level activities using context information from the MWM system and geographic information providers, and to provide the semantic trajectory information back to the MWM system in order to support business intelligence processes. The rest of this paper is organized as follows. Section 2 describes the annotation methodology and the activity taxonomies that form the basis of the methodology. Then, Sect. 3 describes the activity pattern specification language that is used on the taxonomy to decide which activity is performed. Finally, Sect. 4 presents the functional architecture of the working system and Sect. 5 presents the conclusions and future work.

2   Annotation Methodology

The purpose of the annotation process is to divide the *raw data* captured by the mobile device during the working day into a collection of activities, each one consisting of a start time, an end time and a label that describes the activity performed by the worker. For example, Fig. 1 shows an annotated trajectory in which the worker was performing the activity *driving on a planned route* between 09:00 and 09:10.

The raw data used to build and annotate the trajectory is retrieved from three different sources: *the MWM system, the sensors of the mobile device*, and *the geographical information of the domain*. Regarding the *MWM system*, the conceptual model of the Fig. 2 shows the minimum information required by the annotation process. First, it is necessary to know the information of all the workers of the company (represented in the class `Worker`). In addition, we must know all the locations to which the employees have to go in their work day (represented in the class `Location`). Each location is described by the name of the client, the name and the geographic position of the location, and a boolean value to indicate whether the location is a facility of our own company or it is a facility of a client. Finally, the daily schedule of each worker is represented by the `Schedule` class. This class describes, for each task that must be performed by each worker, the scheduled start and end time, the type of task (from a catalog

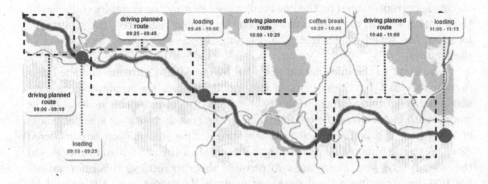

Fig. 1. Trajectory annotated with semantic activities

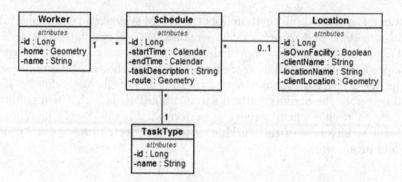

Fig. 2. Minimum information required from the MWM system

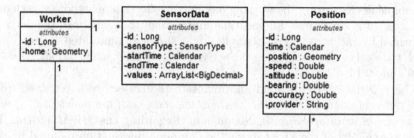

Fig. 3. Raw data collected from the mobile device

represented by `TaskType`), a description of the task, and the planned route that the employee must follow to reach the location.

Figure 3 shows a conceptual model of the information collected by the sensors of the mobile device. Each worker (represented by the `Worker` class) is related to all the values collected by the sensors. The sensor information is represented by the `SensorData` class, which stores the sensor type, the time interval when the value was collected, and the value itself. In addition, we keep all the locations of the workers (represented by the `Position` class) storing the variables collected by the location sensor: the time instant when the value is registered, the geographic location, the speed, the height, the heading, the precision and the provider of the location.

In addition to the information provided by the MWM software and the information collected by the sensors of the mobile device, the annotation process needs the geographic information of the domain to compare the location of the worker with elements of the context such as the road network, or specific points of interest of the domain such as gas stations. This information is considered external to the annotation system, but it is used in the annotation process and the system retrieves. There are two possible ways to retrieve this information: the first by accessing a local database using SQL queries, and the second by

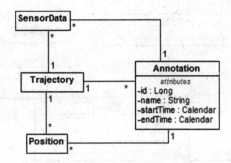

Fig. 4. Annotated trajectory

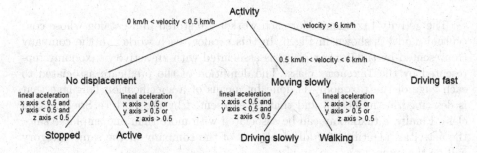

Fig. 5. Example of an activity taxonomy

querying OpenStreetMap using the Overpass API[1]. In both cases, the result is a set of geographic objects that can be used in the evaluation of the activity pattern.

The conceptual model in Fig. 4 shows the expected result of the annotation process. A raw trajectory is a set of raw data represented by the `SensorData` and `Position` classes. An annotated trajectory consists of a set of annotations represented by the class `Annotation`. Each annotation stores the activity name, the start and end time of the activity, and it references the raw data that compose the activity.

The basis of the annotation process is the *activity taxonomy*. For each of the worker types in the company an activity taxonomy must be defined that includes all the activities that can be performed by the worker type and that includes the rules for deciding what activity is performed at each time interval. The Fig. 5 shows an example of an activity taxonomy. The leaf nodes of the taxonomy are the activities that can be performed by a worker (e.g., *stopped, active, driving slowly, walking, driving fast*). Each intermediate node is formed by a set of edges. Each taxonomy edge is tagged with an *activity pattern* that represents the expected values for the variables that are collected in the system (e.g., $0\,\text{km/h} < velocity < 0.5\,\text{km/h}$).

---

[1] https://overpass-api.de/.

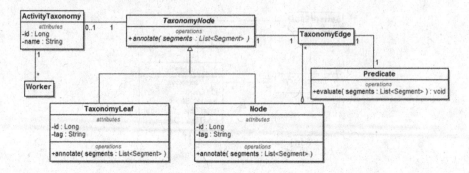

Fig. 6. Catalog of activity taxonomies

The activity taxonomies for each worker are stored in a catalog whose conceptual model is shown in Fig. 6. In this catalog, each worker in the company (represented by the `Worker` class) is associated with an activity taxonomy represented by the `Taxonomy` class. The definition of the predicate associated to each edge of the taxonomy is done by means of a specification language that is described in the Sect. 3 and that is represented by the Pattern Specification class. Finally, a taxonomy can be associated with more than one employee since the activities identified for all employees of the company in the same category will be the same.

The procedure for annotating the trajectories is described in Algorithm 1. The first step is to obtain all the workers of the company. Then, for each worker, the activity taxonomy corresponding to the worker type is retrieved. After that, the raw data is retrieved for the worker. As shown in Fig. 3, the sensor data consists of a collection of `SensorData` objects, each of them consisting of a time interval and a sensor value. Similarly, the location data consists of a collection of `Position` objects, each of them consisting of a timestamp and the GPS variables. However, these data may not be *aligned* in the sense that the start and end times of the intervals are not necessarily the same for all sensor types, and the location timestamps may not coincide with any time interval. Therefore, it is necessary a step in the algorithm to homogenize the time intervals. The result is a collection of `TrajectorySegment` objects, each of them consisting of a time interval, a sensor value for each sensor type, a `Position`.

In the next step, the activity taxonomy is evaluated against the segmented trajectory. Algorithm 2 shows the algorithm used for the evaluation. The process starts at the root of the taxonomy. The first taxonomy edge is retrieved and its activity pattern is evaluated against the trajectory segments. All segments that evaluate to true are passed to the taxonomy edge child node to be evaluated recursively. This recursive procedure ends when a taxonomy leaf node is reached. In this case, all the segments received are annotated using the activity name in the leaf node. All the segments that do not evaluate to true in an internal node are evaluated against the next taxonomy edge. The segments that remain after all taxonomy edges are annotated as *undefined*.

Algorithm 1. Algorithm to annotate trajectories

---

function ANNOTATETRAJECTORIES(currentDate: Timestamp)
   workers ← retrieveWorkers()
   for all aWorker ∈ workers **do**
      ▷ *Retrieve the activity taxonomy*
      activityTaxonomy ← retrieveActivityTaxonomy(aWorker)
      rootNode ← activityTaxonomy.getRootNode()
      ▷ *Retrieve and segment the trajectory*
      rawTrajectory ← retrieveTrajectoryData(aWorker, currentDate)
      segmentedTrajectory ← segmentTrajectory(rawTrajectory)
      ▷ *Annotate the trajectory (see Algorithm 2)*
      rawAnnotation ← annotate(segmentedTrajectory, rootNode)
      ▷ *Aggregate contiguous segments of the same activity*
      annotation ← aggregateSegments(rawAnnotation)
      ▷ *Store the annotated trajectory*
      for all segment ∈ annotation **do**
         annotate(rawTrajectory, segment)
      end for
   end for
end function

Algorithm 2. Algorithm to evaluate a trajectory in a taxonomy node

---

function ANNOTATE(segmentedTrajectory: List of segments, node: TaxonomyNode)
   if node.getType() ≠ "leaf" **then**
      ▷ *It is an intermediate node*
      edges ← note.getTaxonomyEdges()
      for all anEdge ∈ edges **do**
         ▷ *The predicate of the edge is evaluated*
         evaluation ← anEdge.getPredicate().evaluate(segmentedTrajectory)
         ▷ *The segments that evaluate to* true *are passed to the child node*
         trueSegments ← removeTrueSegments(evaluation, segmentedTrajectory)
         annotate(trueSegments, anEdge.getChildNode())
         ▷ *Only the segments that evaluate to* false *are kept in segmentedTrajectory*
         removeFalseSegments(evaluation, segmentedTrajectory)
      end for
      ▷ *The remaining segments are annotated as* undefined
      annotate(segmentedTrajectory, *undefined*)
   else
      ▷ *It is a leaf node*
      for all segment ∈ segmentedTrajectory **do**
         ▷ *All segments are annotated with the activity of the node*
         segment.activity ← node.getActivityName()
      end for
   end if
end function

After evaluating the activity taxonomy against the segmented trajectory it may happen that many segments contiguous in time are annotated with the same activity. The next step of Algorithm 1 aggregates all these segments to a single one. The final step of the algorithm stores the annotation in a database following the conceptual model described in Fig. 4.

3   Pattern Specification Language

As described in Sect. 2, each edge of the activity taxonomy is associated with a predicate that is used to evaluate each trajectory segment and decide the concrete activity that is used to annotate the segment. Each predicate is defined using a *pattern specification language* that describes the expected values for each of the variables that are collected in the system. The language consists of seven different types of predicates that receive a trajectory represented as a list of segments and return the result of evaluating the predicate as a list of boolean value annotated with a time interval. The different types of predicates are the following and are grouped into two levels, primary level and composite level, this last level allows to combine simple predicates to build relationships between them.

Primary Predicates

- SensorPredicate: It returns true if the sensor values in the segment satisfies a comparison operator.
  - sensorname: The name of the device sensor used.
  - operator: A list of comparison operators used to check the sensor value against the threshold (one operator for each sensor dimension). Each operator may be one of $<, >, =, \leq, \geq, \neq$.
  - threshold: A list of threshold values used in the comparison (one value for each sensor dimension).
  - isOr: A boolean value determining whether it is enough that one sensor dimension fulfills the comparison (true), or all sensor dimensions are required to fulfill the comparison (false).
  - time: The minimum time interval that the sensor value must not fulfill the comparison in order to render the predicate false. This attribute is used to that short changes in the sensor values turn the predicate false (e.g., a sudden and short movement of the device should not be considered relevant if the device has been static for a long period of time).
- GPSPredicate: It returns true if the GPS position in the segment satisfies a comparison operator.
  - gpsattribute: The GPS attribute used in the predicate. It may be one of *speed, altitude, bearing, precission,* or *location provider.*
  - operator: A comparison operator used to check the GPS against the threshold. The operator may be one of $<, >, =, \leq, \geq, \neq$.
  - threshold: A threshold value used in the comparison.

- **time**: The minimum time interval that the GPS attribute must not fulfill the comparison in order to render the predicate false.
- **SpatialPredicate**: It evaluates whether the GPS position satisfies a spatial relationship with the context geographical information.
  - **operator**: The spatial relationship predicate used to compare the GPS position against the collection of spatial features. It may be any of the predicates defined by the Open Geospatial Consortium Simple Features Specification (i.e., *equals, disjoint, overlaps, touches, within, contains, intersects*).
  - **features**: A list of spatial features retrieved from the context geographic information.
  - **time**: The minimum time interval that the GPS position must not fulfill the spatial predicate in order to render the predicate false.
- **SchedulePredicate**: It returns true if the schedule information in the MWM for the worker satisfies a comparison operator.
  - **operator**: The comparison operator used between the task name provided in the predicate and the task scheduled in the MWM. It may be one of *equals, distinct, like, any* (returns true as long as there is an scheduled task).
  - **taskname**: The name of the task. It may use SQL-like wildcards.

Composite Predicates

- **LogicPredicate**: It allows to combine different predicates through logical operators.
  - **operator**: The logic operator used to combine the child predicates. It may be one of *and, or* or *not*.
  - **childpredicates**: A list of child predicates to be evaluated and combined.
- **DecisionPredicate**: It can be used to create a decision tree.
  - **condition**: The predicate that is evaluated and that is used to decide which value must be returned.
  - **isTrue**: The predicate that is returned when the condition predicate returns true.
  - **isFalse**: The predicate that is returned when the condition predicate returns false.
  - **isUndefined**: The predicate that is returned when the condition predicate returns undefined.
- **ConstantPredicate**: It returns a constant value (either true, false or undefined) regardless of the segment values. It is useful as a child predicate of a **DecisionPredicate**.
  - **value**: The value that is always returned by the predicate. It may be either *true, true,* or *undefined*.

Figures 7 and 8 show a conceptual model of these predicates. Each predicate is a specialization of the abstract class **Predicate**, which defines a method to evaluate the predicate on a list of trajectory segments. Each subclass of **Predicate** defines specific attributes for the concrete predicate and it overrides the method

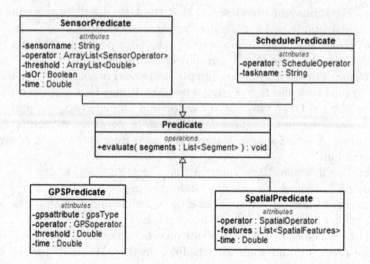

Fig. 7. Predicate types

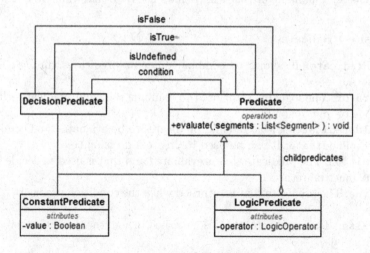

Fig. 8. Predicate types

evaluate to implement a different evaluation procedure. Finally, `LogicPredicate` and `DecisionPredicate` are special because they require a set of child predicates (the arguments of the logical operator in the first case, the decision predicate and the predicates for each decision result).

Figure 9 shows in a conceptual way the result of evaluating some predicates. The top part of the figure shows the GPS positions of the trajectory and a spatial feature used for the evaluation. The bottom part of the figure shows the results of the predicate evaluation. The horizontal axis represents time, the vertical axis

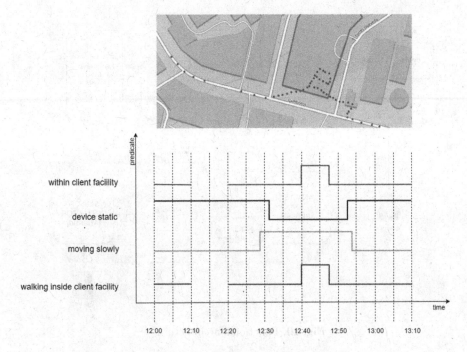

Fig. 9. Evaluation of the predicate *walking inside client facility*

represents the result of the evaluation of the predicate using a the value zero
if the evaluation is false, the value one if the evaluation is false, and no value
if the evaluation is undefined. The topmost predicate, *within client facility*, is a
`SpatialPredicate` that returns true when the GPS position is within the spatial
feature of the client facility (i.e., between 12:40 and 12:47) and false otherwise. It
also returns *undefined* from 12:10 to 12:20 because there are no GPS data. The
second predicate, *device static*, is a `SensorPredicate` that returns true when
the values returned by the linear accelerometer of the device are below $1\,\mathrm{m/s^2}$
(hence, the device is relatively static and the user is not walking or running). The
following predicate, *moving slowly*, is defined using a `GPSPredicate` that returns
true when the speed recorded by the GPS is less than $10\,\mathrm{km/h}$. Finally, the
predicate *walking inside client facility* is defined using a `LogicPredicate` that
combines the previous predicates using the logical operator *and* and negating
the predicate *device static* as follows:

walking inside client facility = within client facility $\wedge$

$\wedge\neg$ device static $\wedge$ moving slowly

4   System Architecture

Figure 10 shows the functional architecture of the system. On the left side of
the figure we show the MWM system with the minimal information that we

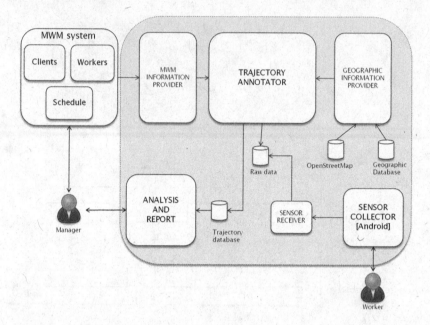

Fig. 10. Functional architecture

expect to retrieve: information regarding the clients of the company, the workers of the company, and their daily schedules. The right side of the figure shows the system that we have built, which is composed of a module that is deployed as an Android application on the worker mobile devices (i.e., *Sensor Collector*) and a collection of server-side modules (i.e., *Sensor Receiver, Geographic Information Provider, MWM Information Provider, Trajectory Annotator*, and *Analysis and Report*). The modules in the architecture are used by three different user roles: *workers* uses the *Sensor Collector* in their mobile devices, *company managers* review the information computed by the *Trajectory Annotator* using the *Analysis and Report* module, and *analysts* configure the different modules to suit the company needs (e.g., they define the activity taxonomies, define the geographic data sources, or configure the *Sensor Collector* sampling rate).

The Android sensor framework supports 13 types of sensors. An application monitoring sensor events decides the desired sampling rate ranging from 5 events per second to real-time (i.e., as fast as possible). Each sensor event consists of a timestamp, the reading accuracy and the sensor's data as an array of float values. The meaning of each element in the array depends on the sensor type, but typically each value represents the measurement in a specific dimension. For example, a linear acceleration sensor returns an acceleration measure on each of the three axes. Furthermore, each sensor reports about its capabilities, such as its maximum range, manufacturer, power requirements, and more importantly, its resolution.

The *Sensor Collector* module is an Android application that collects information from the devices of the workers and sends it to the server-side. The module can be configured to select which sensor types will be captured and the sampling rate used. In order to reduce the volume of data that must be stored in the mobile device and transmitted over the network, instead of storing every sampled value from the sensor, the data is stored aggregated in *sensor segments* that consist of a time interval (i.e., start time and end time) and a sensor event value array. When the Sensor Collector module receives a new sensor event, if the difference between the new sensor value and the value in the current sensor segment is smaller than the sensor resolution (i.e., the sensor event can be considered noise) the sensor event is discarded. Otherwise, the current sensor segment end time is set to the current timestamp and a new sensor segment is started.

The location sensor works differently in Android because the developer must configure a distance and a time threshold that must be exceeded in order to receive a location event. Therefore, the Android framework does the work of avoiding excessive location events. For example, a developer may indicate that a location event must only occur if the distance from the last position is larger than 10 m and the time passed is larger than 10 s. Hence, considering that the data rate from the location sensor is lower than the data rate from the other sensors, the *Sensor Collector* does not have to discard data from the location sensor.

Given that sending data through the mobile network is expensive in terms of battery life, and considering that the worker may not be connected at all times, the *Sensor Collector* uses two data queues to optimize the network usage. When a sensor event occurs, the data is stored in the *ready for packing* queue. Even though this task is executed frequently, it is simple and it does not consume much battery. At regular time intervals (e.g., every five minutes, although this time interval is configurable by the developer) all elements in the *ready for packing* queue are removed, compressed in a single data package using the ZIP file format, and stored in the *ready for sending* queue. A different process retrieves data packets from the *ready for sending* queue and tries to deliver them to the server-side. If the sending process is successful, the data packets are removed from the queue. Otherwise, the data packets in the queue to retry sending them later. These two strategies allow the *Sensor Collector* to save battery and to be resistant to network problems.

The sensor information is received in the server-side by the *Sensor Receiver*, which is a simple REST web service that receives the sensor data packets and stores them in the *raw data repository*, whose conceptual data model can be seen in Fig. 3.

The *Geographic Information Provider* retrieves geographic information from different data sources and makes it available to the trajectory annotator. This module currently supports two different types of geographic data sources: *spatial databases* (i.e., databases that support the Simple Features for SQL standard) and *OpenStreetMap* (i.e., using the Overpass API). A developer defines a geographic data source in this module providing a name for the data source and the query that must be executed (i.e., a JDBC connection string and a SQL query for spatial database, or an overpass query for OpenStreetMap). The spatial features in the geographic data sources are available to the trajectory annotator as a named list that can be used in the predicates.

The *MWM Information Provider* retrieves the information from the MWM system. The minimum information we expect to retrieve from the MWM system is described in the conceptual model of Fig. 2. This module is the only one that must be adapted for different MWM systems from different vendors. In some cases it may be a simple proxy that retrieves information from the web services provided by the MWM system, but in other cases it may be a complex module that retrieves information from the MWM data repositories.

The *Trajectory Annotator* module uses the raw data collected from the device sensors, the information retrieved from the MWM system, the context geographic information, and the activity taxonomies to annotate the trajectories of the workers and store them in the *trajectory database*, as described in Sect. 2.

Finally, the *Analysis and Report* module uses the annotated trajectories to provide useful information to the company managers, such as delays on the schedules, that can be used to improve future schedules.

5   Conclusions

We have presented in this paper a new methodology to turn raw data collected from the sensors of mobile devices into trajectories annotated with semantic activities of a high level of abstraction. The methodology is based on the concept of *activity taxonomies* that make the system is highly flexible because they can be adapted easily to the needs of any company. Furthermore, the activity taxonomies describe the expected values for each of the variables that are collected in the system using predicates defined in a *pattern specification language*, which is very expressive and takes into account not only the raw sensor data but also data retrieved from a *MWM system*, and from *domain-related context geographical information*. Finally, we describe the functional architecture of a module that can be easily integrated in MWM systems and in the workflow of any company.

As future work, we are finishing the implementation of all the modules and we plan to do a full-fledged experimental evaluation with two real companies in the context of a research project.

References

1. Baglioni, M., Macedo, J., Renso, C., Wachowicz, M.: An ontology-based approach for the semantic modelling and reasoning on trajectories. In: Song, I.-Y., et al. (eds.) ER 2008. LNCS, vol. 5232, pp. 344–353. Springer, Heidelberg (2008). doi:10.1007/978-3-540-87991-6_41
2. Bayat, A., Pomplun, M., Tran, D.A.: A study on human activity recognition using accelerometer data from smartphones. Procedia Comput. Sci. **34**, 450–457 (2014). The 11th International Conference on Mobile Systems and Pervasive Computing (MobiSPC 2014)

3. Bogorny, V., Kuijpers, B., Alvares, L.O.: ST-DMQL: a semantic trajectory data mining query language. Int. J. Geogr. Inf. Sci. **23**(10), 1245–1276 (2009)
4. Güting, R.H., Valdés, F., Damiani, M.L.: Symbolic trajectories. ACM Trans. Spat. Algorithms Syst. **1**(2), 7:1–7:51 (2015)
5. Ilarri, S., Stojanovic, D., Ray, C.: Semantic management of moving objects. Expert Syst. Appl. **42**(3), 1418–1435 (2015)
6. Parent, C., Spaccapietra, S., Renso, C., Andrienko, G., Andrienko, N., Bogorny, V., Damiani, M.L., Gkoulalas-Divanis, A., Macedo, J., Pelekis, N., Theodoridis, Y., Yan, Z.: Semantic trajectories modeling and analysis. ACM Comput. Surv. **45**(4), 42:1–42:32 (2013)
7. Pew Research Center: Smartphone ownership and internet usage continues to climb in emerging economies. http://www.pewglobal.org/2016/02/22/smartphone-owner ship-and-internet-usage-continues-to-climb-in-emerging-economies/. Accessed 12 Dec 2016
8. Read, J., Žliobaitė, I., Hollmén, J.: Labeling sensing data for mobility modeling. Inf. Syst. **57**, 207–222 (2016)
9. Rehman, M.H., Liew, C.S., Wah, T.Y., Shuja, J., Daghighi, B.: Mining personal data using smartphones and wearable devices: a survey. Sensors **15**(2), 4430 (2015)
10. Spaccapietra, S., Parent, C., Damiani, M.L., de Macedo, J.A., Porto, F., Vangenot, C.: A conceptual view on trajectories. Data Knowl. Eng. **65**(1), 126–146 (2008)
11. Yan, Z., Spremic, L., Chakraborty, D., Parent, C., Spaccapietra, S., Aberer, K.: Automatic construction and multi-level visualization of semantic trajectories. In: Proceedings of the 18th SIGSPATIAL International Conference on Advances in Geographic Information Systems, GIS 2010, pp. 524–525. ACM, New York (2010)

Web Visualization

Towards GPU-Accelerated Web-GIS for Query-Driven Visual Exploration

Jianting Zhang[1,2]([✉]), Simin You[2], and Le Gruenwald[3]

[1] Department of Computer Science, City College, City University of New York,
138th Convent Avenue, New York, NY 10031, USA
jzhang@cs.ccny.cuny.edu
[2] Department of Computer Science, Graduate Center, City University of New York,
365 Fifth Avenue, New York, NY 10016, USA
syou@gradcenter.cuny.edu
[3] Department of Computer Science, The University of Oklahoma,
110 W. Boyd Street, Norman, OK 73019, USA
ggruenwald@ou.edu

Abstract. Web-GIS has played an important role in supporting accesses, visualization and analysis of geospatial data over the Web for the past two decades. However, most of existing WebGIS software stacks are not able to exploit increasingly available parallel computing power and provide the desired high performance to support more complex applications on large-scale geospatial data. Built on top our past works on developing high-performance spatial query processing techniques on Graphics Processing Units (GPUs), we propose a novel yet practical framework on developing a GPU-accelerated Web-GIS environment to support Query-Driven Visual Explorations (QDVE) on Big Spatial Data. An application case on visually exploring global biodiversity data is presented to demonstrate the feasibility and the efficiency of the proposed framework and related techniques on both the frontend and backend of the prototype system.

Keywords: Web-GIS · GPU · QDVE · Spatial join · Biodiversity

1 Introduction

Since the inception of Web-GIS more than two decades ago, Web-GIS systems have played important roles in extending desktop GIS functionality to Web environments that allow users to visualize and query geographical information anywhere and anytime. In the coming Big Data era, the volume, variety and velocity (3Vs) of geo-referenced data increase proportionally, if not more rapidly, when compared with the mainstream relational data. However, although considerable new techniques have been developed for relational Big Data by exploiting newly emerging hardware, platforms and algorithms for higher performance, it seems that Web-GIS systems are still largely relying on the frameworks and techniques matured decades ago. As such, Web-GIS users are often forced to limit their applications to pre-aggregated data generated by third-party systems

© Springer International Publishing AG 2017
D. Brosset et al. (Eds.): W2GIS 2017, LNCS 10181, pp. 119–136, 2017.
DOI: 10.1007/978-3-319-55998-8_8

before feeding them to existing Web-GIS systems. This not only significantly increases end-to-end system complexity but also makes the overall performance very poor, as data exchanges among multiple systems through disks and network interfaces are known to be expensive. The low performance likely makes more performance demanding applications in Web-GIS environments impractical, such as query-driven visual exploration on large-scale geo-referenced data.

Although HTML5 has been quickly adopted and new Web techniques are increasingly feature-rich, the development of server side techniques for large-scale geospatial data is more complicated. Existing leading Big Data techniques, such as Hadoop and Spark, are mostly designed for offline batch processing on cluster computers. Although those techniques have been extended to process large-scale geospatial data (e.g. [1–4]), the technical complexity, hardware cost and high-latency make them generally unattractive for Web-GIS applications. Parallel techniques on multiple processors [5], such as multi-core CPUs and many-core Graphics Processing Units (GPUs), offer alternative solutions to cluster-based distributed computing techniques, although those two categories of techniques can be combined in principle. While efforts on parallelizing geospatial operations on multi-core CPUs for higher performance can be dated back to decades ago, using GPUs for general computing did not come into being until 2007 when Compute Unified Device Architecture (CUDA) was announced by Nvidia [6]. There have been growing interests in using the massively data parallel processing power provided by GPUs for geospatial processing (see Sect. 2 for more details), however, to the best of our knowledge, there have been little systematic efforts on using GPUs to speed up Web-GIS applications on large-scale geo-referenced data.

In this study, we propose to exploit parallel processing power on modern processors, adopt new parallel designs and implementations of spatial join query processing and refactor existing Web-GIS processing pipelines to support visual query exploration on large-scale geo-referenced data. Our specific contributions in this paper are the following. First, we present a novel yet practical framework on integrating GPU techniques, geospatial techniques and Web-GIS pipelines to enable query driven visual explorations on large-scale geo-reference data to achieve the desired high performance. Second, we design and implement the relevant components and develop a prototype system for feasibility and performance studies. Third, we perform experiments on a real world large-scale geospatial dataset at global scale to demonstrate its feasibility and realizable performance. The rest of the paper is arranged as follows. Section 2 introduces background, motivation and related work. Section 3 presents system architecture and the design and implementation details. Section 4 reports experiments and results. Finally, Sect. 5 is the conclusion and future work directions.

2   Background and Related Work

2.1   Web-GIS and Parallel and Distributed Processing

A Web-GIS can be considered as a distributed computing system that allows visualizing and querying geo-referenced data in Web browsers. Standards such

as Web Map Services (WMS) and Web Feature Services (WFS) are developed
to standardize data communication protocols between server side and client side
in a Web-GIS application. While it is desirable to expose as many desktop
GIS functionalities to Web browsers as possible, functionalities that are supported by WebGIS are typically limited when compared with desktop GIS, due
to security restrictions and limited accesses to native or raw computing power
through Web browsers in the browser-server computing model whose strength
and weakness are well understood. Query-Driven Visual Explorations (QDVE)
integrates dynamic queries with traditional visualization techniques to support
users explore large-scale datasets interactively (e.g. [7]). There have been growing interests in enabling QDVE in a Web environment. We consider Web-based
QDVE on large-scale geospatial data a special application of Web-GIS and is a
natural extension to traditional Web-GIS applications that primarily focus on
mapping and simple queries. It is easy to see that QDVE imposes significant
performance challenges on both client and server sides of Web-GIS systems in
this setting.

While client machines (including both PCs and mobile devices) hosting Web
browsers have significantly improved their processing power due to hardware progresses on single processors, the hardware performance improvements on server
side are mostly due to the increased parallelisms, including multi-core CPUs
and many-core GPUs. Indeed, while parallelizing a sophisticated general-purpose
browser program is very difficult, it is relatively easier to parallelize individual
server programs which are very often domain-specific and with abundant parallelisms to exploit. Unfortunately, most of existing Web-GIS applications are built
on top of legacy commercial or open-source Web-GIS systems that are aware of
neither application parallelisms nor the underlying parallel hardware. It is thus
both conceptually interesting and practically useful to match the intrinsic parallelisms in processing large-scale geospatial data with the increasingly available
parallel hardware for desired high performance in Web-GIS applications, especially for QDVE applications that demand interactive responses in real time.

Parallel processing of geospatial data is not a new idea and can be traced back
to at least two decades ago (see the dedicated book by Healey [8] for details).
However, as discussed in [9], research on parallel and distributed processing of
geospatial data prior to 2003 has very little impact on mainstream geospatial
data processing applications, possibly due to the accessibility of hardware and
infrastructures in the past. The past ten years have seen two major technical trends in scaling up large-scale data processing, one is MapReduce/Hadoop
based techniques for distributed computing and the other is GPU related techniques for parallel computing on a single computing node. MapReduce/Hadoop
based techniques provide a distributed execution engine and a runtime system to
automatically distribute Map and Reduce tasks to distributed computing nodes
and assemble results. So long as users can decompose their problems into independent Map and Reduce tasks, they do not need to write sophisticated and
error-prone distributed programs while are able to achieve significant speedups.
More efficient successors, such as Spark-based techniques that utilize in-memory

processing, are likely to play a leading role in Big Data market in the near future. Although there were attempts to integrate MapReduce/Hadoop based techniques for interactive visualization (e.g. [2]), their inherent high latency (due to start-up delay and batch-oriented processing schema) has made the attempts largely unsuccessful. Although Spark-based techniques are generally more efficient, there are still significant gaps between hardware potential and realizable capabilities. Our focus in this work is to maximize the utilization of increasing parallel computing power on a single computing node and understand its realizable performance on commodity hardware in the context of Web-GIS applications.

A typical modern computing node is equipped with 2–4 CPUs each with 4–16 processing cores (totaling 8–64 CPU cores) and multiple hardware accelerators, such as Nvidia GPUs [6]. While multi-core CPUs feature large-memory capacity and multi-level large caches to accommodate tasks with complex logics and irregular data accesses, GPUs typically have much larger number of cores ($10^2 - 10^4$), higher memory bandwidth ($10^2 - 10^3$ GB/s) and significantly higher floating point computing power (10+ TFLOPs) than multi-core CPUs [5]. Although a single CPU core may only have a few to a few tens of GFLOPs computing power, a modern computing node can easily achieve several tens of TFLOPs when SIMD computing power of both GPUs and multi-core CPUs are fully utilized. When properly used, the three orders higher computing power may produce orders of magnitude of higher performance.

Towards this end, we have been working on data parallel designs of major operations that support spatial query processing and we refer to an invited ACM SIGSPATIAL Special contribution [11] for a summary. Preliminary results have demonstrated thousands of times of speedups over traditional techniques that reflect the combined improvements of data structures, algorithms, in-memory process and GPU accelerations on a single computing node. This effectively reduces processing time from tens of hours to tens of seconds on several real world datasets on GPUs (e.g. [12,14]). However, as runtimes are not crucially important to offline processing, we believe that interactive applications, especially for QDVE on large-scale geospatial data in a Web-GIS environment where real time response is essential, are better suited for the newly developed high-performance geospatial techniques. While most of the data parallel designs and implementations utilized in this study were initially developed for offline applications as improvements to traditional single-node and cluster computing environments, we believe adopting and adapting these techniques for Web-GIS applications to support interactive QDVE is reasonably novel and could be interesting to the Web-GIS community, especially at the tipping point that hardware progresses demand software renovations due to the changed cost models, to better support real world applications.

2.2 Spatial Joins on GPUs

Spatial joins techniques are fundamental to spatial query processing in spatial databases [17,18], which are typically the core of a Web-GIS application backend, especially when working with vector geo-referenced data. For example, both MapServer and ESRI ArcGIS Server can delegate spatial operations written in SQL to major database systems that support spatial data, such as PostgreSQL (with PostGIS), Oracle and Microsoft SQLServer. Compared with point/location query and window/range query that involve querying a point/box against a single dataset which typically only incurs linear complexity at most, spatial joins typically involve multiple datasets and their tuples need to be related based on certain spatial operations. The indexing and query processing capabilities provided by such database systems are fundamental to the performance of Web-GIS applications when datasets are getting large. The efficiencies of indexing schemes and query execution plans, which may vary significantly among aforementioned spatially-enhanced database systems, have been one of the primary driving forces for spatial databases research. While hundreds of spatial indexing techniques and numerous query processing techniques have been proposed [19,20], most of them are designed for serial executions on uniprocessors.

Our efforts on developing spatial indexing and query processing techniques on GPU-accelerated machines are largely based data parallel deigns and implementations [11]. By carefully identifying parallelisms on spatial indexing (including grid-file based, quadtree based and R-Tree based) and spatial joins (including point-to-polyline/polygon distance based, point-in-polygon test based and polyline-intersection test based), we are able to chain parallel primitives [36], such as map/transform scan, reduce and sort, to partition spatial data into blocks (partitioning), index the Minimum Bounding Boxes (MBBs) of these blocks (indexing) and join them based on spatial intersections (filtering) before developing fine-grained parallel designs for geometric computation on GPUs (refinement). The behavior of the underlying parallel primitives is well understood and their efficient implementations on multiple parallel hardware (including both multi-core CPUs and GPUs) are available either by hardware vendors or parallel computing research community. Since spatial partitioning and indexing are typically one-time cost and spatial filtering are typically cheaper than refinement, the design choice represents a reasonable tradeoff between complexity and efficiency. On the other hand, spatial refinement generally involves floating-point intensive geometric computation and very often dominates the overall cost in spatial joins. As such, it is crucial to maximize its performance by exploiting GPU specific hardware features and we refer to our individual reports on computing point-to-polyline distance (NN) [13], point-to-polygon distance (KNN) [12], point-in-polygon test [10,14] and polyline intersection [16] based relationships. As a general strategy, in spatial refinement, we allocate a joined pair (P, Q) to a GPU thread block and let all the basic elements in P (e.g., points in a quadrant or a grid cell and vertices of a polyline or a polygon) loop through all the basic elements in Q to achieve coalesced memory accesses and reduce control divergence, both are important in maximizing GPU performance. We have also developed efficient lightweight data structures (e.g., array-based queues) on block-specific shared memory (fast but with very limited size [6]) and use atomic operations whereas appropriate to further maximize GPU hardware utilization.

While our data parallel spatial join techniques were motivated by GPU hardware, we have found that our in-memory columnar data layouts using flat arrays [12] have contributed significantly to the orders of magnitude of performance improvement when compared with traditional spatial databases that are typically row/tuple based and disk resident. By storing columns or column groups as arrays and only load columns that are relevant into CPU memory (and subsequently transferred to GPU memory), both disk I/Os and memory footprints can be significantly reduced. Furthermore, since array offsets can be used in lieu of pointers and data accesses in data parallel deigns are well behaved, the columnar layouts are cache friendly on CPUs and memory accesses are largely coalesced on GPUs, both are highly desirable with respect to memory system performance, which are becoming increasingly important on modern hardware.

2.3   Previous Efforts on WebGIS for QDVE on Large-Scale Geospatial Data

Our previous efforts on supporting QDVE in a WebGIS framework mostly focus on improving spatial indexing and query processing in traditional disk-resident systems (PostgreSQL in particular) and main-memory systems. In [21], we decompose millions of polygons from thousands of bird species range maps into linear quadtree nodes and represent them as strings. Subsequently, we use the LTREE module available in PostgreSQL[1] to index the strings and support window/range queries based on string matching. By using a same quadtree based spatial tessellation for both polygons and query windows, the technique essentially transforms a spatial query into a string query. While it does not seem to be elegant from a spatial databases research perspective, experiments have demonstrated the desired high performance than querying PostgreSQL/PostGIS directly with 6–9.5X speedups.

To further improve performance, we have developed a memory-resident Multi-Attributed Quadtree (MAQ-Tree) structure by re-using the linear quadtree nodes derived previously [22]. Basically, individual linear quadtree nodes that represent range maps of thousands of bird species were spatially aggregated based on binary linear codes. As such, polygon identifies are now associated with both intermediate and leaf quadtree nodes. A window/range query can be efficiently processed by traversing the multi-attributed quadtree while evaluating the query in memory at each quadtree node. The new technique, which was integrated with a OpenLayers based WebGIS, has reduced the end-to-end response time from high tens of seconds to below a second in a Web environment and is suitable for interactive location/window query processing.

We have also experimented a simple brute-force based technique to support simple QDVE in a WebGIS environment [15]. By adopting the columnar based design for point and polygon data discussed previously and utilizing multi-core

---

[1] http://www.sai.msu.su/~megera/postgres/gist/ltree/.

CPU parallel processing power, we have successfully demonstrated that interactively querying hundreds of millions of taxi trip records that fall within a few Regions of Interests (ROIs) that are defined by users interactively in a Web environment (using Google Map client APIs) while achieving sub-second end-to-end performance without sophisticated indexing is possible. It is conceivable that a WebGIS backend that can leverage both spatial indexing and parallel processing is essential to provide desired performance when handling more complex QDVE tasks on more complex spatial data types such as polygons and polylines.

Similar to indexing and querying vector data on GPUs, we have also developed a server side indexing technique called Binned Min-Max Quadtree (BMMQ-Tree) to support efficient query processing on large-scale raster data [23]. The technique was integrated with an ArcGIS Server for QDVE on monthly climate data using the 1-km global WorldClim datasets [24]. The BMMQ-Tree construction algorithm was later parallelized on GPUs with significant performance improvements [25, 26]. We further have developed a technique that converts query results on a BMMQ-Tree to tiled images to be overlaid with base map data at the client side for highlighting purposes [27]. As the on-the-fly derived query results are provided as dynamic WMS services, the technique imposes virtually no data management overhead to the server side (the CPU overhead of generating binary image tiles along with query processing is negligible) and is easy to use on client side (by using conventional XYZ tile request).

2.4   Other Related Work

It is beyond the scope of this paper to provide a comprehensive review of large bodies of related works on spatial databases, parallel processing of geospatial data, WebGIS and QDVE applications in various application contexts. Besides what have been discussed in the previous section and subsections, we refer to the SP-GIST project [28] for developing a general index framework for space partitioning trees and its implementation in PostgreSQL. Several research groups have developed GPU-based techniques for large scale geospatial data for different purposes [29, 30]. However, to the best of our knowledge, these techniques have not been applied to Web-GIS environment. There are several works that integrate high-end computing facilities at supercomputer centers and visualization software (e.g., ParaView[2]) to facilitate identifying and understanding patterns from large-scale geospatial data, such as weather and climate data [7]. A hybrid architecture that integrates the data storage and processing power from remote Cloud resources (Microsoft Azure in particular) and visual analytics functionality of local workstations is demonstrated to be beneficial for visual explorations of large-scale ocean data [2]. However, these systems are typically developed for domain experts that have accesses to supercomputer resources and are not available to the general public. Furthermore, the techniques behind are significantly different from those that Web-GIS applications are built upon.

---

[2] http://www.paraview.org/.

3   System Design and Prototyping

The prototype system being presented in this work integrates several techniques we have developed previously, including spatial indexing and spatial joins on GPUs, dynamic tiled map services and client side geometry APIs for query optimization. In this section, we will first introduce the overall system design and then present details of the relevant modules. Due to time limit, not all modules discussed have been tested and they are left for future work. The overall system design follows a typical Web-GIS framework: a server side backend for data processing, a client side frontend runs in Web browsers and the backend and the frontend communicate using WMS, WFS and other relevant Web services. Different from classic WebGIS backends that delegates spatial query processing to spatial databases, our prototype integrates spatial query processing with the backend to conveniently exploit parallel processing power on modern hardware. While the frontend can be implemented on top of various Web Map Javascript libraries, we have chosen Google Map API for popularity, ease-of-use (API) and performance (fast base map loading). The overall system architecture is shown in Fig. 1.

The left side of Fig. 1 illustrates the major modules of the proposed Web-GIS backend: data storage, spatial indexing, spatial filtering and spatial refinement. The right side of the figure also shows the major modules of our WebGIS frontend for QDVE applications. While the frontend and the backend communicate through conventional Web standards, including WMS, WFS and JSON, both the backend and the frontend are enhanced with the targeted application: QDVE on large-scale geospatial data. As discussed previously, the backend is accelerated by GPU hardware which requires a complete new set of techniques for data storage, indexing, filtering and refinement. While the backend is designed to support major geospatial data types (point, polyline and polygons) and popular spatial operations (e.g., point-to-polyline distance computation, point-to-polyline/polygon distance computation, polyline-to-polyline distance computation and point-in-polygon topological test), we will focus on point-in-polygon test based spatial operation in this study. The frontend is enhanced with customized Graphics User Interface (GUI) to facilitate realizing typical QDVE schemes (see below for details) and a simple yet effective Javascript geometry for performance optimization. We next present more design and implementation details on the relevant modules.

3.1   On-Demand Data Parallel Spatial Joins on GPUs

As discussed in Sect. 2.2, spatial join processing is indispensable in supporting query-driven visual explorations on large-scale data. Our previous works have developed data parallel spatial indexing, filtering and refinement techniques on GPUs, including utilizing quadtree indexing for point and rasters and grid-file and R-Tree indexing for MBRs of polylines and polygons, which have demonstrated excellent performance. However, these techniques were developed for static data and offline processing. In this study, we adapt these techniques for online interactive QDVE with a set of strategies to effectively support QDVE for the following considerations.

First, queries in QDVE are typically ad-hoc and it is impractical to pre-build indices for all possible queries for both raw and intermediate data. On the other hand, as long as the response time is in the order of sub-second to a few seconds, users on QDVE tasks would hardly perceive major differences. As such, for QDVE tasks, it is possible to more aggressively exploit the concept of "disposable indexing" for on-demand spatial joins. The idea is that, instead of loading pre-built index from disks and use it for the subsequent spatial filtering

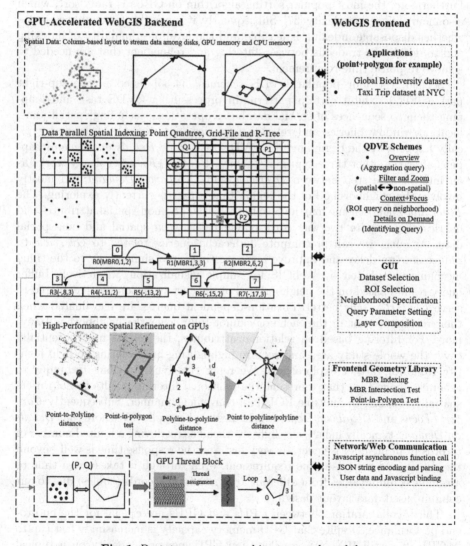

Fig. 1. Prototype system architecture and modules.

(as in traditional databases), we build index on the data partitions of interests in real time and use it to relate relevant data partitions on both sides of a spatial join for the final spatial refinement based on the desired spatial operation (e.g., point-in-polygon test). While the end-to-end runtime of a spatial join significantly depends on the spatial distributions of the underlying spatial datasets to be joined, the average performance of each of the three steps in a spatial join (indexing, filtering and refinement) with respect to the number of data items can be roughly estimated based on historical experiments. This is because our implementations are based on data parallel designs which mostly involve element-wise operations that include transform (map), scan, reduce and binary search [36]. Furthermore, the most popular sorting algorithm on GPUs is radix sort, which also incurs linear complexity [37]. Subsequently, it is possible to roughly estimate whether disposable indexing is feasible and the level of granularity of indexing and to decide the tradeoffs between filtering and refinement that are needed to achieve response time requirement.

Second, the four popular QVDE schemes [34,35] listed in the top-right part of Fig. 1 exhibit certain patterns in processing a QVDE task and mapping them to sequences of spatial databases operations, including spatial joins, location/window queries and relational queries. For example, *Overview* typically happens at the beginning of a QVDE task while *Details on Demand* happens after the other three types of schemes. *Context+Focus*, typically works as an intermediate step between *Overview* and *Details on Demand* and mostly involves the neighborhood of the region that a user is currently exploring. The *Filter and Zoom* scheme may involve both spatial and non-spatial attributes and queries may require two-way correspondence between spatial and non-spatial data. As such, we can precompute and cache queries related to *Overview* to reduce startup delay and improve response time. In a similar way to the tiling mechanism exploited by WebGIS for simple visualization, we actively buffer query results based on the neighborhood of the current region being explored to serve *Context+Focus* better. Location-dependent queries are reevaluated when their results are not in the cache or cannot fully cover the neighborhood anymore. For filtering based on relational attributes, the results may potentially cover the whole study area and require highlighting and coloring to help identify ROIs for further explorations. We reuse the dynamic tiling technique to generate image tiles that represent the relational filtering results to help users spatially zooming to multiple ROIs in a convenient manner. Subsequently *Context+Focus* and *Details on Demand* schemes can be applied. We note that *Details on Demand* typically incurs very light overhead as retrieving a limited number of records from memory is generally very fast and the response time is well beyond the sub-second response time requirement, even through it takes extra time to assemble column values from different arrays to form records (tuples) due to our column-based data layout design.

Third, collaborations between CPUs and GPUs are crucial for the end-to-end performance. Despite that GPU memory capacity is increasingly fast (up to 24 GB), it is still 10X–50X smaller than CPU memory capacity on a typical machine. The data transfer speed between CPU memory and GPU memory is limited to PCI-E bandwidth (16/32 GB/s). Fortunately, all our spatial indexing and spatial filtering techniques designed for GPUs are implemented based on data parallel primitives that are also supported on multi-core CPUs. Even though our spatial refinement implementations are GPU specific, we have developed multi-core CPU implementations on top of Intel TBB parallel library [36] with the same interfaces. As such, it is both desirable and feasible to execute certain queries on multi-core CPUs to avoid the data transfer overhead between CPUs and GPUs, which naturally improves the overall performance. The large CPU memory capacity also makes it suitable to cache GPU results as discussed above.

3.2 WebGIS Frontend Optimized for QDVE

Different from our previous works on Web-GIS applications using OpenLayers [22] and ESRI ArcGIS API for Flex [23], we have chosen to use Google Map Javascript API for our WebGIS frontend in this study. Several modules listed in the lower-right part of Fig. 1 are inherited from our previous work on visual analytics of taxi trip Origin-Destination (OD) data in a Web environment [15] with enhancements which will be described shortly.

The GUI module is the interfaces to interact with users which is largely application specific. Nevertheless, there are several interfaces that are common to many applications, including selecting dataset(s) to start a QVDE task, choosing/switching base map layers and turning on/off auxiliary and cosmetic layers, tools to interactively specifying ROIs and neighborhood, and dynamic interfaces to set both mandatory and optional parameters for spatial queries during a QVDE task. Those interfaces can be relatively easily implemented using Javascript and HTML and we skip the details due to space limit. The network/Web Communication modules listed in the bottom-right part of Fig. 1, while important, are quite standard in implementation and whose details are also skipped for the same reason. We note that the preference of JSON over GML or KML as a data format to communicate between the WebGIS backend and the frontend is mostly due to efficiency concerns, although other data formats including GML and KML can also be used with an additional conversion step before the parsed data can be used by Javascript APIs. We next focus on the frontend geometry API module which is unique to the targeted QDVE applications.

The optional *GetFeatureInfo* operation defined in the WMS specification allows to retrieve the underlying data including geometry and attribute values for a pixel location on a map. Since the operation can also return unique FeatureID, it is possible to combine it with the *GetFeature* operation defined in the WFS specification to retrieve specific attribute values to support visualization and information display at the Web frontend. However, while those techniques work reasonably well for a small number of features in traditional WebGIS applications, working at the individual feature level through WMS/WFS is not likely to be efficient for QEDV tasks where a large number of features can be involved, such as results of queries for *Overview, Filter and Zoom* and *Context+Focus* schemes. While dynamically generating WMS/WFS layers at the backend side and make them ready to be pulled by the frontend is a practically useful solution, efficiently filtering features at the frontend (to reduce the backend overhead of generating and maintaining a large number of dynamic WMS/WFS layers) is complementarily beneficial. Towards this end, we reuse the MBR intersection test and point-in-polygon test Javascript code initially implemented in [15] to spatially filter out FeatureIDs at the Web frontend that cannot be part of queries, such as those involve ROIs that are interactively drawn by users and those involve neighborhood dynamically set by users, before the queries are sent for server side processing. We note that the server side processing of such filtering can be several orders of magnitude faster than the performance of the Javascript code performance at the frontend. However, the benefit here is mostly on reducing data transmission overhead over the Web and reducing the associated encoding/decoding overhead, which could be much more costly than spatial filtering on the frontend using Javascript code.

We are aware of the techniques and applications of integrating Google Map and Google BigQuery[3] APIs to spatially visualize "small" query results from "big" relational tables in Cloud where the number of features (after combining geometry and relational attribute values) is limited. However, we believe these techniques are generally incapable of handling QEDV tasks on large-scale geospatial datasets where the features can be large in quantity and complex in topology and thus a pure Web frontend solution is inapplicable. Our strategy is to hybridize the traditional WMS/WFS based techniques that mostly rely on backend processing and the Google Map/BigQuery based techniques that mostly rely on frontend processing. The idea is to use the size of the set of unique FeatureIDs to determine whether a backend or a frontend processing is more beneficial. When size is large, we generate dynamic WMS/WFS layers so that query results in different visual representations can be pulled by the frontend. On the other hand, when the size is small, we choose to request feature data (including both geometry and attribute values) and create cosmetic layer(s). Either the dynamic layers, the cosmetic layers or their combinations can be composited with existing layers for better visualization and visual explorations.

4   Application Case, Experiments and Results

Quantifying species-environment relationships, i.e., analyzing how species are distributed on the Earth has been one of the fundamental questions studied by biogeographers and ecologists for a long time [33]. Several enabling technologies have made biodiversity data available at much finer scales in the past decade [32]. The complex relationships among environmental variables and species distribution patterns make query-driven visual explorations desirable. The uninterrupted exploration processes are likely to facilitate novel scientific discoveries effectively. As discussed in [22,31], the relevant data for large-scale biodiversity exploration can be categorized into three types: taxonomic (T), geographical (G)

---

[3] https://cloud.google.com/bigquery/.

and environmental (E). Taxonomic data are the classifications of organisms (e.g., Family, Genus and Species) and environmental data are the measurements of environmental variables (e.g., precipitation and temperature) on the Earth. The geographical data defines the spatial tessellation of how the taxonomic data and the environmental data are observed/measured, which can be based on either the vector polygonal or the raster grid tessellation [31]. The potential research in exploring species distributions and their relationships with the environment is virtually countless given the possible combinations of geographic/ecological regions, species groups and environmental variables [31]. Previously, we have developed a desktop application called Linked Environment for Exploratory Analysis of Large-Scale Species Distribution Data (LEEASP, [31]) to visually explore 4000+ birds species range maps in the West hemisphere and 19 World-Clim environmental variables [24]. The taxonomic hierarchy is represented as a tree and visualized using Prefuse[4] with rich user interaction functionality. The software has several sophisticated mechanisms to coordinate the multiple views representing the three types of biodiversity data. A subset of the functionality of the desktop application has been provided by a WebGIS application supported by a main-memory database engine using MAQ-Tree data structure to represent rasterized polygons [22], as discussed in Sect. 2.2.

In this study, as an application case of the proposed framework and techniques for QDVE on large-scale geospatial data in a WebGIS environment discussed in the previous three sections, we use a different set of species distribution data and geographical data to explore global biodiversity patterns (linking with environmental data will be added in future work). For the species distribution data, we use the Global Biodiversity Information Facility (GBIF[5]) global species occurrence dataset which has 375+ million species occurrences records (as of 2012). Our preprocessing results have shown that the dataset contains 1,487,496 species, 168,280 genus, 1,142 families in 262 classes, 109 phyla and 9 kingdoms. Different from LEEASP that uses a raster grid tessellation which exploits polygon rasterization in a preprocessing step to improve response time during a QDVE task with reduced accuracy (as limited by raster grid cell size), in this study, we use vector tessellation to achieve a maximum possible spatial accuracy. Towards this end, although virtually any global administrative data (e.g., country boundary) or ecological zone data can be used for tessellation, we have chosen the World Wild Fund (WWF) ecoregion dataset[6] for such a purpose. The WWF ecoregion data has 14,458 polygons, 16,838 rings and 4,028,622 points. Linking the point species distribution data and the polygonal geographical data largely depends on the functionality and efficiency of spatial joins based on the point-in-polygon test spatial operation (known as Zonal Summation). Our previous work on the spatial join using both the full species occurrence and the WWF ecoregion datasets indicate that it takes less than 100 s on a Nvidia Quadro 6000 GPU (released in 2010), which represents a 4–5 orders of magnitude

---

[4] http://www.prefuse.org/.

[5] http://www.gbif.org/.

[6] http://www.worldwildlife.org/biomes.

of higher performance than a standalone program using libspatialindex[7]for spatial indexing and GDAL[8] for point-in-polygon test on a single CPU core [14]. The offline GPU processing performance also suggests that it may be possible to reduce the processing time to sub-second level when processing a subset of species distribution data. This is often the case for the majority of queries in QDVE tasks and the conjecture largely motivated this work.

Our experiments in this application case has several goals. First, as a WebGIS application, to examine that each component is implemented correctly and data flows among different components as expected. Second, to check that GUI interfaces work properly and ensure that users are able to use the interfaces to complete their desired QDVE tasks. Third, to demonstrate the desired efficiency and high performance by using GPU acceleration. Among the three goals, the first two goals are realized by using traditional Web techniques, such as Javascript/PHP/Python programming and HTML/XML/JSON for coding/encoding and we leave their verifications for interactive tests. We next focus on the experiments for the third goal on real time spatial join performance, which focus on backend side GPU design and implementations and are unique to this study.

Towards this end, we have randomly picked five groups of species in two selected categories, although users are allowed to pick up any combinations of species by clicking on the taxonomic tree, to evaluate the performance of spatial joins on these five species groups. The spatial join result, which tells the number of occurrences of the species in the group in each ecoregion, will be used to generate dynamic image tiles for the WebGIS frontend, as introduced in Sect. 3.2. Conceptually, this is an example of applying the *Filter and Zoom* scheme in QDVE where species identifications are used for filtering the full species occurrence dataset. On the other hand, this example can also be considered as an application of the *Overview* scheme to help users understand the distributions of the species occurrence records of the subset of the species occurrence dataset with respect to the species in the chosen group.

For notation convenience, the two categories are named as C34, where the number of occurrence records of a species is between 1000 and 10,000, and C45, where the number of occurrence records of a species is between 10,000 and 100,000, respectively. There are 22,421 species in C34 and 3223 in C45, out of the 1,487,496 total species in the full dataset. Species in the two categories represent the most widely distributed ones. In our experiments, three groups of species are randomly chosen in C34 with 100, 50 and 20 species, and, two groups of species are randomly chosen in C45 with 25 and 10 species, respectively. We have chosen to use a 8192*8192 grid for grid-file based spatial indexing which seems to be appropriate. Note that using grid-file for spatial indexing is different from rasterization as used in our previous works [21,22,31] and does not sacrifice spatial accuracy. The experiment results of the four groups are shown in Table 1

---

[7] https://libspatialindex.github.io/.
[8] http://www.gdal.org/.

using a 2013 Nvidia GTX Titan GPU with 2688 cores and 6 GB memory[9]. All experiments are repeated several times to ensure that the results are consistent. The runtimes reported in the table are end-to-end times that include the runtimes of all the three modules in a spatial join (indexing for both points and polygons, filtering and refinement) but excluding disk I/O times as we assume all data are memory-resident for QDVE. Note that the polygon indexing times are the same as the WWF ecoregion data is used for all the five groups.

Table 1. Runtimes of experimenting five selected species groups on GPUs (in milliseconds)

Group	1($C34$)	2($C34$)	3($C34$)	4($C45$)	5($C45$)
#of species	100	50	20	25	10
# of records	264,917	114,883	58,332	746,302	279,808
Point Indexing Time (ms)	3.0	2.4	2.0	4.5	3.1
Polygon MBR Indexing Time (ms)	29	29	29	29	29
Filtering Time (ms)	595	285	259	759	399
Refinement Time (ms)	785	329	163	860	590
Total Time (ms)	1412	645	453	1653	1021

From Table 1 we can see that there are two groups that have a total runtime significantly below one second and there are two groups that have a total runtime around 1.5 s. The average of the runtimes is around 1.0 s, which is very close to the desired sub-second level. Note that the GPU we use in the experiment was released in 2013. As more powerful GPUs are available in the past three years and the near future, we expect the average runtime can be further reduced to below 0.5 s on these GPUs. The results suggest that QDVE on global biodiversity data with support from a GPU-accelerated WebGIS backend is quite possible on a commodity personal workstation. While we have not had a chance to compare with the performance of a conventional spatial database directly for the subsets of the species occurrence data we have chosen, based on the performance on the full species occurrence dataset [14], we believe that the performance can be orders of magnitude higher and we leave a full comparison for future work.

5   Conclusions and Ongoing Work

In this study, motived by the increasingly available parallel hardware and the low performance of the traditional WebGIS software stacks, we have proposed a new WebGIS framework and the techniques to leverage GPU-accelerated spatial join techniques for query driven visual explorations on large-scale geospatial data. The design and implementation considerations are discussed in details and an

---

[9] http://www.geforce.com/hardware/desktop-gpus/geforce-gtx-titan/specifications.

application case on exploring global biodiversity data is presented. The experiment results have demonstrated the feasibility of the proposed framework and the desired high performance on exploring large-scale geospatial data through extensive queries.

The presented work is preliminary in nature from a system development perspective. While the major components, including query processing on the backend and QDVE related GUIs on the frontend have been designed and implemented, our prototype currently is largely geared towards the specific application case. Evolving the prototype towards a more mature system that can serve as a generic platform to accommodate more application cases certainly requires significant amount of efforts in the future. Furthermore, as CPUs are also getting more powerful with significantly larger number of cores and memory capacities, integrating both CPUs and GPUs to further enhance backend performance is not only interesting but practically useful. Finally, compared with traditional WebGIS applications, QDVE workflows are significantly more complex and require novel ideas on designing effective GUI interfaces and the direction is also left for our future work.

References

1. Cary, A., Sun, Z., Hristidis, V., Rishe, N.: Experiences on processing spatial data with MapReduce. In: Winslett, M. (ed.) SSDBM 2009. LNCS, vol. 5566, pp. 302–319. Springer, Heidelberg (2009). doi:10.1007/978-3-642-02279-1_24
2. Grochow, K., Howe, B., Stoermer, M., Barga, R., Lazowska, E.: Client + cloud: Evaluating seamless architectures for visual data analytics in the ocean sciences. In: Gertz, M., Ludäscher, B. (eds.) SSDBM 2010. LNCS, vol. 6187, pp. 114–131. Springer, Heidelberg (2010). doi:10.1007/978-3-642-13818-8_10
3. Aji, A., Wang, F., et al.: HadoopGIS: A high performance spatial data warehousing system over MapReduce. Proc. VLDB Endow. **6**(11), 1009–1020 (2013)
4. Eldawy, A., Mokbel, M.F., Jonathan, C.: HadoopViz: A MapReduce framework for extensible visualization of big spatial data. In: Proceedings of the ICDE 2016, pp. 601–612 (2016)
5. Hennessy, J.L., Patterson, D.A.: Computer Architecture: A Quantitative Approach, 5th edn. Morgan Kaufmann, Burlington (2011)
6. Kirk, D.B., Hwu, W.W.: Programming Massively Parallel Processors: A Hands-on Approach, 2nd edn. Morgan Kaufmann, Burlington (2012)
7. Kendall, W., Glatter, M., et al.: Terascale data organization for discovering multivariate climatic trends. In: SuperComputing 2009, pp. 1–12 (2009)
8. Healey, R., Dowers, S., et al.: Parallel Processing Algorithms for GIS. CRC, Boca Raton (1997)
9. Clematis, A., Mineter, M., Marciano, R.: High performance computing with geographical data. Parallel Comput. **29**(10), 1275–1279 (2003)
10. You, S., Zhang, J., Gruenwald, L.: Parallel spatial query processing on GPUs using R-trees. In: Proceedings of the BigSpatial@SIGSPATIAL, pp. 23–31 (2013)
11. Zhang, J., You, S., Gruenwald, L.: Large-scale spatial data processing on GPUs and GPU-accelerated clusters. ACM SIGSPATIAL Spec. **6**(3), 27–34 (2014)
12. Zhang, J., You, S., Gruenwald, L.: High-performance spatial query processing on big taxi trip data using GPGPUs. In: Proceedings of the IEEE International Congress on Big Data, pp. 72–79 (2014)

13. Zhang, J., You, S., Gruenwald, L.: Parallel online spatial and temporal aggregations on multi-core CPUs and many-core GPUs. Inf. Syst. **44**, 134–154 (2014)
14. Zhang, J., You, S., Gruenwald, L.: Efficient parallel zonal statistics on large-scale global biodiversity data on GPUs. In: Proceedings of the BigSpatial@SIGSPATIAL, pp. 35–44 (2015)
15. Zhang, J., You, S., Xia, Y.: Prototyping a web-based high-performance visual analytics platform for origin-destination data: A case study of NYC taxi trip records. In: Proceedings of the UrbanGIS@SIGSPATIAL, pp. 16–23 (2015)
16. You, S., Zhang, J., Gruenwald, L.: High-performance polyline intersection based spatial join on GPU-accelerated clusters. In: Proceedings of the BigSpatial@SIGSPATIAL, pp. 42–49 (2016)
17. Shekhar, S., Chawla, S.: Spatial Databases: A Tour. Pearson, London (2003)
18. Jacox, E.H., Samet, H.: Spatial join techniques. ACM TODS **32**(1), 7 (2007)
19. Gaede, V., Gunther, O.: Multidimensional access methods. Comput. Surv. **30**(2), 170–231 (1998)
20. Samet, H.: Foundations of Multidimensional and Metric Data Structures. Morgan Kaufmann Publishers Inc., Burlington (2005)
21. Zhang, J., Gertz, M., Gruenwald, L.: Efficiently managing large-scale raster species distribution data in PostgreSQL. In: Proceedings of the ACM-GIS 2009, pp. 316–325 (2009)
22. Zhang, J.: A high-performance web-based information system for publishing large-scale species range maps in support of biodiversity studies. Ecol. Inform. **8**, 68–77 (2012)
23. Zhang, J., You, S.: Supporting web-based visual exploration of large-scale raster geospatial data using binned min-max quadtree. In: Gertz, M., Ludäscher, B. (eds.) SSDBM 2010. LNCS, vol. 6187, pp. 379–396. Springer, Heidelberg (2010). doi:10.1007/978-3-642-13818-8_27
24. Hijmans, R.J., Cameron, S.E., et al.: Very high resolution interpolated climate surfaces for global land areas. Int. J. Climatol. **25**(15), 1965–1978 (2005). http://www.worldclim.org/current
25. Zhang, J., You, S., Gruenwald, L.: Parallel quadtree coding of large-scale raster geospatial data on GPGPUs. In: Proceedings ACM-GIS 2011, pp. 457–460 (2011)
26. Zhang, J., You, S., Gruenwald, L.: High-performance quadtree constructions on large-scale geospatial rasters using GPGPU parallel primitives. IJGIS **27**(11), 2207–2226 (2013)
27. Zhang, J., You, S.: Dynamic tiled map services: Supporting query-based visualization of large-scale raster geospatial data. In: Proceedings of the COM.GEO 2010 (2010)
28. Aref, G.A., Ilyas, I.F.: SP-GiST: an extensible database index for supporting space partitioning trees. J. Intell. Inf. Syst. (JIIS) **17**(2/3), 215–240 (2001)
29. Aji, A., Teodoro, G., Wang, F.: Haggis: turbocharge a MapReduce based spatial data warehousing system with GPU engine. In: Proceedings of the ACM BigSpatial@SIGSPATIAL, pp. 15–20 (2014)
30. Chavan, H., Alghamdi, R., Mokbel, M.F.: Towards a GPU accelerated spatial computing framework. In: Proceedings of the ICDE Workshops, pp. 135–142 (2016)
31. Zhang, J., Gruenwald, L.: Embedding and extending GIS for exploratory analysis of large-scale species distribution data. In: Proceedings of the ACM-GIS 2008, article no. 28 (2008)
32. Bisby, F.A.: The quiet revolution: Biodiversity informatics and the Internet. Science **289**(5488), 2309–2312 (2000)

33. Cox, C., Moore, P.: Biogeography: An Ecological and Evolutionary Approach, 7th edn. Wiley, New York (2005)
34. Shneiderman, B.: The eyes have it: A task by data type taxonomy for information visualizations. In: Proceedings of the IEEE Symposium on Visual Languages, pp. 336–343 (1996)
35. Keim, D.A., Mansmann, F., et al.: Challenges in visual data analysis. In: Proceedings of the IEEE Conference on Information Visualization, pp. 9–16 (2006)
36. McCool, M., Robison, A.D., Reinders, J.: Structured Parallel Programming: Patterns for Efficient Computation. Morgan Kaufmann, Burlington (2012)
37. Merrill, D., Grimshaw, A.S.: High performance and scalable radix sorting: a case study of implementing dynamic parallelism for GPU computing. Parallel Process. Lett. $21(2)$, 245–272 (2011)

Visualization of Spatio-Temporal Events in Geo-Tagged Social Media

Yuanyuan Wang[1]([✉]), Muhammad Syafiq Mohd Pozi[2], Goki Yasui[2],
Yukiko Kawai[2], Kazutoshi Sumiya[3], and Toyokazu Akiyama[2]

[1] Yamaguchi University, Ube City 755-8611, Japan
y.wang@yamaguchi-u.ac.jp
[2] Kyoto Sangyo University, Kyoto City 603-8555, Japan
{syafiq,kawai,akiyama}@cc.kyoto-su.ac.jp, gxyasui@gmail.com
[3] Kwansei Gakuin University, Sanda City 669-1337, Japan
sumiya@kwansei.ac.jp

Abstract. This paper presents a spatio-temporal mapping system for visualizing a summary of geo-tagged social media as tags in a cloud, and it is associated with a web page by detecting spatio-temporal events. Through it, users can grasp events at anytime from anywhere while they browse any web pages. In order to detect spatio-temporal events from social media such as tweets, the system extracts expected events (e.g., crowded restaurants) by using machine learning algorithms to classify tweets through space and time, and it also extracts unexpected or seasonal events (e.g., time sales) by comparing the current situation to those normal regularities. Thus, the system presents a social tag cloud of tweets to help users gain a quick overview of spatio-temporal events while they browse a web page, and it also presents a tweet list to help users obtain more details about events. Furthermore, users can freely specify a time period or a tag to view its related tweets. Finally, we discuss our proposed social tag cloud generation method's effectiveness using dense geo-tagged tweets at multi-functional buildings in urban areas.

Keywords: Social tag cloud · Visualization · Geo-tagged tweets · Web pages · Spatial and temporal information

1 Introduction

Twitter and other social media are frequently used to express personal opinions or to share massive updates of events such as daily life activities and incidents. Previous works assumed that tweets mainly describe "what and where happens now," they have a common target for detecting real-world events based on geographical areas or location mentions, such as a twitter-based event detection system [4] and an earthquake reporting system [22]. Other examples of newly visualization applications on social media include a system for aggregating and visualizing spatial attention over time in Twitter [2], and a system for querying, analyzing and visualizing geo-tagged microblogs [14]. However, these works

© Springer International Publishing AG 2017
D. Brosset et al. (Eds.): W2GIS 2017, LNCS 10181, pp. 137–152, 2017.
DOI: 10.1007/978-3-319-55998-8_9

focused on city-level locations on social media, they did not detect events by considering locations with height information within buildings or small areas of multi-functional buildings. Actually, there are many events happening at any time such as crowded restaurants and time sales on different floors or shops at multi-functional buildings in urban areas. While browsing web pages, since these are not updated in real time, it is difficult for users to obtain latest events or current situation from social media senders. Therefore, it is important to detect spatio-temporal events including both expected and unexpected events to help us to better understand dense related social media through space and time [11]. To achieve them, not only a location-based social media analysis method but also a spatio-temporal analysis method of social media is necessary.

In this paper, we advocate a novel system for visualizing social media (tweets) in a tag cloud is associated with web pages based on detected spatio-temporal events. Although several social media analysis techniques have been studied in the existing works [18,24], they have focused on location-based social media analysis by using latitude and longitude only, they do not solve the mentioned issues about height information and temporal information of social media. Figure 1 illustrates an example of streaming tweets describe about different floors of a large shopping mall nearby Osaka station in Japan, called "LUCUA Osaka," a tweet "Yummy!" may report a comment about foods on the restaurant floor, a tweet "Interesting book!" may report an impression on the lifestyle floor, and a tweet "I love this dress! I will buy it." may report an activity of shopping on the fashion floor.

For this, we first collect geo-tagged tweets based on content analysis and region selection. Then, we can acquire tweets that are related to target locations even though the tweets do not include location names, and we can also filter out the tweets from target locations for which content is not related to the target locations. This allows us to map acquired tweets to web pages by matching location names extracted from the acquired tweets and the web pages. We then detect events by adopting machine learning algorithms to classify tweets into different categories of small-scale facility information (e.g., floors, attraction areas) from web pages in different time frames of a day. Thus, we can generate a social tag cloud by using *TF-IDF*-based feature words from tweets. To sum up, the system has two main features:

- Detecting and analyzing geo-tagged social media (tweets) based on the spatial and temporal information.
- Generating and presenting a social tag cloud of social media (tweets) with web pages that can be changed over different time periods.

The next section provides an overview of our system, and Sect. 3 reviews related work. Section 4 explains how to analyze tweets based on the spatial and temporal information. Section 5 describes how to generate a social tag cloud of tweets. Section 6 illustrates the experimental results obtained by using a real dataset of streamed geo-tagged tweets at urban areas in Japan and web pages. Finally, Sect. 7 concludes the paper and outlines our future work.

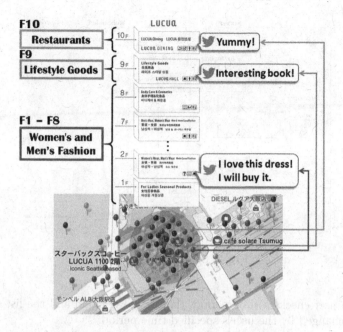

Fig. 1. An example of tweets of LUCUA Osaka.

2   A Spatio-Temporal Mapping System

The processing flow of our spatio-temporal mapping system for visualizing a summary of tweets in a social tag cloud is shown in Fig. 2. To use this system, users are required to install a toolbar (a browser plug-in). The system acquires geo-tagged tweets from a certain region by using Twitter Streaming API[1]. The certain region is determined by a northeast point and a southwest point, we then obtain tweets in a rectangular region surrounding these two points. The system acquires URLs of web pages that users are browsing with the installed toolbar in a Web browser. Once a user browses a web page with the installed toolbar, the system records the information into a database, which is used for mapping tweets to the web page based on a location name detected from the tweets and the web page, and classifying the tweets based on category names of small-scale facility information from the web page in different time frames of a day. The system then returns a social tag cloud of *TF-IDF*-based words in tweets is associated with the web page during different time periods. In our system, anonymous of all messages (tweets) can be maintained through Twitter services and a WebSocket server[2].

The flow of our system is described as follows:

– After a user selects a web page to browse, the system then returns a social tag cloud of tweets and a list of tweets are associated with the web page.

---

[1] https://dev.twitter.com/streaming/overview.

[2] https://html.spec.whatwg.org/multipage/comms.html#network.

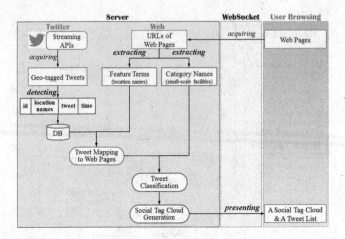

Fig. 2. System architecture.

- When a user checks a time period, the social tag cloud and the list of tweets can be changed by the user's specified time period.
- When a user clicks a tag, the system then presents a list of its most related tweets.

3   Related Work

Recently, event detection on social media has been a very popular research area with many applications, such as a trend detection system by identifying bursty words [13], tracked events by applying a locality sensitive hashing (LSH) [19], a map generation of small sub-events around big, popular events by using conditional random fields (CRFs) [10], the discovery of breaking events by using hashtags in Twitter [5], and an open-domain calendar of significant events extracted from Twitter [21], and topic detection by using tag correlations [1]. Our work is unique from these studies because our analysis aims to explore spatio-temporal events from tweets that may help in providing users with more complete and useful information.

Several studies have focused on problems such as the summarization and detection of topics in tweets as well as the mass clustering of tweets. TweetMotif took an unsupervised approach for tweet clustering [16]. Our goal is similar to this work, we utilize a clustering method to classify tweets based on the spatial and temporal information. To detect location information of tweets, Yamaguchi et al. [26] proposed an online location inference method that exploits the spatiotemporal correlation over social streams to predict users' locations without geo-tagged data. In our study, we utilized geo-tagged tweets and web pages to identify locations that users are currently checking, even the tweets do not contain local words.

Numerous research works have shown the usefulness of tweet classification in many domains, ranging from detecting novel, newsworthy topics/events [9], news photos from tweets [8], user communities are recommended to advertisers in Twitter [20], and real-time geospatial event features from tweets to enhance event awareness [12]. Another application extracts event characterization in microblog posts via the use of hashtags (#) [3]. These works focused on topics on Twitter, in order to classify tweets into small-scale facilities in different time periods, we focused on spatio-temporal information of tweets.

4 Spatio-Temporal Analysis of Tweets

4.1 Tweet Acquisition

To acquire tweets, our proposed method that got a good performance about tweet acquisition [23], we first detect location names within a radius r of a region by using Google Places API v3[3], from latitude and longitude of collected geo-tagged tweets. Then, our server database manages {Twitter user ID, icon URL, latitude, longitude, location name, tweet, word set, acquisition time} (central part of Fig. 2). Next, we determine tweets that relate to the detected location names, it is necessary to analyze the content of tweets and to filter out tweets that have a low relation to their locations by a morphological analysis of nouns and adjectives. Therefore, we select tweets that contain many feature terms (high-frequency words) describe locations. In particular, we acquire a total amount n of tweets based on a given location, and calculate the average frequency of each word i that appears in each tweet t. Moreover, we use a standard sigmoid function $1/(1 + e^{-x_i})$ for weighting each word i related to location names.

$$\sum_{i=1}^{m} \left(x_i \times \frac{1}{1 + e^{-x_i}} \right) \times \frac{1}{m} \tag{1}$$

$$x_i = \frac{\#\text{tweets with } i}{n} \tag{2}$$

Here, m denotes the total number of words that appear in tweet t. If Eq. (1) is more than a threshold value, t is related to its location. x_i as a DF value of i is calculated by Eq. (2).

4.2 Web Page Acquisition

To analyze web pages, we first extract high-frequency nouns from snippets of the acquired URLs of web pages by using Yahoo! Web API[4]. Next, we detect feature terms like location names from extracted high-frequency proper nouns by using a morphological analyzer, called JUMAN[5]. Then, all location names on

---

[3] https://developers.google.com/place.

[4] http://developer.yahoo.co.jp/.

[5] http://nlp.ist.i.kyoto-u.ac.jp/EN/index.php?JUMAN.

each web page can be geocoded to latitude and longitude information by using Google Places API v3. Also, we extract category names of small-scale facilities (e.g., floors, attraction areas), which are labeled referring to guide information of multi-functional buildings in web pages.

4.3 Tweet Classification

Since k-NN (k-nearest neighbor algorithm) got a good result about tweet classification by comparing with naïve Bayes classifier and SVM (support vector machine) with linear and RBF kernels [25], in this work, we classify tweets based on category names of multi-functional buildings from web pages by adopting k-NN refer to 8 time periods (before dawn, at dawn, morning, before noon, past noon, past noon, evening, early at night, late at night) are divided by each 3 h of a day.

k-**NN** is a simple classification algorithm based on a similarity of a target data and a training data by using Euclidean distance. We calculate a vector of each tweet by using the DF value of each word (noun or adjective) in the tweet with Eq. (2) into a target set. Also, we assign a class (category name) for each tweet into a training set. For fitting the DF values of all words in each tweet, if the number of words appear in all tweets without duplication is q, vectors of each tweet are represented by an q-dimensional space. The similarity $sim(F, L)$ of a target set F and a training set L is calculated by $\sqrt{\sum_{i=1}^{q}(F_i - L_i)^2}$ using vectors of tweets. Therefore, we can extract the class of each training data with the highest similarity. Then, each target data is assigned to the most common class of its nearest training data by a majority vote.

$$class = \begin{cases} j & where\,\{c_j\} = max\{c_1, ..., c_k\} \\ reject & where\,\{c_i, ..., c_j\} = max\{c_1, ..., c_k\} \end{cases}$$

Here, $k = 8$ classes of the training data are acquired. If the most common class is a class j from the acquired classes, then, the class of the target data is identified as j. However, if there are multiple most common classes, the class has the highest similarity with the target data is determined as the class of the target data.

5 Tweet Visualization

Users can browse a web page and simultaneously obtain a social tag cloud of tweets referring to all time periods and a list of streaming tweets which are related to the web page. Furthermore, users can freely specify a time period and click a tag to view its related tweets. Users will be able to freely interact with our system as explained in the following scenarios.

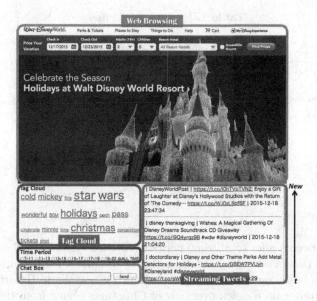

Fig. 3. The user interface of our system.

5.1 Social Tag Cloud Generation

To generate a social tag cloud, we apply a *TF-IDF* method for extracting feature words of the classified tweets in 8 time periods. We calculate *TF-IDF* values of each word i that appears in tweets by using *TF* and *IDF* as follows:

$$TF = \frac{\#i \text{ in each time period}}{\text{total } \#words \text{ in each time period}}$$

$$IDF = \frac{\text{total } \#categories \text{ in all time periods}}{\#categories \text{ with } i}$$

Therefore, we can generate a social tag cloud of tweets by adjusting font sizes of feature words based on their *TF-IDF* values. Although the positions of words are important in a tag cloud, in this paper, we provide an intuitive interface by changing font sizes only in different time periods.

5.2 Visualization Interface

The user interface of our system has three parts in a Web browser: a web page browsing part on the top, a social tag cloud with a time period selection bar on the bottom left, and a tweet list on the bottom right (see Fig. 3). Users can easily grasp an overview or detailed information about events from tweets refer to both space and time while they browse web pages. Furthermore, users can freely specify a time period and click a tag to view its related tweets.

As an example in Fig. 3, which depicts a user browsing an official website of Walt Disney World Resort in the Web browser, the system presents a social

Table 1. Experimental dataset

Time period	#Tweets	
	LUCUA	TDR
06:00–09:00 (morning)	847	965
09:00–12:00 (before noon)	1007	1745
12:00–15:00 (past noon)	1209	1538
15:00–18:00 (evening)	1496	1518
18:00–21:00 (early at night)	1734	1498
21:00–24:00 (late at night)	1073	1144
All Time	7366	8399

tag cloud of tweets refer to all time periods (checked **ALL TIME** as a default) and a list of tweets sorted by the time (latest to earliest) which are related to the web page based on a location name, "Walt Disney World Resort," the user can immediately gain a quick overview of Christmas events from the social tag cloud, e.g., Star Wars, during the holiday season.

6   Evaluation

6.1   Dataset

The dataset has been built retrieving 31.6 million geo-tagged tweets between 2015/7/13–12/17 of all Japan. In order to evaluate the accuracy of tweet classification and verify the social tag cloud generation, we narrowed down the test dataset in (1) a large shopping mall "LUCUA Osaka" (Lat.34.703289, Lon.135.496242) nearby Osaka station with a radius $r = 200$ m, totally 7,366 tweets during 2015/10/1–31; and (2) a large theme park "Tokyo Disney Resort (TDR)" (Lat.35.6290692, Lon.139.8829573) with a radius $r = 800$ m, totally 8,399 tweets during 2015/8/1–31 as shown in Table 1, respectively. Table 2 shows category names based on floors which are extracted from the web page of LUCUA Osaka. Since some floors in a composite facility are the same genre, we grouped some floors into the same category, e.g., 1F to 8F can be grouped into "Women's and Men's Fashion". Figure 4 shows category names based on 14 attraction areas of Tokyo Disneyland (TDL) and Tokyo DisneySEA (TDS) which are extracted from the web page of Tokyo Disney Resort (TDR).

6.2   Experiment 1: Verification of Feature Words Changed over Time

The purpose of this experiment is to verify whether extracted feature words are changed over different time periods. Thirteen subjects participated in this experiment by using the test dataset of LUCUA Osaka and Tokyo Disneyland

Table 2. Category names of floors in LUCUA Osaka.

Floor	Category name
10F	Restaurants
9F	Books, Lifestyle Goods
1F-8F	Women's and Men's Fashion
B1F	Sweets, Food, and Cosmetics
No Relation	Others

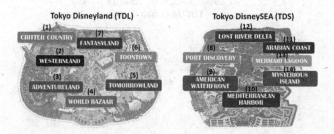

Fig. 4. Category names of 14 attraction areas in Tokyo Disney Resort (TDR).

(TDL) of Tokyo Disney Resort (TDR). We calculated a *TF-IDF* ranking of feature words in each category with k-NN in each time period.

In order to verify how about feature words in a social tag cloud are changed over time, we compared top-30 feature words of the rankings between (a) morning and before noon (06:00–09:00 and 09:00–12:00), (b) before noon and past noon (09:00–12:00 and 12:00–15:00), (c) past noon and evening (12:00–15:00 and 15:00–18:00), (d) evening and early at night (15:00–18:00 and 18:00–21:00), (e) early at night and late at night (18:00–21:00 and 21:00–24:00), by using Spearman's rank correlation coefficient. Figure 5 shows the correlations between every two adjacent time periods of LUCUA Osaka and Tokyo Disneyland (TDL), respectively. The results and findings are shown as follows:

- In categories "Books, Lifestyle Goods" and "Restaurants" of LUCUA Osaka, the correlations between every two adjacent time periods becomes high from past noon. For example, no feature words about foods appear in the morning because there are no tweets related to restaurants before opening.
- In category "Women's and Men's Fashion" of LUCUA Osaka, the correlations between all every two adjacent time periods are below 0.4.
- In category "Sweets, Food, and Cosmetics" of LUCUA Osaka, the correlations between (a) morning and before noon, (e) early at night and late at night are about 0.4. Others' correlations are below 0.4.
- In category "CRITTER COUNTRY" of Tokyo Disneyland, the correlations between all every two adjacent time periods are about 0.4.
- In all categories except "CRITTER COUNTRY" of Tokyo Disneyland, the correlations between all every two adjacent time periods are below 0.2.

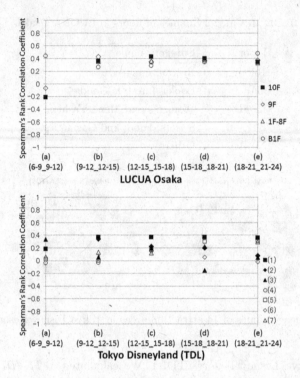

Fig. 5. The correlations based on adjacent time periods.

Based on the above, there are low correlations of feature words in each category between every two adjacent time periods. We could confirm that the feature words in a social tag cloud are greatly changed between every two adjacent time periods. In addition, we also compared top-30 feature words of the rankings between (f) morning and past noon, (g) morning and early at night, (h) morning and late at night, (i) past noon and early at night, (j) past noon and late at night, by using Spearman's rank correlation coefficient. Figure 6 shows the correlations between day and evening of LUCUA Osaka and Tokyo Disneyland (TDL), respectively. The results and findings are shown as follows:

- In categories "Books, Lifestyle Goods" and "Restaurants" of LUCUA Osaka, the correlations between the morning and others are low, and the correlations of other categories are about 0.3.
- In category "CRITTER COUNTRY" of Tokyo Disneyland, the correlations between day and evening are low, almost no correlations in other categories.
- In category "WESTERNLAND" of Tokyo Disneyland, the correlation between (f) morning and past noon is high, since same topics in a few tweets.

Based on the above, there are low correlations of feature words in each category between day and evening. We could confirm that the feature words are changed in different categories between different time periods.

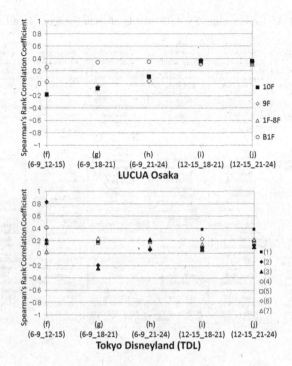

Fig. 6. The correlations based on day and evening.

6.3   Experiment 2: Accuracy of Feature Word Extraction

The purpose of this experiment is to evaluate the accuracy of *TF-IDF*-based feature words for generating a social tag cloud. We compared top-15 high *TF-IDF* words of each category in different time periods and calculated their precisions[6], the results of LUCUA Osaka and Tokyo Disneyland (TDL) are shown in Tables 3 and 4, respectively. There are ten subjects identified feature words are "related to its category", "unsure", or "not related to its category" in each time period. Correct answers of feature words are defined if the evaluation ratio[7] of "related to it category" and "not related to its category" is over 1.0. In Tables 3 and 4, underlined words denote the same feature words of each category appear in different time periods, and bold words are related to their categories.

- The precisions of all categories of LUCUA Osaka are about 0.7. Especially, the precision of the category "Women's and Men's Fashion" reached 0.72. Some high *TF-IDF* words (e.g., strawberry, smoothie) about drinks can be extracted because there are some coffee shops on each floor.
- The precisions of all time periods except past noon of LUCUA Osaka are about 0.7. We could confirm that many feature words about coffee appear in

---

[6] Precision = $\dfrac{\text{\#correct answers}}{\text{total \#feature words of each category}}$.

[7] EvaluationRatio = $\dfrac{\text{\#answers of "related to its category"}}{\text{\#answers of "not related to its category"}}$.

Table 3. LUCUA: Top-15 high *TF-IDF* words of each category in all time periods

Time / Category	06:00-09:00 (morning)	09:00-12:00 (before noon)	12:00-15:00 (past noon)	15:00-18:00 (evening)	18:00-21:00 (early at night)	21:00-24:00 (late at night)	Precision
Restaurants (10F)	kitchen, LUCUA, north, Osaka	engagement ring, piece, exhibition garden, Meguro, art, full, staff, way back, last night, enjoyed, birth, sa, diamond, chain	have a mfullal, sundubu, yam, Korea, octopus dumplings, bush, flow, refresh, bamboo, pot, Khao Man Kai, kitchen, tree, mango, cuisine	Volga, pone, refresh, have a meal, pity, accessories, pearl, hopeless, condition, lower right, destiny, octopus dumplings, green onion, well, reception	rotation, sushi, Capricciosa, zumi, octopus dumplings, win, sweet, vicinity, hot, people, asnas, boss, reviews, managing director, president	chair, village, jump, exercise, Satsuma, cooking, studio, pasta, lasagna, holiday, experience, classroom, cuisine, South Korea, sashimi	0.709
Books, Lifestyle Goods (9F)	outside, time, multimedia, Yodobashi Camera, use, Umeda, Osaka	fried chicken, sky, classical, two, opponent, sincerity, ku, char, Kinokuniya, marche, design, friendly, happiness, ume, SLOTH	Kinokuniya, floppy disk, beach, art, detour, home, shito, raw, earphone, show, gym, enter hospital, procedure, EVOLTA, anniversary	hammer, pliers, clumsy, finish, tassel, fur, elegant, claim, season, early spring, well, short, bread, head office, eye	light bulb, noisy, pity, burn, speaker, customer, broadcast, usually, kid, fried chicken, winner, crowning glory, shopping, kaya, garlic	top, food, ume, cable, corde, Tully's, satisfaction, plain clothes, cosiness, lens, bamboo, help, cold, he, sleepy	0.683
Women's and Men's Fashion (1F-8F)	—	dessert, Halloween, sweet, after the meal, agar, correct, earring, this time, aquatic, train, miscellaneous goods, selection, period, now, design	light, week, pork buns, valet, seminar, brother, sister, semester, school, support, lesson, new, east, Satsuma, EVISU	strawberry, sally, juice, smoothie, Banana, money, Uniqlo, Chaplin, heart, everyone, girls, customer, safety, guy, navy	gym, loose, dark, marshmallow, soup, poisoning, shop, Daikan, yama, sense, beauty, position, sword, implication, groom	Mi-chan, next, call, earring, girls, collection, event, just now, arrival, number, limitation, su, everyone, bow, type	0.720
Sweets, Food, and Cosmetics (B1F)	the bulls, rock, matter, open, Starbucks, Starbucks Coffee, status, terrace, next week, man, warawara, series, entree, court, central	Minas, Luminarie, roux, stall, gold, every time, shoes, shoeshine, pear, pot, top, hand, period, clothes, activity	morning, house, orchid, image, staff, chance, FamilyMart, Star Festival, this month, Milky Way, exist, weekday, strong, new moon, male	like, everyone, under, dream, couple, bookstore, mischievous, weekly, alloy, Khao Man Kai, fire, moments, Earl Grey, egg, tart	Maru, cafe, Tajima, feast, paradise, ease, fortune, supermarket, camp, special, spoon, visit, Burden, counselling, space	tourism, fortune, stressful, origin, highball, market, tension, Burden, specialty, Craft, hobby, counter, Tokyu, occasion, pancake	0.678
Precision	0.707	0.677	0.595	0.723	0.742	0.692	

the morning, and many feature words about foods appear from noon to night. The precision of past noon is below 0.6. Several tweets are wrongly classified because Twitter users often post some tweets about lunch before they moving to the restaurants.
- The precision of the category "CRITTER COUNTRY" of Tokyo Disneyland is 0.655, and the precisions of other categories are more than 0.7. Since a few tweets in the category "WORLD BAZAAR", they are almost related to its category, the precision of it reached 0.935.
- The precisions of all time periods of Tokyo Disneyland are more than 0.7. Especially, the precision of morning (06:00–09:00) reached 0.9.

Based on the above, we confirmed that feature words can be extracted in each category between different time periods. Compared the results of LUCUA Osaka to Tokyo Disneyland, we confirmed that the number of the relevant high *TF-IDF* words of Tokyo Disneyland is more than that of LUCUA Osaka. In addition, the number of the same feature words of each category in different time periods of Tokyo Disneyland is more than that of LUCUA Osaka. Since all subjects have been to Tokyo Disneyland and fewer subjects have been to LUCUA Osaka, some shops and products in LUCUA Osaka are not identified.

In summary, we confirmed that our social tag cloud generation method could extract feature words of tweets in different categories and different time periods, and topics of tweets of each category are changed over different time periods.

Table 4. TDL: Top-15 high *TF-IDF* words of each category in all time periods

Time / Category	06:00-09:00 (morning)	09:00-12:00 (before noon)	12:00-15:00 (past noon)	15:00-18:00 (evening)	18:00-21:00 (early at night)	21:00-24:00 (late at night)	Precision
(1) CRITTER COUNTRY	fuss, counter, a large amount, human, three, my, shirt, two, many, one, Stitch, people	closed, believer, last week, around, word, wide, drowning, oneself, carpet, jasmine, flying, don, surroundings, cafe, banana	recent, along, calypso, cool, limit, bayeux, river, expedition, dangerous, location, tyo, what, hand, sebastian, kid	umbrella, hindrance, Keisei, new, pond, sai, bro, behind, appreciation, up, brother, cloudy, Hideo, still, Splash Mountain	nephew, cost, length, up, claim, fierce, beauty, valley, neck, Sinbad, stand-by, book, trump, rash, seabed	shrimp, snack, stand-by, peanuts, dangerous, doing well, criticism, mountain, knotweed, caste, fan, law, check, wood, pig	0.655
(2) WESTERNLAND	big, thunder, mountain, Chiba, Urayasu	big, terrible, thunder, fast, pass, mountain, of, Chiba, Urayasu	big, thunder, mountain	big, last, thunder, before, attraction	bride, dangerous, you, presents, monger, now, child, thunder, big, minute	grass, big, thunder, mountain, Chiba, Urayasu	0.816
(3) ADVENTURELAND	aloha, presents, fascination, cruise, jungle, caribbean, my, Stitch	15, caribbean, pirate, today, stand-by, cruise, stairs, Splash	fool, parent, late, ying, village, on, broom, crystal, palace, clean, puddle, counter, Turtle Talk, edition, eldest son	cup, souvenir, excursion, crystal, palace, presents, fascination, ran, mouse, universe, pirate, aloha, first, caribbean, Stitch	adventure, crystal, Jones, palace, devil, presents, fascination, aloha, my, Indy, cruise, jungle, Stitch	wrapping, consultation, line, jungle, pirate, tag, caribbean, black, adventure, Indy, crystal, Jones, palace, devil, muscle	0.770
(4) WORLD BAZAAR	parade, root, castle, Chiba, Urayasu	partner, figure, waiting, way, root, parade, back, absent, castle, lottery, Chiba, Urayasu	drainage, root, parade, now, castle, summar, happy, Chiba, Urayasu	root, parade, castle, Urayasu, Chiba	—	—	0.935
(5) TOMORROWLAND	inc, monster, land, continue, star, encounter, an, Stitch, entrance, Chiba, Urayasu	hall, Astro, year, blaster, case, light, encounter, lunch, sky, tomorrow, space, tan	about, crash, Darth Vader, priestess, physical fitness, graduate, abroad, tomorrow, beauty, handsome, high, inc, terrace, monster, land	mom, tomorrow, year, point, inc, monster, land, encounter, continue, Theater Orleans, star, space, Astro, blaster, light	tomorrow, food, Astro, year, blaster, Enoshima, destination, continue, from, fashionable, gorilla, pattern, Hyadain, first, work	space, Astro, year, blaster, nursing, article for sale, disqualification, position, inc, continue, monster, land, mountain, light, tomorrow	0.795
(6) TOONTOWN	—	today, year, country, dream, Disney, Disneyland, Tokyo	want, stomach, gadgets, cartoon, spin, Roger Rabbit, home, Minnie, Chiba, Urayasu	gadgets, daughter, Chiba, Urayasu	request, gadgets, ride, wind, happy, country, one, rain, dream, good, Disney, Disneyland, Tokyo, Chiba, Urayasu	prompt decision, gadgets, let's go, contact, bad, daughter, country, dream, tomorrow, Disney, Disneyland, Tokyo, Chiba, Urayasu	0.784
(7) FANTASYLAND	honey, hunt, pooh, Haunted Mansion, small, world, minute, Chiba, Urayasu	short, interesting, fool, horrible, watching, human, money, Kazuya, will, Yokohama, explosion, Fujita, field, soul, Pinocchio	adventure, small, Pinocchio, travel, queen, heart, Ket, Van, world, hall, Cinderella, honey, hunt, pooh	honey, hunt, forehead, now, pooh, barb, hidden, chum, youth, fantasy, Haunted Mansion, small, world	posture, bazaar, Joe, adventure, world, Pinocchio, horrible, family, Haunted Mansion, honey, hunt, before, me	bee, thanks, queen, gate, snow, game, running, low rank, penalty, number, honey, hunt, loop, charge, wind	0.734
Precision	0.900	0.718	0.753	0.819	0.753	0.691	

6.4 Experiment 3: Verification of Social Tag Cloud Visualization

The purpose of this experiment is to verify whether the proposed social tag cloud visualization is useful for helping users to grasp events from tweets. The user interface of our developed prototype system is shown in Fig. 3, and a demonstration video is shown in [6]. The system could present tweets from the Twitter users with the web page within 1.6 s. Users can freely interact with the system by specifying a time period or clicking a tag to view its related tweets. When the user checks a time period **7–11**, the system then returns a tag cloud of tweets located on **Walt Disney World Resort** in the time period of 7:00–11:00 (see Fig. 7), e.g., the font sizes of "mickey" and "minnie" are decreased, and the font sizes of "fine" and "pass" are increased around morning (7:00–11:00) from a tag cloud of tweets in all time periods (see Fig. 3). In addition, when the user clicks a tag **entrance**, the system shows a list of most related tweets about "entrance" sorted by the time (latest to earliest) (see Fig. 8), the user can easily obtain more detailed situation about entrance information of all theme parks from the tweet list.

Based on the above, we confirmed that users can grasp topics of tweets in that time period, and they can obtain a summary of tweets about their interesting topics.

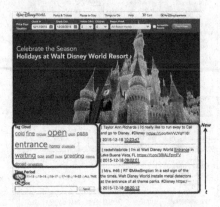

Fig. 7. Check a time period (**7–11**).

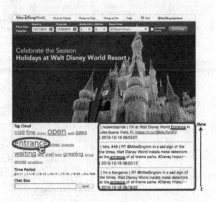

Fig. 8. Click a tag (**entrance**).

7   Conclusions

In this paper, we developed a spatio-temporal mapping system for visualizing a summary of social media in a cloud. Through it, users can grasp events from tweets through both the contents of tweets and web pages based on the spatio-temporal analysis. The system maps tweets to web pages by matching location names and detects events by utilizing machine learning algorithms to classify tweets into different categories of small-scale facility information from web pages in different time frames of a day.

Experimental results show that our system can effectively detect related tweets of small-scale facilities in composite multi-functional buildings, and it also can generate a social tag cloud for visualizing a summary of tweets, to help users gain a quick overview of current situation about each small-scale facility in different time periods.

For future work, we plan to enhance our system based on experimental results and verification experiments will be carried out for many types of multi-functional buildings with many more subjects. Then, we enumerate several directions for future research.

Enhanced spatio-temporal analysis. The addition of time expressions and location mentions appear in tweets to the analysis should help to more precisely detect and classify tweets of various types of facilities. We could also investigate time-space orthogonality through the comparative analysis of the temporal and spatial attention with NLP techniques.

Cross-media user communication. As mentioned before, a summary of tweets is synchronized with web pages, it can support simultaneous communication between Twitter users and users who browse web pages to extend our prototype as a function of TWinChat [24].

Indoor navigation. Based on classified tweets of each small-scale facility (e.g., floor, attraction area) of multi-functional buildings, our system could better suggest indoor navigation help users find popular areas or avoid crowded places based on current situations referring to [7].

Visualization. It should be possible to visualize a summary of tweets based on generic platforms with visualization tools to portray time perspectives [15]. This should be useful for E-commerce to help users (e.g., travelers, customers) to understand the social data easily and efficiently as a store visualization system for shopping mall [17].

Recommendation. As future work, we plan to extend our system to accept any datasets, e.g., services and products, for discovering topics over tweets. This should be useful to recommend particular activities, products, services, events, or places to visit.

Acknowledgments. This work was partially supported by MIC SCOPE (150201013), and JSPS KAKENHI Grant Numbers 26280042, 15K00162, 16H01722, and Grants for Women Researchers of Yamaguchi University.

References

1. Alvanaki, F., Sebastian, M., Ramamritham, K., Weikum, G.: Enblogue: emergent topic detection in web 2.0 streams. In: SIGMOD 2011, pp. 1271–1273 (2011). doi:10.1145/1989323.1989473
2. Antoine, E., Jatowt, A., Wakamiya, S., Kawai, Y., Akiyama, T.: Portraying collective spatial attention in twitter. In: KDD 2015, pp. 39–48 (2015). doi:10.1145/2783258.2783418
3. Carter, S., Tsagkias, M., Weerkamp, W.: Twitter hashtags: joint translation and clustering. In: Web Science 2011, pp. 1–3 (2011)
4. Cheng, T., Wicks, T.: Event detection using twitter: a spatio-temporal approach. PloS One 9(6), e97,807 (2014). doi:10.1371/journal.pone.0097807
5. Cui, A., Zhang, M., Liu, Y., Ma, S., Zhang, K.: Discover breaking events with popular hashtags in twitter. In: CIKM 2012, pp. 1794–1798 (2012). doi:10.1145/2396761.2398519
6. Demostration Video Page of Prototype System. http://www.wie.csse.yamaguchi-u.ac.jp/share/Demo2016.mp4
7. Fallah, N., Apostolopoulos, I., Bekris, K., Folmer, E.: Indoor human navigation systems: a survey. Interact. Comput. **25**(1), 21–33 (2013). doi:10.1093/iwc/iws010
8. Fruin, B.C., Samet, H., Sankaranarayanan, J.: Tweetphoto: photos from news tweets. In: SIGSPATIAL 2012, pp. 582–585 (2012)
9. Ifrim, G., Shi, B., Brigadir, I.: Event detection in twitter using aggressive filtering and hierarchical tweet clustering. In: SNOW-DC@WWW 2014, pp. 33–40 (2016)
10. Khurdiya, A., Dey, L., Mahajan, D., Verma, I.: Extraction and compilation of events and sub-events from twitter. In: WI-IAT 2012, pp. 504–508 (2012). doi:10.1109/WI-IAT.2012.192

11. Lansley, G., Longley, P.A.: The geography of twitter topics in london. Comput. Environ. Urban Syst. **58**, 85–96 (2016). doi:10.1016/j.compenvurbsys.2016.04.002

12. Lee, C.H.: Mining spatio-temporal information on microblogging streams using a density-based online clustering method. Expert Syst. Appl. **39**(10), 9623–9641 (2012). doi:10.1016/j.eswa.2012.02.136

13. Li, C., Sun, A., Datta, A.: Twevent: Segment-based event detection from tweets. In: CIKM 2012, pp. 155–164 (2012). doi:10.1145/2396761.2396785

14. Magdy, A., Alarabi, L., Al-Harthi, S., Musleh, M., Ghanem, T.M., Ghani, S., Mokbel, M.F.: Taghreed: A system for querying, analyzing, and visualizing geo-tagged microblogs. In: SIGSPATIAL 2014, pp. 163–172 (2014). doi:10.1145/2666310.2666397

15. Musleh, M.: Spatio-temporal visual analysis for event-specific tweets. In: SIGMOD 2014, pp. 1611–1612 (2014). doi:10.1145/2588555.2612666

16. O'Connor, B., Krieger, M., Ahn, D.: Tweetmotif: exploratory search and topic summarization for twitter. In: ICWSM 2010, pp. 384–385 (2010)

17. Ookawara, K., Hirano, H., Masuko, S., Hoshino, J.: Store visualization system for shopping mall type e-commerce [in Japanese]. J. Inf. Process. (JIP) **56**(3), 847–855 (2015)

18. Pat, B., Kanza, Y., Naaman, M.: Geosocial search: Finding places based on geo-tagged social-media posts. In: WWW Companion, pp. 231–234 (2015). doi:10.1145/2740908.2742847

19. Petrović, S., Osborne, M., Lavrenko, V.: Streaming first story detection with application to twitter. In: HLT 2010, pp. 181–189 (2010)

20. Poomagal, S., Visalakshi, P., Hamsapriya, T.: A novel method for clustering tweets in twitter. Int. J. Web Based Communities **11**(2), 170–187 (2015). doi:10.1504/IJWBC.2015.068540

21. Ritter, A., Etzioni, O., Clark, S., et al.: Open domain event extraction from twitter. In: SIGKDD 2012, pp. 1104–1112 (2012). doi:10.1145/2339530.2339704

22. Sakaki, T., Okazaki, M., Matsuo, Y.: Tweet analysis for real-time event detection and earthquake reporting system development. IEEE Trans. Knowl. Data Eng. **25**(4), 919–931 (2013). doi:10.1109/TKDE.2012.29

23. Wang, Y., Yasui, G., Hosokawa, Y., Kawai, Y., Akiyama, T., Sumiya, K.: Location-based microblog viewing system synchronized with web pages. In: FTSIS 2014, pp. 70–75 (2014). doi:10.1109/SRDSW.2014.18

24. Wang, Y., Yasui, G., Hosokawa, Y., Kawai, Y., Akiyama, T., Sumiya, K.: Twinchat: A twitter and web user interactive chat system. In: CIKM 2014, pp. 2045–2047 (2014). doi:10.1145/2661829.2661844

25. Wang, Y., Yasui, G., Kawai, Y., Akiyama, T., Sumiya, K., Ishikawa, Y.: Dynamic mapping of dense geo-tweets and web pages based on spatio-temporal analysis. In: SAC 2016, pp. 1170–1173 (2016). doi:10.1145/2851613.2851985

26. Yamaguchi, Y., Amagasa, T., Kitagawa, H., Ikawa, Y.: Online user location inference exploiting spatiotemporal correlations in social streams. In: CIKM 2014, pp. 1139–1148 (2014). doi:10.1145/2661829.2662039

Quality Measures for Visual Point Clustering in Geospatial Mapping

Christian Beilschmidt[✉], Thomas Fober, Michael Mattig,
and Bernhard Seeger

Department of Mathematics and Computer Science, University of Marburg,
Marburg, Germany
{beilschmidt,thomas,mattig,seeger}@mathematik.uni-marburg.de

Abstract. Visualizing large amounts of point data in a way that resembles the density of the distribution is a complex problem if the size of the drawing area is constrained. Naïvely drawing points on top of each other leads to occlusion and therefore a loss of information. An intuitive approach is combining close points as clusters that resemble their size as well as their geographic location. However, traditional clustering algorithms are not designed for visual clusterings rather than minimizing an error function independent of a graphical representation. This paper introduces measures for the quality of circle representations based on clustering outputs. Our experimental evaluation revealed that all methods had weaknesses regarding at least one of these criteria.

Keywords: Geographic visualization · Point clustering · Evaluation

1 Introduction

The amount of geospatial data generated by mobile sensors and cell phones are rapidly increasing today. These data items consist of a two- or three-dimensional point related to a spatial reference system and one or multiple observational measurements. In order to address the current and future data deluge like the one in the biodiversity domain [1], it is of utmost importance to develop new methods for visual analytics that allow inspecting the data distribution, detecting hot spots and spatially correlating environmental variables. Despite the challenge of big data sets, end-users often prefer to visualize data on low-cost devices like commodity hardware, tablets and mobiles rather than on high-end devices like visualization walls. In addition, it is very appealing for end-users to run the visualization in a web browser avoiding the burden of managing special-purpose software. For example, browser-based tools like Map-of-Life [2] are already popular visualization tools in the scientific biodiversity domain.

The visualization of very large point data sets in web browsers on commodity hardware causes at least three serious problems related to the (i) visualization space, (ii) rendering capabilities, and (iii) transfer rates. First, the visualization space on such a device is very limited leading to an occlusion of points in the drawing area. Considering a common HD resolution of 1920×1080 pixels, there is a

© Springer International Publishing AG 2017
D. Brosset et al. (Eds.): W2GIS 2017, LNCS 10181, pp. 153–168, 2017.
DOI: 10.1007/978-3-319-55998-8_10

natural limitation of about 2 million points on a display. However, a point is not just a pixel, but refers to a circle with a certain radius occupying a larger area on the display. In addition, a boundary around a circle is required to separate points from each other. Thus, the actual maximum number of points is below 100 000, but the chance of an overlap among these circles is still very high. Second, there is also a limitation on the display rate of browsers to avoid time lags when users are interacting with the system. Even for an up-to-date desktop computer (without any high-end graphic card) tens of thousands of points already cause severe display problems and hence, impairments in the user experience. It is therefore common to rasterize point plots. However, much of the information of the points like the individual measurements are then lost in the raster layer. In addition, it is not possible anymore to select individual points on the display. Third, the transfer rate of mobile devices is fairly limited. Since data is kept on a powerful server while visualization is performed on a thin browser, the amount of data to be transferred from the server to the browser should be as small as possible. For instance, already 20 000 points with 20 textual and numeric attributes represented in the popular GeoJSON format result in 15 MB of raw data. Though a loss-less compression already helps in reducing the data to be transferred, it is desirable to avoid transferring data that does not have an impact on the visualization.

This paper deals with removing point occlusion in maps via aggregation by applying clustering methods. Clustering addresses the three problems mentioned above as it fuses individual points to dense clusters. This removes spatial clutter, it leads to fewer shapes to be displayed and the data transfer is reduced as well (if the clustering is computed on the server). There is a plethora of clustering techniques, but almost all of them are neither specially designed nor thoroughly examined for the purpose of visualization. It is thus unclear whether particular clustering methods are applicable to visualization and how well they perform in this special setting. Our work does not only compare many clustering techniques by visual inspection, but introduces first quality measures that are suitable for comparing visual clustering techniques.

The contributions are: (i) to the best of our knowledge the first comprehensive set of quality measures for visual clustering, (ii) a survey of state-of-the-art point aggregation methods with focus on clustering, and (iii) experiments with different domain data sets to inspect the validity of the quality measures and to find the best-suited method.

The rest of this paper is structured as follows. Section 2 defines the problem and presents real-world applications. Section 3 gives an overview of approaches for point clustering and visualization. In Sect. 4 we present a set of quality measures for comparing circle representations for point sets. In Sect. 5 we compare the algorithms of Sect. 3 by applying the measures of Sect. 4. Finally, Sect. 6 concludes this paper and gives an outlook for further research.

2   Problems and Applications

This section describes the problem to specify the setting and the desired solution. It motivates the importance by presenting current, relevant applications of multiple domains. Finally, it discusses an extension to comparative visualization and further dimensions.

2.1 Problem Definition

We are given a set of n points in a two-dimensional coordinate system which represent arbitrary objects like observations. Without loss of generality we consider a quadratic Web Mercator reference system using meters as unit. In order to draw them onto a map on screen, we need to project them to pixel coordinates. We determine the bounds of the map by considering a zoom level $z \in \mathbb{N}_0^+$ and calculate the side length $l := 256 \cdot 2^z$, leading to

$$P := \{(x_1, y_1), \ldots, (x_n, y_n) \mid x_i, y_i \in [0, l]\}.$$

The goal is to compute a set C of circles $(x_i, y_i, r_i) \in [0, l]^2 \times (0, l/2]$ which do not overlap. C should represent P *best* regarding the user's perception of the geographic distribution and frequency of the points in P. Note that the cardinality of C is not specified or known in advance. However, we will use $m := |C|$ throughout this paper. C must represent outliers as well as hot spots of P. Moreover, C must contain circles which are distinguishable and recognizable. The latter requirement is realized by fixing a minimum circle radius $r_{\min}$ and the former one by specifying a minimum inter-circle distance δ.

In the next section we provide a concrete example. Section 4 introduces novel quality measures that specify these requirements mathematically.

2.2 Applications

There are tremendously many applications that include spatial data and rely on point data visualization. We point out two trending applications that emphasize the relevance of visual clustering.

Biodiversity Research. In biodiversity research, scientists investigate the state of ecosystem and species variety. The so-called Millenium Ecosystem Assessment [3] revealed the impact of the degradation of the earth's ecosystems on human well-being. In order to counteract those developments it is crucial to first assess the current state and then model possible actions. For gathering data, the whole field utilizes diverse sensors and heavily relies on collecting human observations. This results in a high volume of interesting data, e.g. observations of species distributions which are usually visualized as points on a map.

In GFBio [4], a German infrastructure project for the management, provision and exploration of biodiversity data, the goal is to provide a central repository for data of research projects. Within this project, we are developing the VAT system [5,6], a system for visualizing, analyzing and transforming spatio-temporal data. It is a tool for interactive exploration of the project data that incorporates other publicly available data sets. The visualization relies heavily on spatially

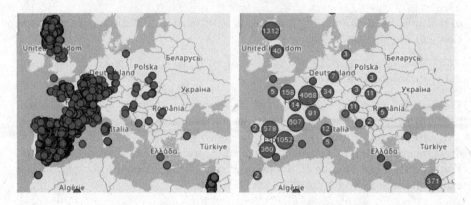

Fig. 1. The images show a comparison of an original (left) and an aggregated (right) point visualization of the species distribution of the European wildcat.

aggregated data representations for detecting and evaluating interesting subsets of the data. VAT makes it possible to investigate outliers and to find hot spots for instance for data cleansing. Figure 1 shows an example of the European wildcat distribution. While the left plot shows raw observations, the right one represents the same data set in an aggregated form. The left image is obviously congested and the top-most points hide most of the data set. This makes it impossible to find regions where wildcats appear very frequently. Considering the plot on the right-hand side one can e.g. recognize very easily that within Europe wildcats appear very frequently in Catalonia (east of Spain) whereas there are only few observations in Galicia (north-west of Spain).

Points of Interest. Aggregating points of interest (POIs) allows finding relevant hot spots for tourism and travel. This allows addressing tasks like planning service workloads for companies. There are local data sets, for instance *Points of Interest* for Great Britain, and global data sets like *OpenStreetMap*. Contemporary augmented reality games like Pokémon GO have locations that correspond to traditional POIs. This allows investigating for instance their mutual impact or correlations with data of other domains like transport. Moreover, POIs of games can be analyzed solely inside the game's world.

2.3 Thematic Demarcation

In this paper we omit investigating comparative visualization as well as handling miscellaneous parameters like timestamps. For the former concept it is possible to modify the visualized circles either as pie charts or use circle packings that put multiple circles of different data sets into the area of a unifying circle. Both approaches are discussed thoroughly in literature [7,8]. However, it is sufficient for us to investigate the visualization for a single data set because we can apply these techniques after finding a global representation for all point data. The inclusion of miscellaneous parameters is also not scope of this paper. Commonly, applications use secondary views like a table of aggregates or a timeline rather than visualizing more than two parameters at once [9].

3 Related Work

This section presents an overview of techniques for visualizing large sets of geospatial point data. It has a clear focus on clustering techniques, but also briefly discusses sampling and space partitioning.

3.1 Sampling

Sampling is a widespread technique to reduce the size of a data set by a factor $\rho \in [0, 1]$. There are several strategies like linear sampling or rejection sampling to select either each $\frac{n}{\rho \cdot n}$'s element or each element by a certain probability. The factor ρ is crucial to the quality of the result. Though it is easy to comply with a maximum output size, sampling does not guarantee an overlap-free representation at all. Choosing a too small sample causes loss of information, e.g. outliers, and a too large one can fail to remove clutter. Using non-uniform sampling like sampling from a systematic grid, it is possible to avoid clutter at the expense of losing information about the spatial density of the data.

Sarma et al. [10] uses the notion of *thinning* to present different layers of detail regarding the user's zoom level. Their greedy algorithm for point data runs in linear time in terms of the number of points and the number of zoom levels. However, they use an importance function that does not exist in each application scenario. For cities, there are comprehensible differences of importance between capitals, megacities and rather smaller cities and villages. Biodiversity data for instance does not have a clear hierarchy in the case of species observations.

3.2 Clustering

Clustering is a technique to partition a data set into k groups with respect to one or more criteria, e.g. a similarity or a distance function, respectively. There are several concepts how to group data and how to find an optimal amount of partitions. Most problems are NP-hard in general [11]. However, there exist many greedy algorithms that approximate a good solution and provide a solution to the visual clustering problem.

Hierarchical Clustering. Hierarchical clustering groups data based on a distance value. It builds a tree structure of merge operations by choosing iteratively the smallest distance as a so-called dendrogram. A cut of the dendrogram produces a resulting data partitioning. There exist several inter-cluster-distance functions in the literature that influence the result as well as the computational complexity [12]. Common ones are *single linkage* and *complete linkage* that computes the distance between the two closest representatives of two clusters or the farthest ones, respectively. The *centroid* linkage utilizes a distance function between the cluster centers.

Jänicke et al. [13] presented an adaptation to cope with visual clustering that uses a growing circle (with respect to the individual cluster size) for distance calculations. The volume of the circle intersection yields the next merge candidate. This leads to an effective overlap removal and a precise cut in the dendrogram for creating the result. They exploit the dimensionality of two in the geospatial context to incorporate Delaunay triangulations into their algorithm. This makes it possible to compute the clustering in $O(n \cdot \log n)$ time. However, they did not formulate any quality criteria for their solution.

Bereuter and Weibel [14] presented a quadtree-based framework for point generalization. Besides discussing means for simplification and displacement they considered aggregations on subtrees with respect to different zoom levels. We consider quadtree-based subdividing the space a hierarchical method to differentiate dense and sparse regions. For each subtree partition, there is the possibility to apply simple averaging or more complex clustering strategies.

Partitional Clustering. The core idea of partitional clustering is to start with a random partitioning that has representative points for each partition with respect to nearest-neighbor classification. Expectation-Maximization (EM), k-Means and k-Medoid are prominent algorithms in this field [15]. Their computation converges by re-setting the representative point to the groups' centers in every iteration. The differences are that k-Medoid uses existing representative points while k-Means uses novel points, and EM uses a *mixture of gaussians* model.

While k-Means and EM have a expected time complexity of $O(n \cdot k)$, k-Medoid performs in quadratic running time which is not efficient with respect to exploratory visualization. k-Means finds clusters in the form of Voronoi cells that can be seen as a rough discretization of a circle. This facilitates visualizing dense spots as circles. *EM* is a fuzzy approach that allows finding more round shapes when restricting it to a spherical variance but clusters can overlap in general. In both cases, the optimal amount of clusters k is not tackled by the algorithm. So, finding a parametrization for a clutter free, minimal clustering that maximizes the information density is up to further research.

Density Based Clustering. The prominent DBSCAN [16] (Density-Based Spatial Clustering of Applications with Noise) algorithm forms groups of data based on their density. It takes the two parameters $MinPts$ and ϵ, where ϵ is the density criterion based on a distance function. $MinPts$ is a boundary condition that marks data as noise.

For the case of two-dimensional geospatial point data, there exists an $O(n \cdot \log n)$ algorithm. Based hereon, Gan and Tau [17] developed a linear running time approximation. This fits well in an exploratory visual analytics scenario.

DBSCAN is able to find clusters of unrestricted shape. This can be very good in general but inconvenient in our use problem setting where we want to output circular representatives of the data.

3.3 Space Partitioning

While cluster algorithms tackle our problem by partitioning the data, there are strategies to partition the space and provide density information within the partition. Prominent examples are heat maps and isopleth (contour) maps, where the former one represents frequencies of points in an equally-sized grid (or by using other shapes like hexagons) and the latter one describes regions of equally-frequent counts [18]. Commonly, application-specific color schemes indicate the value differences (in this domain the frequency). Other approaches use density estimators to generate hot spot maps. Then, there are more complex partitioning techniques like Voronoi or Tree Maps [19]. These methods provide an irregular partitioning based on either the Voronoi Diagram or a leaf representation of a multidimensional tree structure (like the R-tree). Both visualizations have in common that dense spots have more partitions. This is however contrary to our problem setting where we want to provide density information by differently-sized circles where a larger circle means more dense.

4 Quality Measures

This section introduces quality measures for assessing sets of circles that visualize a set of points as described in the problem specification in Sect. 2.1. Due to different zoom levels we have to evaluate circles on differently sized maps. As a result, our quality measures would be influenced by the zoom level. We chose a very efficient solution to tackle this problem, i.e., we use a linear transformation to map the points in P into $[0, 1]^2$. This results in a decrease of the circle radii with the factor $1/2^z$. As the mapping is linear, there is no distortion of distances or positioning. Independent of the zoom level, the minimum Euclidean distance between two points or circle centers is 0 and the maximum distance is $\sqrt{1^2 + 1^2} = \sqrt{2}$, respectively.

4.1 Preliminaries

Here, we define some essential notations and functions that we will need throughout the rest of this paper. For a point p we use $p.x$ and $p.y$, respectively, to address the x and y coordinate. In the case of a circle c we have moreover the radius r which we address by $c.r$. To measure distances between circle centers and points, we only consider the coordinates (ignoring the radius of the circle), leading to $pdist(c, p) := \sqrt{(c.x - p.x)^2 + (c.y - p.y)^2}$. The function

$$centroid(P') := \left(\frac{1}{|P'|} \sum_{p \in P'} p.x, \frac{1}{|P'|} \sum_{p \in P'} p.y \right)$$

calculates the geometrical center of a set of points $P' \subseteq P$. For calculating the area of an arbitrary object o, we use the function $A(o)$. If the object is a circle c, we can make use of the well-known formula $(c.r)^2 \cdot \pi$. Otherwise, we use a Monte Carlo simulation to approximate the area due to efficiency reasons or absence of an analytical solution. Finally, the associative operators $c_i \cap c_j$ and $c_i \cup c_j$ define, respectively, the geometric intersection and union of circles c_i and c_j.

4.2   Visual Assignment

When measuring the quality of a circle representation of a point set, each quality measure needs to consider the original points that are attached to the circles. This leads to an assignment as in clustering such that each point belongs to a cluster. As clustering algorithms output assignments, it could come natural to use these for further investigation. However, our quality measures have to address the visual quality of these clusterings. Therefore, it is necessary to measure the perception rather than the intent (the output of a clustering algorithm) such that the visual assignment of points to a representative circle must be independent of the output of the algorithm. With this in mind, the traditional clustering measures relate to the intent and are not applicable here. Subsequently, there are two variants to assign the points of P to the circles of C.

Nearest Neighbor. The nearest neighbor assignment $\mathcal{N}$ of $c_i \in C$ is defined as

$$\mathcal{N}_{c_i} := \{p \in P \mid c_i = \arg\min_{c \in C} dist(c, p)\}$$

with

$$dist(c, p) := \begin{cases} pdist(c, p) - c.r & \text{if } c.r \geq pdist(c, p) \\ -\sqrt{2} + pdist(c, p) & \text{else} \end{cases}.$$

It assigns the points to the closest circle. If a point is outside of a circle, the assignment uses the distance to the perimeter. Otherwise, the circle contains the point and the assignment considers the distance to the center (which can be at maximum $\sqrt{2}$). This leads to the natural assignment of a point to the most inner (containing) circle in the case of overlapping circles.

Enclosing. The enclosing assignment $\mathcal{E}$ of $c_i \in C$ is defined as

$$\mathcal{E}_{c_i} := \{p \in P \mid contains(c_i, p)\}$$

with the predicate $contains(c, p) := pdist(c, p) \leq c.r$. Moreover, a residual assignment $\mathcal{E}_\emptyset = P \setminus (\mathcal{E}_{c_1} \cup \ldots \cup \mathcal{E}_{c_m})$ exists.

This assignment attaches each point to an enclosing circle. Note that in contrast to the nearest neighbor assignment, points can be attached to multiple circles in the case of circle overlap.

4.3   Measures

In the following we define a set of quality measures, assessing as a whole the quality of a circle representation C for a set of points P. The measure μ_i tackles the requirement i. Given this requirement, we measure the deviation ν_i of C to the optimal solution. To ensure intercomparability of requirements, we want to enforce all measures to be in the interval $(0, 1]$ which is accomplished by mapping ν_i onto $e^{-\nu_i} =: \mu_i$. By this mapping we ensure that for deviations of zero a quality of one is obtained whereas the quality decreases exponentially to zero with increasing deviation.

As a result, it is sufficient to define in the following the requirements i and the deviations ν_i only. As will turn out later, some ν_i values have an upper bound of one. This means, putting them as negative value into the exponential function results in outcomes in the interval $[0.36, 1]$. Then, a linear stretch function is applied to utilize the full range again.

Area Proportionality. The area of circles should be proportional to the number of points they represent. For this, we require the densities of all circles to be almost equal. We define the density for circle c_i as $d_i := |\mathcal{N}_{c_i}|/A(c_i)$. To quantify *almost equal* we make use of the variance coefficient

$$\nu_{area} := \frac{\sqrt{Var(\{d_1, \ldots, d_m\})}}{E(\{d_1, \ldots, d_m\})}.$$

This measure obviously penalizes strong variations in the d_i values which is the desired property of the measure.

Circle Points Centered. The centroid of the points assigned to a circle should be close to the circle's center. For each circle we calculate the distance between its center and the centroid of the points assigned to the circle. We aggregate the m distances by taking the average.

$$\nu_{centered} := \frac{1}{m} \sum_{i=1}^{m} pdist(c_i, centroid(\mathcal{N}_{c_i}))$$

Circle Overlap. The optimal solution does not contain overlaps and thus no occlusion. We measure the deviation from the optimum therefore by

$$\nu_{overlap} := \frac{A(C_1 \cap \ldots \cap C_m)}{A(C_1 \cup \ldots \cup C_m)},$$

which is to some extent a modification of the well known Jaccard-coefficient.

Circle Point Distance. Points outside its representative circle are unintended. Therefore, we measure how far points on average are outside their representing circle. Concretely, this is done by

$$\nu_{distance} := \frac{1}{m} \sum_{c \in C} \sum_{p \in \mathcal{N}_c} \mathcal{I}_{c,p} \cdot (pdist(c, p) - c.r).$$

To evaluate $\nu_{distance}$ we incorporate all points that are not enclosed by their representative circle by the indicator function $\mathcal{I}_{c,p}$ that returns 1 if $pdist(c,p) - c.r > 0$ and 0 otherwise.

Unassigned Points. Points in P that are not contained within a circle are undesired. Hence, the more points a solution C does not cover, the more C deviates from an optimal solution. We assess this with the following measure: $\nu_{unassigned} := |\mathcal{E}_\emptyset|/n$. It makes use of the residual assignment and calculates the fraction of points that are not enclosed by a circle with respect to the total amount of points n.

Uniform Point Distribution. The optimal distribution of points within their representing circle should be uniform. We measure the deviation of this optimal distribution as follows: We partition a circle c_i into a grid of $\sqrt{|\mathcal{E}_i|}$ square buckets by applying the function $histogram(c_i)$. For each bucket we count the number of points that fall into the bucket[1]. Similarly to the measure ν_{area}, we employ the variance coefficient to measure the deviations of the individual bucket counts. Equal counts in all buckets correspond to uniform distributions, hence, the variance coefficient is an appropriate measure to check this property. We aggregate results for individual circles by taking the average of the variance coefficients and define $\nu_{uniform}$ as

$$\nu_{uniform} := \frac{1}{m} \sum_{c_i \in C} \frac{\sqrt{Var(histogram(c_i))}}{E(histogram(c_i))}.$$

Alternatively, a Kolmogorov-Smirnov-Test [20] allows measuring the deviation. However, the spatial histogram turned out to be more robust for smaller amounts of points within a circle.

Zoom Consistency. Zooming into an area should break up clusters and give a more detailed view on the point distribution. This means, we expect that smaller circles are located in all regions which are covered by bigger circles from the previous zoom level. This measure is an adaptation of the zoom consistency defined by Sarma et al. [21]. We define the set of circles at zoom level z as $C^{(z)}$. To check the zoom consistency property for an individual circle $c \in C^{(z)}$ we measure the relative overlap with the next zoom level $z+1$. Averaging over all circles in $C^{(z)}$ leads finally to

$$\nu_{zoom} := \frac{1}{m} \sum_{c \in C^{(z)}} \frac{A\left(\left(\bigcup_{c' \in C^{(z+1)}} c'\right) \cap c\right)}{A(c)}.$$

Due to the scaling to the unit interval there is no need to adjust the sizes between contiguous zoom levels. Note that this measure is the only one which requires two sets of circles and no points as arguments.

---

[1] Our counting also considers the case where a bucket is only partially contained by a circle. In this case we interpolate the count by the fraction of its contained part.

5   Experimental Evaluation

We performed experiments on five data sets to assess in how far selected methods of Sect. 3 are applicable for our problem setting. As almost all approaches calculate a clustering rather than an aggregation, a transformation is inevitable. We considered three approaches for transformation and combined them with the methods. Moreover, each method has certain parameters that influence the final solution. The combination of method settings and the choice of the transformation function forms the final set of parameters.

5.1   Methods

As already mentioned, the output of the methods used is an assignment of n points to m clusters. Let $G_i := \{p \in P \mid p$ is assigned to Cluster $i\}$ be the ith assignment. For generating circles, it is necessary to apply a transformation function τ to each cluster that maps it to a circle. We used three methods:

Circumcircle. This mapping function uses the centroid of the assigned points for calculating the circle center. For defining the radius we use the farthermost point to the center. Thus we obtain

$$\tau_{cc}(G_i) := \left(centroid(G_i), \max_{p' \in G_i} \left(pdist\left(centroid(G_i), p'\right)\right)\right).$$

Log2. Jänicke et al. [13] presented a mapping function that uses the cluster centroid and scales the radius with regard to the amount of assigned points. They used an empirical maximum circle area $A_{max} := (4 \log_2(n+1))^2 \cdot \pi$ and a minimal circle area $A_{min} := r_{min}^2 \cdot \pi$ with a fixed r_{min} based on the proposal in [13]. Using these two values leads finally to

$$\tau_{Log2}(G_i) := \left(centroid(G_i), \sqrt{\frac{A_{min} + \frac{|G_i|-1}{n-1}(A_{max} - A_{min})}{\pi}}\right).$$

Log10. As their findings were empirical, we added another maximum area function using the decimal logarithm. This implies a doubling of the size by an increase of an order of magnitude of points. We define $A_{max} := (\log_{10}(n) \cdot r_{min})^2 \cdot \pi$ and use the same transformation function as defined above.

Above, we presented how a clustering can be transformed into circle representation. In the following we present the required methods to assign points to clusters. These methods can be grouped into three categories (cf. Sect. 3). For each category we consider certain representatives.

Partitional Clustering. We evaluated k-Means and EM by using the implementation k-Means++ of Apache Commons Math[2] and EM of OpenCV[3],

---

[2] commons.apache.org/proper/commons-math/.
[3] www.opencv.org.

respectively. Both methods exhibit the parameter k (which equals to m in our case), giving the number of clusters one wants to detect.

Hierarchical Clustering. We applied single-link ($SLINK$), complete-link (C-$LINK$) and *centroid* clustering, provided by the ELKI library [22] (the last one uses `AnderbergHierarchicalClustering`). Additionally, we implemented the Delaunay-based algorithm *GeoTemCo* of Jänicke et al. [13]. The first three methods output a dendrogram which we utilize to extract clusters of cardinality m. *GeoTemCo*, on the other hand, directly outputs circles using circle sizes identically to those generated by the *Log2* transformation.

Density-Based Clustering. We used *DBSCAN* of ELKI to generate density-based clusters. The parameters to specify are $MinPts$ and ϵ which were already described in Sect. 3.

5.2   Data Sets

We chose five differently sized data sets. Four address the domain of biodiversity research and concern species observations from gbif.org. These are *Loxodonta cyclotis* (African forest elephant) with 23 points, *Puma concolor* (cougar) with 1 992 points, *Macropus giganteus* (eastern grey kangaroo) with 23 039 points and *Alnus Glutinosa* (common alder) with 185 259 points. Another one (*german libraries*) settles in the domain of points of interest. It shows 3 383 points that display library locations in Germany (taken from openstreetmap.org).

5.3   Evaluation

In our experimental study, we used the proposed clustering methods which exhibit certain internal parameters. The choice of the transformation function represents another parameter. The optimal parametrization is unclear. To guarantee a fair comparison of approaches, we performed a grid search on the parameters of each clustering method. The parameters were investigated as follows: $m \in [1, 15\,000]$, $\epsilon \in [2.5, 25]$, $MinPts \in [1, 10]$ and $\tau \in \{\log2, \log10, cc\}$. Thus, we retrieved a large set of circle representations for each data set, each of which we evaluated by applying our potentially conflicting quality measures.

Clustering Approaches. For this experiment we considered only the first six quality measures, omitting zoom consistency (which will be considered later). For each clustering method we discarded dominated solutions and obtained a Pareto frontier (skyline). Using these frontiers, we can assure a fair comparison independent of parametrization. For instance, if a Pareto frontier of a method is completely above the Pareto frontier of another method, it indicates that the former method outperforms the latter one. Figure 2 presents the results in a plot-matrix on the Alnus glutinosa data set. The results for the other four data sets could not be presented in this paper due to space limitations. They are, however, accessible via http://uni-marburg.de/vqANd. The diagonal of the plot matrix depicts individual criteria. The criteria *distance, overlap, centered* and *unassigned* can be fulfilled completely by all approaches – there is at least one parametrization located at position $(1, 1)$ indicating a perfect result. The criterion

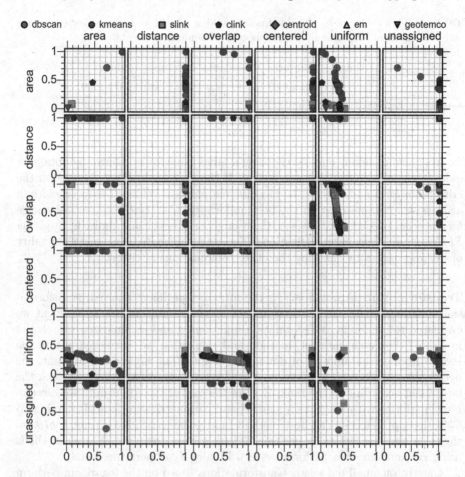

Fig. 2. This plot matrix shows all pairwise Pareto frontiers on data set Alnus glutinosa.

area can be fulfilled completely only by k-Means. The other approaches perform worse. *DBSCAN* suffers from non-convex clusters, while *SLINK* is much more prone to tubular clusters which are hardly approximated by any circle. *CLINK*, on the other hand, has a better quality due to the different distance function which outputs rather circular clusters. Even though *GeoTemCo* performs worse on this criterion, it is much better on all the other data sets which are significantly smaller. Obviously, the *log2*-scaling poses a problem. Therefore, it will be subject to another experiment. The *uniform* criterion is not sufficiently fulfilled by any method. We interpret this due to the lack of uniform distributions in the underlying point data set. Thus, it is hard to fit uniform areas. *GeoTemCo* seems to have a slight drift from the optimum due to the displacement of the circle in each step of the algorithm. The plots that are not on the diagonal of the matrix show combinations of different criteria. The *uniform-overlap* plot shows an interesting curve that indicates that relaxing the overlap-constraint allows for fitting the circles better to the uniform spots of the point data.

Table 1. This table shows the dominance ranking for the projections for each data set. The numbers in braces show the amounts of dominated points.

τ	Alnus	Libraries	Loxodonta	Macropus	Puma
cc	1 (574)	91 (306)	-	209 (2343)	137 (1660)
log2	139 (395)	5 (372)	-	1 (4182)	1 (2901)
log10	22 (528)	1 (512)	1 (1489)	29 (3176)	84 (1823)

Such a phenomenon occurs by choosing a large value for m, hence, by obtaining more circles that allow this adaptation. If the user for instance focuses on the criteria *uniform* and *overlap*, he has different choices: While *SLINK* provides in at least one parametrization the best uniformity, *GeoTemCo* is the best choice for the criterion *overlap*. However, the user gets the best compromise by applying *SLINK* in different parametrizations. The reader is invited to assess the quality of the approaches by checking the other combinations of criteria.

Transformation Functions. As the former experiment showed, transformation functions might have a deep impact on the results. In this experiment we evaluated the different transformation functions τ and summarized the results in Table 1. For each data set, method and τ function we calculated within the Pareto frontier the amount of dominated points. The higher this amount, the better the transformation function. Then, for each transformation, we took the best result according to the rank. E.g., in the case of the Alnus data set *circumcircle* performs within a certain method and parametrization best. It dominated 574 other approaches. The best method (and parametrization) using *Log10*, on the other hand, is ranked on position 22 (this means, there are 21 other methods using *circumcircle* that perform better). Finally, *Log2* performs worst.

Clearly, on small data sets, transformations based on the logarithm perform very well. However, if the data set size increases, even the logarithm does not yield appropriate radii for the circles – they become too large a number. In such scenarios, the *circumcircle* approach performs best, as in the case of the Alnus data set. This clearly indicates that the maximal circle areas have to incorporate the drawing area rather than just relying on the number of input points.

Zoom Consistency. Finally, we investigated also the important property of zoom consistency. We chose three zoom levels for measuring the zoom consistency. Three zoom levels are sufficient for assessing the zoom consistency due to transitivity. Figure 3 shows the results in terms of boxplots. We can observe, that all approaches are able to produce very good results, since there is at least one parametrization for each approach that gets quality values of around 1. However, the majority of results is located within the boxes, indicating, that many parametrizations of *DBSCAN* lead to bad zoom consistencies. Since parametrization is a crucial point for users, *DBSCAN* seems hard to use. Other approaches are much more robust in this regard. *GeoTemCo* leads, independent of

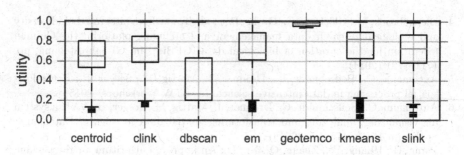

Fig. 3. This boxplot shows the different quality values regarding the zoom consistency.

parametrization, to almost perfect results. This is an important finding since it shows that this approach allows for comfortable usage.

6   Conclusion and Outlook

In this paper we addressed the important problem of visualizing geographic point data in order to remove clutter. We investigated this by applying clustering techniques. These techniques, however, are rather designed to assign classes to data instances than serving as a tool for visualization. We introduced novel criteria to evaluate circle representations that derive from clusterings. These measures cover important properties and we were able to show that state-of-the art methods are not fully appropriate for this kind of problem. Moreover, we showed insights of the weaknesses of the approaches. As we believe, this problem needs more consideration and there are many opportunities for future work.

One possibility is to generate optimal visual clusterings by using for instance evolutionary algorithms with our quality measures. Besides using multi-objective optimization, an appropriate combination of the quality measures to a single-criterion fitness function (e.g. a linear combination) would allow defining a total order and using single-objective optimization for finding the single best solution. To find a weighted combination, it is possible to utilize techniques from preference learning [23] and conduct a user study to gather valid results. A user study also allows assessing the comprehensiveness of the measures.

Acknowledgement. This work was supported by DFG grant no. SE 553/7-2.

References

1. Kelling, S., Hochachka, W., Fink, D., et al.: Data-intensive science: a new paradigm for biodiversity studies. BioScience **59**(7), 613–620 (2009)
2. Jetz, W., McPherson, J., Guralnick, R.: Integrating biodiversity distribution knowledge: toward a global map of life. Trends Ecol. Evol. **27**(3), 151–159 (2012)
3. Corvalan, C., Hales, S., McMichael, A.: Ecosystems and Human Well-Being: Health Synthesis. World Health Organization, Geneva (2005)

4. Diepenbroek, M., Glöckner, F., Grobe, P., et al.: Towards an integrated biodiversity and ecological research data management and archiving platform: the German federation for the curation of biological data (GFBio). In: GI-Jahrestagung, pp. 1711–1721 (2014)
5. Authmann, C., Beilschmidt, C., Drönner, J., Mattig, M., Seeger, B.: Rethinking spatial processing in data-intensive science. In: BTW Workshops (2015)
6. Authmann, C., Beilschmidt, C., Drönner, J., Mattig, M., Seeger, B.: VAT: a system for visualizing, analyzing and transforming spatial data in science. Datenbank-Spektrum 15(3), 175–184 (2015)
7. Wang, H., Huang, W., Zhang, Q., Xu, D.: An improved algorithm for the packing of unequal circles within a larger containing circle. Eur. J. Oper. Res. 141(2), 440–453 (2002)
8. Jänicke, S., Heine, C., Stockmann, R., Scheuermann, G.: Comparative visualization of geospatial-temporal data. In: Proceedings of IVAPP, pp. 613–625 (2012)
9. Mazza, R.: Introduction to Information Visualization. Springer, New York (2009)
10. Das Sarma, A., Lee, H., Gonzalez, H., Madhavan, J., Halevy, A.: Consistent thinning of large geographical data for map visualization. ACM Trans. Database Syst. (TODS) 38(4), 22 (2013)
11. Hansen, P., Jaumard, B.: Cluster analysis and mathematical programming. Math. Program. 79(1–3), 191–215 (1997)
12. Murtagh, F., Contreras, P.: Algorithms for hierarchical clustering: an overview. Wiley Interdiscip. Rev. Data Min. Knowl. Discov. 2(1), 86–97 (2012)
13. Jänicke, S., Heine, C., Scheuermann, G.: GeoTemCo: comparative visualization of geospatial-temporal data with clutter removal based on dynamic delaunay triangulations. In: Csurka, G., Kraus, M., Laramee, R.S., Richard, P., Braz, J. (eds.) VISI-GRAPP 2012. CCIS, vol. 359, pp. 160–175. Springer, Heidelberg (2013). doi:10.1007/978-3-642-38241-3_11
14. Bereuter, P., Weibel, R.: Real-time generalization of point data in mobile and web mapping using quadtrees. Cartogr. Geogr. Inf. Sci. 40(4), 271–281 (2013)
15. Xu, R., Wunsch, D.: Survey of clustering algorithms. IEEE Trans. Neural Netw. Learn. Syst. 16(3), 645–678 (2005)
16. Ester, M., Kriegel, H., Sander, J., Xu, X.: A density-based algorithm for discovering clusters in large spatial databases with noise. In: Proceedings of International Conference on Knowledge Discovery and Data Mining (KDD), pp. 226–231 (1996)
17. Gan, J., Tao, Y.: DBSCAN revisited: mis-claim, un-fixability, and approximation. In: Proceedings of ACM SIGMOD, pp. 519–530. ACM (2015)
18. Slocum, T., McMaster, R., Kessler, F., Howard, H.: Thematic Cartography and Geovisualization. Pearson Prentice Hall, Upper Saddle River (2009)
19. Herman, I., Melançon, G., Marshall, M.: Graph visualization and navigation in information visualization: a survey. IEEE Trans. Vis. Comput. Graph. 6(1), 24–43 (2000)
20. Lopes, R., Reid, I., Hobson, P.: The two-dimensional kolmogorov-smirnov test. In: Proceedings of Science (2007)
21. Das Sarma, A., Lee, H., Gonzalez, H., Madhavan, J., Halevy, A.: Efficient spatial sampling of large geographical tables categories and subject descriptors. In: Proceedings of ACM SIGMOD, pp. 193–204 (2012)
22. Achtert, E., Goldhofer, S., Kriegel, H., Schubert, E., Zimek, A.: Evaluation of clusterings - metrics and visual support. In: ICDE, pp. 1285–1288. IEEE CS (2012)
23. Fober, T., Cheng, W., Hüllermeier, E.: Focusing search in multiobjective evolutionary optimization through preference learning from user feedback. In: Proceedings of Workshop Computational Intelligence, vol. 40, p. 107 (2011)

Offshore Wind Turbines Visual Impact Estimation

Nicolas Maslov[1(✉)], Tianzhen Wang[1], Tianhao Tang[1], and Christophe Claramunt[2]

[1] Shanghai Maritime University, Shanghai, China
nico.maslov@gmail.com, {tzwang,thtang}@shmtu.edu.cn
[2] Naval Academy Research Institute, Brest, France
christophe.claramunt@ecole-navale.fr

Abstract. The objective of this paper is to present a method that qualifies the degree of visibility of an offshore wind farm from an observer located along the coast. In many cases, the deployment of an offshore wind farm leads to public opposition. This entails the need for the development of appropriate methods that might present in the most intelligible way the impacts of an offshore wind farm. Amongst many factors to take into account, the visual impact of such farms is surely a factor to take into account. We introduce a visual operator that integrates several parameters that mainly depend on the distance of the wind farm to the cost. We apply a measure that evaluates the horizon surface impact modulated by the number of distinguishable turbines and an aesthetic index based on turbine alignments. The whole method is implemented on top of a Geographical Information System (GIS) and provides a decision-aid mechanism oriented to decision-makers. The whole approach is experimented in the context of a wind farm in North West France.

Keywords: Visual impact · Offshore wind turbine · GIS · Seascape · Aesthetic · Decision-aid system

1 Introduction

It has been long observed that marine renewable energy could make a significant contribution to energy production [1, 2]. The technological development of offshore wind turbines has rapidly increased this generating many economic challenges [3], novel approaches for the ocean management [4], as well as public concerns regarding possible environmental impacts [5–7].

The management of the maritime and littoral environments generates many conflicting issues due to rapid development and pressure on these areas. Indeed, any new activity close to the coast might generate many socioeconomic conflicts. Among the principal reasons of social reluctance, the visual impact on the seascape could entail the successful development of a marine renewable energy project. In fact, seascape protection has become an important issue in many countries [8]. An appropriate evaluation of the visual impact of a wind farm project is one of the first steps to develop for engaging discussions with the general public and local stakeholders in order to study and even decrease any visual damage that may constitute the deployment of an offshore wind farm in the seascape.

D. Brosset et al. (Eds.): W2GIS 2017, LNCS 10181, pp. 169–177, 2017.
DOI: 10.1007/978-3-319-55998-8_11

The objective of the research presented in this paper is to introduce a method that quantifies the visual impact on the seascape of an offshore wind farm. The problem is not completely new at hand as many researches have been recently oriented to this issue [9]. However, the main challenge that still arises comes from the subjective part of problem. One might apply a series of surveys on population samples. This has been done using photo-montages approaches [10, 11] or 3D visualization tools [12]. In this paper, we introduce a computational method that might be qualified as objective, and it can be considered as a preliminary process at the design phase of a given project of a wind farm, as well as a complementary approach to the ones mentioned above.

The technique developed in this paper provides a computational visual impact operator derived from a series of quantifiable indicators. Several parameters are considered such as the surface covered and the arrangement of the wind farm as well as its perception from the horizon as perceived from the coast. The way turbines are potentially perceived and qualified are taken into account and quantified, an aesthetic factor denotes the visual alignment of the turbines. The whole approach is implemented on top of a GIS environment that has the advantage of providing appropriate functions for managing, manipulating and deriving task-oriented operators.

2   Methodology

The methodology developed in this paper is first based on the evaluation the horizon occupation which mainly depends on the distance of the energy farm to the coast, height of the turbines and farm layout. We assume that observers are located along the shore line although the method can be applied to different constraints with some minor adaptations. No obstacles are supposed to alter the farm vision of the observers. The aim is to estimate the horizon occupation of the wind farm considered as a visual plane located at one meter of observer. The number and spatial arrangement of the turbines will be

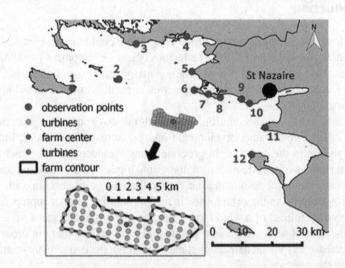

Fig. 1. Offshore wind farm layout planned in the Saint-Nazaire coastal region

the key factor to take into account. In order to illustrate the approach we consider the case of an offshore wind farm project located in Saint-Nazaire in North West France (Fig. 1). The assessment of the visual impact is carried out for 12 observation points located around the farm and in the seacoast.

2.1 Horizon Occupation

Let us consider the wind farm as a whole object of study. The spatial distribution of the wind turbines is considered as a convex polygon. This polygon constitutes the object whose visual occupation is to be estimated. The considered area for the horizon surface occupation is the one derived by the polygon projection on a perpendicular sight direction plan located at one meter of the observer. The sight is supposed in the direction of the farm center. The apparent height of the turbine is derived from the actual hub height which a hidden part has been removed due to the Earth curve when the turbines are located above the horizon distance (Fig. 2). The surface occupied by the farm on the horizon is defined by the area delimited by a convex curve joining the turbine hubs placed at the polygon visible edges. Figure 3 shows the apparent hub height and turbines arrangement for an observer located at different places. The horizon occupation, *HO*, is defined as the surface below the convex envelop.

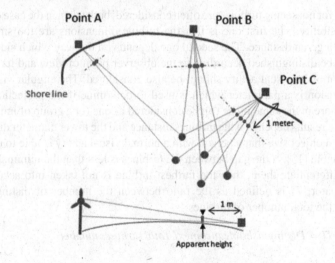

Fig. 2. Schematic illustration of the projection

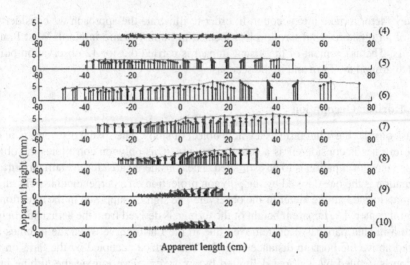

Fig. 3. Visualization of hub height projection for the observation points from 4 to 8

2.2 Distinguishable Turbines

Two reasons for not seeing turbines are often considered, both taken in the case of perfect condition visibility. The first one is that the turbine dimensions are too small to be perceived at a given distance. The second one depends on the way which side-by-side turbines can be distinguished according to the observer point of view and its direction sight. The notion of visual acuity should be also considered. The angular visibility of the human vision is a parameter which is used to determine if the projection of two turbines or more in the same plane can be considered as one (or a group of innumerable turbines). The results depend on the turbines distance and the tower diameter dimension. The minimum object size that a person with a normal visual acuity is able to recognize is one arc minute [13]. If the gap between the turbines is less than the minimal distance needed to differentiate them, then the farthest turbine is not taken into account. The turbine indicator, *TI* is defined as the ratio between the number of distinguishable turbines and the total number of turbines:

$$TI = Distinguishable\ turbines\,/\,Total\ turbines\ number \tag{1}$$

2.3 Aesthetic Indicator

The aesthetic notion has been introduced to describe the continuity and fractal dimension of a visual offshore farm [14]. Here, and as the case study support is mostly oriented towards regular grid turbines, the number of turbine arrangements that can be clearly distinguished is taken into account. The aesthetic is, for the human mind, always dealing with the question of order and symmetry, the idea is to privilege the orientations of the wind farm that display regular distribution of the turbine rather than chaotic distribution (Fig. 4). The aesthetic indicator implies, according to view angle of the observer, to enumerate the number of turbine arrangements that can be clearly dissociated (i.e., not overlaid by other turbines alignments in the projection). The turbine spatial arrangements are composed by the different alignments exhibited by the turbine layout. In a regular grid configuration (composed by L rows and C columns) observed perpendicularly, these turbines are observed as rows, or as diagonals in other cases. Figure 5 shows the possible turbine alignments that can be observed regarding the St-Nazaire wind farm layout.

Fig. 4. View of different wind farm with, (a) chaotic distribution of turbine and (b) regular distributing allowing to distinguished alignments

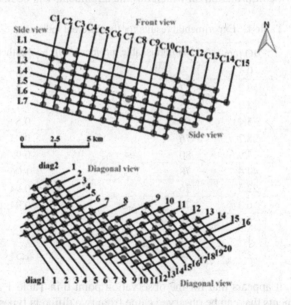

Fig. 5. Wind farm layout and alignments visualization, 'L' row alignments, 'C' column alignments, 'diag' diagonal alignments

The aesthetic parameter (AI) is defined as the ratio between the number of turbine alignments that can be practically distinguished and the maximal number of alignments that can be theoretically observed:

$$AI = Alignement_{seen} / Alignments_{Total} \tag{2}$$

The maximal number of alignments is given by either the maximal number of columns (e.g., 15 as illustrated by Fig. 5), the maximal number of rows (e.g., 7 as illustrated by Fig. 5) or the maximal number of diagonals (i.e., 16 or 20 as illustrated by Fig. 5) depending on the observer point of view. In other words a person rather located in the front view is more likely to perceive the 'column' alignment. In the case illustrated by Fig. 5, the maximal number of alignment is the one given by the number of columns. The aesthetic indicator is linearly scaled from 0.5 to 1.5. An optimal aesthetic arrangement with regular and harmonious turbines arrangements is supposed to reduce the impact, a visual aesthetic indicator of 0.5 is valued in this best case. On the contrary, a chaotic distribution is supposed to decrease the visual acceptance, a valuation of the visual impact of 1.5 is chosen for that worst case.

2.4 Visual Impact Operator

In the case of the Saint-Nazaire farm layout, turbine towers of 80 meters high and 4 meters large are considered. The results for derived for the different indicators are summarized in Table 1. Details of the aesthetic indicator estimation are also given in Table 2 and provide information on which turbine alignments can be discerned.

Table 1. Experimental results for the different indicators

Observation point	HO (cm^2)	Distinguishable turbines (/80)	Aesthetic factor (AI)
1	0	5	/
2	9.2	77	1.3
3	2.9	53	1.1
4	3.4	65	0.5
5	28.7	76	0.83
6	73.9	80	0.97
7	44.4	78	1.06
8	22.5	76	0.94
9	6.3	72	0.94
10	3.7	55	1
11	1.4	31	1.5
12	2.9	44	1.5

In particular, it appears that for the observation point 6 in Table 1 and Fig. 6, the turbine arrangements that can be observed came from two different types of alignments (diagonal and column). Still, the maximal number of arrangements that can be seen theoretically is the one of the observation point 15, in which the observer is then considered in the front area of the wind farm. At the observation point 1, the number of turbines seen is too low to consider the calculation of the aesthetic indicator, it is therefore not taken into account in the evaluation of the visual impact. The visual impact operator is defined as the cross product of the different indicators:

Table 2. Details of aesthetic index calculation

Observation point	Number of alignments seen	Alignments affected[1]		Alignments total[2]
2	4	diag1	1, 2, 3, 4	20
3	8	diag1	11 to 18	20
4	15	C	1 to 15	15
5	10 + 2	C diag2	6 to 15 1, 2	15
6	5 + 3	C diag2	11 to 15 1, 2, 3	15
7	7	diag2	1 to 7	16
8	9	diag2	1 to 9	16
9	9	diag2	3, 4, 5 11 to 16	16
10	8	diag2	4 to 8 14 to 16	16

$$Visual\,Impact \;=\; HO \times TI \times AI \tag{3}$$

where HO denotes the horizon occupation, TI, the turbine indicator and AI the aesthetic indicator.

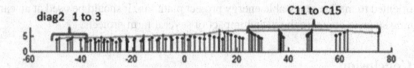

Fig. 6. View at observer point 6 with details of the turbines alignments that can be observed

2.5 Final Results and Discussion

The results for the offshore find farm of Saint-Nazaire at the different observation points are summarized in Fig. 7. The figures that appear confirm that the distance of the farm to the observation point is an important factor in the visual assessment. However, it also appears that the results exhibited show different aesthetic trends. For instance at the observer point 3, the visual impact is less important than at the observation point 4 according only to the horizon occupation indicator.

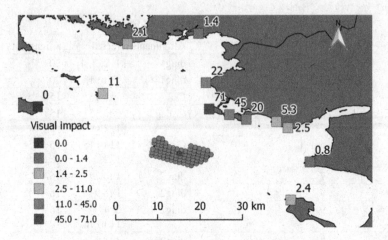

Fig. 7. Visual impacts of the offshore wind farm

Although variations in the results may come from the way the aesthetic coefficient has been rescaled. For a better valuation and understanding of this measure, a complementary study that will evaluate how much the aesthetic indicator influences the visual impact, and therefore the degree of acceptance should be performed. Indeed, this visual impact estimation method should be integrated as part of a more complete decision-aid tool oriented to marine renewable energy project planning. It should be used at an early planning stage to compare the visual impact of several farm projects.

3   Conclusion

The research developed in this paper introduces a computational-based operator for quantifying the visual assessment of an offshore wind farm. This operator is designed as an intelligible and objective function, and can be used in several iterations to estimate the visual impact of different farm projects. This approach also includes a new method for measuring the aesthetic of an offshore wind farm.

The work is preliminary and should be extended to include for instance some additional parameters such as the real density of population land uses closely related to the observation points as defined by the current approach. Accordingly, the seacoast might be segmented into different observation areas. An aggregation of the different variables identified using a multicriteria analysis is another relevant direction to explore in order to match as much as possible decision-making processes, and an appropriate level of subjectivity in the final step of the decision process.

References

1. Horn, M., Krupp, F.: Earth: The Sequel: The Race to Reinvent Energy and Stop Global Warming. WW Norton & Company, New York (2009)
2. Jeffrey, H., Jay, B., Winskel, M.: Accelerating the development of marine energy: exploring the prospects, benefits and challenges. Technol. Forecast. Soc. Change **80**, 1306–1316 (2013)
3. Brown, M.T., Cohen, M.J., Sweeney, S.: Predicting national sustainability: the convergence of energetic, economic and environmental realities. Ecol. Model. **220**, 3424–3438 (2009)
4. Douvere, F.: The importance of marine spatial planning in advancing ecosystem-based sea use management. Mar. Policy **32**, 762–771 (2008)
5. Gill, A.B.: Offshore renewable energy: ecological implications of generating electricity in the coastal zone. J. Appl. Ecol. **42**, 605–615 (2005)
6. Boehlert, G.W., Andrew, B.G.: Environmental and ecological effects of ocean renewable energy development: a current synthesis. J. Oceanogr. **23**, 68–81 (2010)
7. Sullivan, R.G., Kirchler, L.B., Cothren, J., Winters, S.L.: Offshore wind turbine visibility and visual impact threshold distances. Environ. Pract. **15**, 33–49 (2013)
8. Barrow, C. J.: Environmental Impact Assessment: Curring Edge for the Twenty-First Century, A. Gilpin. Cabridge University Press, Cambridge (1995)
9. Bishop, I.D.: What do we really know? A meta-analysis of studies into public responses to wind energy. In: World Renewable Energy Congress, pp. 4161–4169. Linköping University Electronic Press, Linköping (2011)
10. Ladenburg, J.: Visual impact assessment of offshore wind farms and prior experience. Appl. Energy **86**, 380–387 (2009)
11. Molnarova, K., Sklenicka, P., Stiborek, J., Svobodova, K., Salek, M., Brabec, E.: Visual preferences for wind turbines: location, numbers and respondent characteristics. Appl. Energy **92**, 269–278 (2012)
12. Paar, P.: Landscape visualizations: applications and requirements of 3D visualization software for environmental planning. Comput. Environ. Urban Syst. **30**, 815–839 (2006)
13. Shang, H., Bishop, I.D.: Visual thresholds for detection, recognition and visual impact in landscape settings. J. Environ. Psychol. **20**, 125–140 (2000)
14. Sibille, A.C.T., Cloquell-Ballester, V.A., Cloquell-Ballester, V.A., Darton, R.: Development and validation of a multicriteria indicator for the assessment of objective aesthetic impact of wind farms. Renew. Sustain. Energy Rev. **13**, 40–66 (2009)

Author Index

Printed in the United States
By Bookmasters